PERSONALITY ASSESSMENT
AND
PSYCHOLOGICAL
INTERPRETATION

PERSONALITY ASSESSMENT
AND
PSYCHOLOGICAL
INTERPRETATION

By

CAROL L. DEINHARDT, Ph.D.

CHARLES C THOMAS • PUBLISHER
Springfield • Illinois • U.S.A.

Published and Distributed Throughout the World by
CHARLES C THOMAS • PUBLISHER
2600 South First Street
Springfield, Illinois, 62717, U.S.A.

© *1983 by* Carol L. Deinhardt

ISBN 0-398-04752-9

Library of Congress Catalog Card Number: 82-10822

With THOMAS BOOKS *careful attention is given to all details of manufacturing and design. It is the Publisher's desire to present books that are satisfactory as to their physical qualities and artistic possibilities and appropriate for their particular use.* THOMAS BOOKS *will be true to those laws of quality that assure a good name and good will.*

Printed in the United States of America
CU-R-1

Library of Congress Cataloging in Publication Data

Deinhardt, Carol L.
  Personality assessment and psychological interpretation.

  Bibliography: p.
  Includes index.
    1. Personality assessment.   2. Personality tests.   I. Title.
  [DNLM: 1. Personality assessment.   BF 698.4D562p]
  BF698.4.D43   1983   155.2′8   82-10822
  ISBN 0-398-04752-9

PREFACE

A HIGH degree of competence in interpreting clinical data is expected of psychologists who assess personality. Yet, psychological interpretation is a topic that is not covered in depth in either texts for graduate students or in reference books for psychologists engaged in personality assessment and testing. Neither are there definitive or "classical" works that describe the process of interpretation. This volume attempts to fill this gap by articulating the systematic thinking, evaluating, weighing, and analyzing processes that are used to draw interpretive conclusions from clinical data. The book takes the view that the logical processes used in interpretation are basic skills for conducting personality assessment in keeping with the spirit of scientific inquiry.

The goals of the volume are (1) to make explicit the operations used to interpret clinical data, and (2) to demonstrate by a case study the rigorous thinking required to analyze and interpret raw and scored data obtained from a psychological test battery. To do this, the volume covers several topics in detail: It reviews the literature on interpretation; it discusses other literature pertinent to interpretation; it summarizes the operations used in interpretation; and it familiarizes the reader with professional codes of the American Psychological Association and the American Personnel and Guidance Association that bear on interpretation. In addition, a large share of the volume presents a case study that demonstrates how to interpret clinical data as discussed in earlier chapters.

An additional goal of the volume is to clarify the extent to which scientific thinking can and cannot be employed when interpreting data for personality assessment. Personality assessment is referred to by some people as more of an art form than a science, though it is not treated as such here. This volume does not delve into mystical or esoteric doctrines about interpretation, nor does it probe the intuitive aspects of interpretation. Instead, it is limited to discussing the *extent* to which interpretation can be carried out "scientifically."

v

The work contains two parts:

Section I discusses research findings and other literature pertinent to interpretation. It surveys personality assessment textbooks and other training literature on interpretation, and discusses the clinical method, clinical judgment, critical-thinking, problem-solving, decision-making, and ethics as they relate to interpretation. General works on scientific inquiry, inference, and logic are also used to make explicit the scientific standards and methods used in interpretation. A summary lists eighteen logical operations involved in the interpretation process.

Section II uses information in Section I to demonstrate sound interpretation in a case study. The case study uses data from six standard psychological tests which were administered to a subject whose identity is disguised. These six tests, comprised of the Wechsler Adult Intelligence Scale (WAIS), Bender-Gestalt, Rorschach, Draw-A-Person Test, Thematic Apperception Test (TAT), and Minnesota Multiphasic Personality Inventory (MMPI), constitute a test battery such as might be used by many clinicians working with adults. In the case study, empirical literature about each test is reviewed. Then the test data for the subject is presented. Finally, inferences are drawn, hypotheses tested, and interpretations presented in a formulation that accompanies each set of test data.

The case study demonstrates interpretation as a logical and conscious process. For example, it verbalizes implicit hypotheses and shows how alternate hypotheses are rejected. Inferences are traced to their sources in the data, and their theoretical and/or empirical bases are stated. The interpretative hypotheses used in the case study are drawn from a variety of sources, such as, clinical lore, test literature, personality theory, and research literature. An eclectic approach is taken in order to follow, as closely as possible, contemporary approaches to interpretation.

A psychological report similar to those prepared by psychologists in the course of their work with clients is presented in Chapter 13. It integrates the findings from each test into a comprehensive picture of the subject. If the case study is successful, the reader should be able to trace the line of reasoning used to analyze the data, draw inferences, test and cross-validate them, and formulate them into the psychological report.

This book is written for graduate students and professional psychologists. In writing style I have tried to follow Klopfer (1960) by avoiding clinical jargon and instead focusing on simple descriptive language. The volume cites old, new, and many "middle-aged" references. The middle-aged references contain most major findings about personality assessment and testing. Perhaps because these topics were largely developed by people of an older generation, we are apt to dismiss their ideas as dated. Yet, as each new generation seems to learn, its best ideas are often the rediscovery of older thoughts.

I hope this volume will help students of psychology become more conscious of the necessary steps and mental rigors required to achieve high professional standards in their work. I also hope that in the long run, in its own small way, the volume might help to increase the rigor of thought used by clinicians in preparing psychological reports, and thereby enhance the validity of clinical findings and the accuracy of personality descriptions.

INTRODUCTION

MANY psychologists employed in clinical and research settings are routinely called upon to draw up detailed personality profiles of clients. Yet, research findings indicate that the validity of such "clinical assessments" is often very poor and many psychologists lack proper skills in interpretation. The sheer size of the task a personality assessor faces in mentally processing the thousands of bits of information s/he works with for one client while conducting a psychological assessment makes the assessor prone to logical error in view of the fact that, generally speaking, the difficulty of a logical problem increases with its size (Bourne, Ekstrand, and Dominowski, 1971).

Not all invalid findings in assessment result from faulty interpretation, however. They can also derive from poorly constructed tests, faulty data, and inaccurate scoring, to name but a few of the possible sources of error. Nonetheless, faulty interpretation can be the weak link that produces invalid results in an otherwise strong chain of clinical skills.

EVIDENCE OF FAULTY INTERPRETATION SKILLS AMONG CLINICIANS

A high level of skill in interpretation should be mastered before any psychologist attempts to conduct personality assessments or formulate psychological reports professionally. Unfortunately, however, studies of psychological interpretations produced by clinicians indicate that the interpretation skills of many professionals are insufficient or inconsistent. Their interpretations vary greatly in reliability and validity, and fallacious interpretations are not uncommon (Slovic and Lichtenstein, 1971; Slovic, Fischhoff, and Lichtenstein, 1977).

Faulty interpreting has a direct and negative impact on the validity of clinical findings and on the value of psychological reports to mental health workers. For example, in a series of studies in which professional colleagues of clinicians rated the quality of psychological reports prepared by the clinicians, the reports generally received poor ratings on inference and interpretation. Coworkers judged many of the interpretations contained in the reports to be farfetched and consequently questioned the validity and reliability of the psychological reports in general (Tallent and Reiss, 1959a, 1959b, 1959c).

Perhaps, though, the judgment of the coworkers in Tallent and Reiss' study was at fault and not that of the clinicians. Other studies suggest this is unlikely. The fallability of clinicians' judgments has had a long history in psychology (see Goldberg, 1968; and Einhorn and Hogarth, 1978, for reviews). For example, the predictive ability of clinicians has been shown to have as low as zero validity in clinical settings (Einhorn, 1972; Goldberg, 1968, and his references). Moreover, the amount of professional training and clinical experience a clinician has fails to relate to his judgmental accuracy (Goldberg, 1959, 1968, and his references). Nor does the availability of additional information about the subject increase his accuracy (Hunt and Walker, 1966), even though it tends to make his confidence in his ratings soar (Oskamp, 1965). Some clinicians persistently use invalid diagnostic signs (Chapman and Chapman, 1967, 1969); others exhibit a seemingly unshakable confidence in their judgmental ability even when confronted with considerable evidence that invalid conclusions are likely to be produced by them (Lichtenstein, Fischhoff, and Phillips, 1977). This "illusion of validity" persists even when it is recognized as such by clinicians (Kahneman and Tversky, 1973, p. 249).

We cannot assume that psychologists automatically use good logic when they interpret clinical data. Some studies indicate that a lack of rigor is apt to be found even among trained professionals. Sawyer (1966), echoing Meehl (1954), found that clinicians tend to be highly inefficient combiners of data. Unfortunately for clinicians, difficulty with the ability to logically integrate information interferes with the ability to predict performance (Dawes and Corrigan, 1974). Moreover, it is known that the degree of judgmental error increases with the size of the information load to be processed (Lueger and Petzel, 1979). Considering the large volume of information that the clinician must mentally process in a personality assessment (information drawn from behavioral impressions, test scores, research literature, personality theories, and from his past experiences with similar clients) and considering the tremendous exercise in logic this entails, it is not unlikely that the accuracy of an assessment would be dramatically impaired by errors in logic.

Only rarely are data available that permit an analysis of the logical thinking actually followed by the clinician when s/he interprets clinical data (Kelly, 1967, pp. 77-78). That which is available is incomplete, whether the clinician is verbalizing his thoughts into a tape recorder as s/he processes data or whether s/he is using introspection to describe his thinking (Koester, 1951; McArthur, 1954; Parker, 1958). For example, in his noted book *The Clinical Application of Psychological Tests*, Schafer (1948, p. 336) tried to, "verbalize the step-by-step process of interpretation of test results." However, he did not demonstrate hypothesis testing and testing of null and alternate hypotheses, nor did he distinguish hypotheses drawn from theory from those drawn from research literature. His exposition was limited to describing inferences he drew from each test and the extent to which they were supported by results from other tests used. This is insufficient information for the reader to follow Schafer's line of reasoning. A second example of incompleteness in the presentation of the thinking used in interpretation is Fowler and Epting's case study (1976) of a thirty-five-year-old white male who was referred to them for a diagnostic personality evaluation. The authors' stated intention in their article was to describe and demonstrate their methodology for interpreting the data. Yet, Stones (1978), in reviewing Fowler and Epting's article, could not find any breakdown of the logical steps taken in interpreting the data—nor could I.

Evidence of the irrationality of clinicians as expert judges has been reviewed by Einhorn and Hogarth (1978). Their conclusions suggest that the fuzzy thinking and impulsiveness that clinicians may find in their clients are also apt to be present in their own thinking, even when they "think" in a professional capacity. Nonetheless, some clinicians produce highly valid interpretations. Several studies (to be discussed in Chapter 3) have found that a moderate proportion of clinicians, about 20 to 25 percent, make excellent interpretations with high predictive validity. In other words, they tend to be right about their clients. What is their secret? Although at this point little research has been conducted to explain differences in interpretation skill among clinicians, it is known that *proper* training and experience, and the ability to logically integrate large amounts of input data, are critical elements (Wiggins, 1973, p. 180).

Good interpretation skills are necessary for valid and ethical personality assessment. However, no work has been published yet, to my knowledge, whose primary purpose is to describe the logical skills necessary to interpret clinical data properly and to demonstrate the mental processes involved in selecting and testing interpretative hypotheses. Consequently, there is a clear gap in the training literature available to students and psychologists. This volume attempts to address this gap in the literature.

THE NEED FOR A DESCRIPTION OF HOW TO INTERPRET

As long as 1948, Roy Schafer, author of the now classic *The Clinical Application of Psychological Tests* (1948) and co-author of the earlier classic *Diagnostic Psychological Testing* (Rapaport, Gill, and Schafer, 1945-6), called for publications that would make clear the methods of analysis used by psychologists. He wrote (1948, p. 336),

> It is important to the future practice of clinical testing that our methods of analysis be presented in publications with as great care as our conclusions. Only if these analytic principles are exposed to general view and thereby to general criticism can we hope to refine them, render them more communicable, and reclaim them as much as possible from the realm of private insights and "art."

Although Schafer wrote these words speaking as a psychoanalytic thinker, both analytic and nonanalytic thinkers, such as Fowler and Epting (1976), Garfield (1963), Ramzy (1974), and Stones (1978), have echoed his sentiments about the need for clear exposition of the principles of interpretation.

It is surprising, then, that there is no literature in psychology that describes how interpretation is done. A number of different paths have been followed, starting in the 1940s and continuing to the present, in attempts to understand the thinking clinicians use in going from data to final conclusions about a subject. However, the review of literature in Chapter 2 finds no literature that traces step-by-step the rigorous thinking required to analyze and interpret personality assessment data. Let us briefly contemplate why this is so.

Studies of Clinical Thinking

Early attempts to understand clinical thinking in the 1940s were marked by introspection as individual psychologists tried to study their own thinking. However, introspection became increasingly suspect for its lack of a scientific methodology, and research moved to a more objective approach: studying the accuracy of clinical judgments. This research produced a host of findings, summarized by Goldberg (1968, p. 485), that tended to be negative. Clinical judgments were discovered to be:

(a) Rather unreliable, except with regard to the same judge using the same data;

(b) Only minimally related to the confidence and to the amount of experience of the judge;

(c) Relatively unaffected by the amount of information available to the judge;

(d) Rather low in validity.

Consequently, a number of psychologists turned away from the field of personality assessment as far as it employed clinical method, and began to use more formalized psychometric forms of processing data so that the clinician's judgmental role in the process of interpretation would be minimal.

Other psychologists kept research interest alive in the area of clinical thinking by directing their attention away from the poor validity of many clinical findings and toward the process of reaching those findings. Unfortunately, I believe, at this juncture research took an unfortunate turn. Rather than focusing their efforts on discovering the constituent elements of accurate clinical judgment,[1] researchers turned their attention away from good clinical thinking

---

[1] Researchers did not seek a model of clinical thinking which would describe how clinical judgment *should* be done to produce *valid* results. They did not examine the thinking of good judges to determine the make-up of accurate judgment. Perhaps the emphasis of clinical method on intuition and empathy made researchers pessimistic that a rational process could be described.

per se and developed mathematical simulations that could, given the data used by clinicians, produce the same results as the clinicians, regardless of the validity of those judgments. No attempt was made to describe actual mental steps followed by clinicians with *good* judgment who produced accurate results (with the exception of earlier work in the 1950s by Koester, 1951; McArthur, 1954; and Parker, 1958.) Instead, mathematical models were built that could replicate clinical findings and eliminate the need for a human thinker to process the data. Not surprisingly, this research produced a number of models that could perform at least as well as clinicians on predictive and diagnostic tasks and opened the door for more psychometric-research and the development of a plethora of new psychometric technologies and tests, and computerized interpretation services (Hoffman, 1960; Hammond, Hursch, and Todd, 1964; Naylor and Wherry, 1965).

As early as 1960, Paul Meehl in his widely read article in the *American Psychologist*, "The Cognitive Activity of the Clinician" (1960), reiterated the need for literature about clinical processes to distinguish formal *diagnosis* (or the attachment of a nosological label) from *prognosis* (or predictive assertions) and from *personality assessment* (or description), since each performs different functions for the psychologist and depends upon different styles of cognitive activity by him. Yet, "personality assessment" was seldom used by name or distinguished from diagnosis and prediction in clinical literature. Instead, "psychodiagnosis," "prediction," and "psychodiagnostic assessment" became popular terms to describe the activities of clinicians. Somehow, "personality assessment" became subsumed under the others, such that by 1981 Korchin and Schuldberg (1981), in reviewing the current state of clinical assessment, had to note that "psychodiagnosis" had become the word commonly used in psychology literature for personality assessment even though the term is ill-suited and invites confusion about personality assessment.[2]

This problem with language has confounded the literature and made it difficult to distinguish logical methods used for diagnosis and

----

[2]For example, Weiner (1972) defended psychodiagnosis against criticism that it was unsuccessful in predicting behavior on the grounds that, "The purpose of psychodiagnostic assessment is not to predict behavior. Rather its purpose is to appraise personality processes...[it] is a descriptive procedure concerned with appraising personality processes." (p. 535)

prediction from those used for description. Writers would purport they were going to discuss methods for describing personality, but then would restrict their research to predictive and diagnostic outcome (such as, Hoffman, 1960). Nevertheless, they would apply their findings to personality assessment and draw inappropriate conclusions about personality assessment's methodology (such as, Sarbin, Taft, and Bailey, 1960). Consequently, personality assessment and the interpretation methodology used in it have been obscured, misunderstood, and misrepresented in the literature about clinicians and clinical processes. Surely this is an odd state of affairs since the *method of arriving at* interpretations is the cornerstone of personality assessment. Without a description of how to interpret, how can interpretation be studied, improved upon, and conceptually validated? How can interpretation be mastered by psychologists? And without mastery of interpretation, what chance do psychologists' interpretative conclusions have of bearing up to the scrutiny of validity studies? Several possible reasons for this state of affairs are discussed below.

WHY IS A DESCRIPTION OF HOW TO INTERPRET LACKING?

We can only speculate about the lack of information about how to interpret. Part of the explanation may rest with the origins of the term "interpretation," which were psychoanalytic.

Interpretation in Psychoanalysis

Sigmund Freud (1887-1902), the originator of psychoanalysis, was one of the first modern thinkers to apply the methods of logic used in interpretation to enable the mind of one person to infer the personality dynamics of another. William James (1890), another early expert at introspection, did not focus his attention on methodology to the extent that others could replicate his findings about himself. Here lay Freud's genius. He laboriously tried to spell out a new method by which one psychoanalyst could find the same personality dynamics in a client as another psychoanalyst.

Freud's purpose, and his student psychoanalysts' purpose, was not to measure traits or characteristics using standardized measures.

Instead, their aim was to develop a methodology for exploring the human psyche and for discovering how it works, changes, and grows. Using interpretation, they sought to infer the psyche's living activities or "dynamics," a concept dating back to Freud, and to describe each personality in these terms. This was the unique task that made psychoanalysis innovative in modern thinking. The fact that in the process of their examination of psyches, psychoanalysts discovered general principles that held true across many individuals has been criticized as a highly culture-bound finding. This may be the case. Nonetheless, their contribution to psychology of logical tools for inferring personality dynamics stands.

However, psychoanalysis failed to be integrated into the main-stream of science. Steiner (1977) has written about this topic and also about the scientific content of psychoanalysis. Apparently, there has not yet been sufficient perspective on psychoanalysis among its adherents, critics, and commentators, alike, to permit clear state-ments about what is scientific about psychoanalysis and what is not. Part of psychoanalytic methodology uses logical, rational treatment of data; in addition, the psychoanalyst's intuition, empathy, and self-knowledge are also used to interpret data. The latter is not ac-ceptable within the sciences as a basis for drawing conclusions: it can be used for generating ideas or hypotheses, but not for establishing them scientifically. Moreover, concepts regarding the inner struc-ture of personality, such as, ego, id, and defenses, which are employed by psychoanalysts, are of questionable value to scientists who do not think the psyche can be discussed scientifically. Because of its close interweaving of scientific and nonscientific methods, psychoanalysis was never integrated into science, nor were its methods and conclusions, i.e. interpretations, recognized by psy-chologists as scientifically respectable, minimally because by defini-tion science employs the intellect rather than intuition to pursue truths of nature.

In spite of questions about the role of interpretive methodology in psychoanalysis, psychologists began using interpretation in other clinical specialties. Perhaps because of its controversial role in psychoanalysis, interpretation was slow to gain sufficient stature to be treated seriously in scientific journals. Alternatively, perhaps psychologists have been less than eager to have the unscientific parts of their methodology pointed to from fear that a description of the process of interpretation used by many psychologists would evoke criticism of the field.

A second possible reason for the lack of literature about the logical methods used in interpretation may be that it is a very difficult process to describe. Ramzy (1974, 1976), in his reviews of literature that purports to trace or treat the logical steps of the interpretative process, found that that some authors begged the question, and the other authors who struggled to trace the logical operations virtually concluded that the steps would never be verbalized. Ramzy's sources were psychoanalytic and neo-analytic. However, since he included in his reviews such authors as Erik Erikson (1958) and David Rapaport (1967), men who have played prominent roles in shaping the thinking of psychoanalytic and nonanalytic psychologists alike, his findings are significant across psychological specialties. What Ramzy found in surveying a large body of psychology literature is little if any clear expositions regarding the proper use of interpretation by psychoanalysts. He wrote (1974),

> Unbelievable as it may sound, in the whole vast library of psycho-analysis — clinical, theoretical, technical, or applied — there are hardly any references which outline the logical guidelines or the methodological rules which the analyst follows in order to understand the patient.

In psychoanalysis, interpretation weaves together rationality, ideology, and intuition. These ingredients may indeed make it impossible to describe interpretation in general terms because it is consequently idiosyncratic to the analyst. However, interpretation that is used in personality assessment can be viewed as a logical and rational process. This would make it more amenable to description than psychoanalytic interpretation. Let us then look beyond psychoanalysis for reasons why a description of the interpretative process, as a rational process for personality assessment, is lacking in the literature.

Interpretation and Unclear Language

Another possible reason for the lack of literature on interpretation methodology has to do with language usage and the failure of psychology to use language with the same clarity demanded by science. Because obscure language is often used in psychological writing, the idea that interpretation can be a rational process involving more than just inference as Sarbin, Taft, and Bailey's (1960) influential book claimed may have been lost in the verbiage.

The meaning of "interpretation" as it is used in clinical psychology and personality assessment has not been distinguished from its meaning in psychoanalysis. Consequently, the word may evoke images of logical methods in one listener's ear and psychoanalytic symbolism in another's. To one it may connote an arbitrary and subjective process; to another, a rational one.

The word "interpretation" does not have a clearly defined meaning in psychological writing and is frequently used with unclear syntax. It currently can mean:

(1) An interpretative *hypothesis* that may be associated with clinical data;
(2) A *descriptive conclusion* about a person that has been tested and reformulated, if necessary, using interpretive methodology;
(3) The *process* of arriving at descriptive conclusions about a person.

In psychoanalytic and nonpsychoanalytic literature the word "interpretation" is used with all three meanings. Yet, when authors use it, it is often unclear which of the three meanings they intend. For example, the titles of two recent books about interpretation, Gilbert's *Interpreting Psychological Test Data* (1978) and Golden's *Clinical Interpretation of Objective Psychological Tests* (1979), seem to imply the third meaning of "interpretation" and we expect discussions of how to interpret. But the syntax of the titles is misleading. The two books deal with interpretative hypotheses only.

A substantial portion of the literature on psychological interpretation could lead the uncritical reader to think that interpretations listed in such books are interpretative conclusions and that interpreting simply means looking up some possible interpretations to see which ones seem to fit the data best. Alternatively, the unwary reader of clinical inference literature may come to think that interpreting means coming up with interpretive hypotheses to explain the data before him. If our neophyte reader peruses psychoanalytic or thematic psychological literature, s/he may again misconstrue interpretation to mean inventing symbols and metaphors to explain the data. All three ideas, of course, are incomplete oversimplifications. In terms of its broad outlines, interpretation methodology starts with a set of interpretative hypotheses (obtained from reference books, research literature, personality theories, brainstorming, and elsewhere) which are all possible explanations of the data. Then each hypothesis is tested against the data and reformulated (or rejected) as necessary. Only those hypotheses that survive this testing plus many other logical checks and double checks called for in the interpretive process survive to become interpretive conclusions.

To avoid confusion about the meaning of the word "interpretation" in this book, we often use "interpretative hypothesis" to convey the first meaning of interpretation; "interpretative conclusion" for the second meaning; and "interpretation methodology" or "interpretation process" for the third meaning.

DESCRIBING INTERPRETATION METHODOLOGY

So far we have discussed the need for accurate interpretation, evidence of faulty interpreting, and reasons why interpretation methodology has not yet been clearly described in the literature. This brings us back to the purpose of this book: to attempt such a description. How shall we proceed? First we need a clearer idea of what interpretation is. Let us digress briefly and place interpretation in a larger context to gain some perspective on it.

Interpretation is the principal methodology used in personality assessment. Personality assessment is the study of the inner person, the one who experiences life and dwells in the human body. In particular, it is the part of psychology that tries to *describe* the psyche of the *individual*. Personality assessment does not aim to discover general principles of the psyche, or to find out what the psyche is composed of, what energizes it, or how it interfaces with the body (although these could be offshoots of its activities.) These topics are all dealt with in other psychology specialties.

Interpretation is the disciplined type of thinking used in personality assessment to construct accurate descriptive statements from data about a person. Interpretation can thus be seen as the methodology used in psychology when a description of the inner life of an individual is sought.

When psychology functions as a strictly empirical discipline, it approaches being a science, but it is not amenable to studying the inner person: When psychology tackles the psyche head on, it must diverge from scientific inquiry (a) because of the assumptions made about its subject matter (these are discussed in Chapter 1), and (b) because the researcher's mind — not empiricism or experimentation — is the major tool used to draw conclusions from data. The latter can be done using intuition or rationality, or both, as in the clinical method. Yet using intuition arbitrarily divorces psychological methodology from science. In order to retain some kinship with science, intuition may be used in personality assessment to generate ideas and hypotheses. But once the process of interpretation begins, logic is paramount.

With this general context for interpretation in mind, how should we approach describing interpretation methodology in more detail? For starters, we need some criteria about what constitutes a description of the interpretation process. To adequately portray how interpretation is best used in personality assessment, a description of methodology should take into account four topics that bear on interpretation:

> Logical thinking
> Codes of ethics
> Clinical processes
> Scientific inquiry

In addition, to be useful in research and training, a description of interpretation methodology should provide both concepts and a framework for studying, teaching, and analyzing interpretation. These five requirements are formulated below into criteria to use for drawing up a description of interpretation methodology. They form the backbone of Part I of this book, where we attempt to *describe* the interpretive process.

A description of interpretation methodology should:

(1) Describe the extent to which the processes characteristic of science can be applied when interpreting. Examples of scientific methodology which should be discussed are: selecting interpretative hypotheses, testing hypotheses, testing alternate

hypotheses, reformulating hypotheses.

(2) Describe the extent to which disciplined inquiry used in interpreting cannot be done scientifically and must depend upon clinical assumptions and methods.

(3) Be consistent with professional codes of ethics about psychological interpretation, in general, and their employment in personality assessment, in particular.

(4) Provide logical concepts for describing how to move from data about a person to interpretative conclusions about his personality.

(5) Provide a framework for tracking and analyzing the thinking used by personality assessors to draw interpretative conclusions from data.

Before proceeding to Chapter 1, some criteria are also needed for discussing *demonstrations* of how to interpret. In the personality assessment literature reviewed in Chapter 2, a number of authors purport to demonstrate how to interpret clinical data by presenting didactic case studies. But their demonstrations tend to be incomplete with regard to interpretation methodology. They typically provide the data, state their hypotheses and then discuss their interpretative conclusions. Missing is information about the line of thinking and logical processes they used to interpret the data and test their interpretative hypotheses. What, then, are some criteria to use for evaluating case studies that try to demonstrate interpretation methodology? It would be difficult for a demonstration ever to be thoroughly complete because thousands of mental operations are involved in analyzing and interpreting data from just one test like the WAIS, much less from a battery of tests. To allow a reader to generally follow the line of reasoning in an assessment, a demonstration should try to:

(1) Verbalize each interpretative hypothesis used and make explicit reference to the source of each interpretative hypothesis so that the reader may consider the rationale for hypothesis selection. Sources of interpretative hypotheses include:

Personality theory
Test literature
Clinical experience of the assessor

Clinical lore, or the accumulated experience of many assessors

Other empirical literature

(2) Verbalize alternate hypotheses and their sources so that the reader can determine the extent to which alternative explanations of the data were considered.

(3) Verbalize reformulated hypotheses and the logical inconsistencies which caused their reformulation so that the reader can monitor the increasing scope of data that are explained by the hypotheses.

(4) Verbalize the rationale for eliminating hypotheses that were unproductive. This gives the reader a window on the way hypotheses are tested against data and against each other for logical inconsistencies.

(5) Cite the source in the data and any relevant empirical literature for each interpretative conclusion so that the reader can consider the basis for the conclusion. This information lets the reader consider the amount of data explained by hypotheses that were retained versus those that were rejected. It also informs the reader about supplemental information that bears on the assessor's interpretative conclusions.

(6) Demonstrate interpretation on a battery of psychological test data since this is the type of data personality assessment is likely to involve. One great difficulty in learning to interpret is learning to deal with the large quantity of data frequently used in case studies. Demonstrations of interpretation that do not use a battery of test data do not deal with a major difficulty encountered when interpreting data for personality assessment.

These six criteria are the standards used in our attempt to *demonstrate* interpretation methodology in Section II of this book.

CONTENTS

Section I. The Interpretation Process

Section II. Interpretation Demonstrated: A Case Study

LIST OF TABLES

PERSONALITY ASSESSMENT
AND
PSYCHOLOGICAL
INTERPRETATION

SECTION I

The Interpretation Process

CHAPTER 1

INTERPRETATION IN PERSONALITY ASSESSMENT

INTRODUCTORY STATEMENT

PERSONALITY assessment is the study of persons "in depth." Simple as it may be to say, this is a difficult task to accomplish in practice. The current state of personality assessment has been called one of "confusion, misconception, attack, and counter attack" (Sloves, Docherty, and Schneider, 1979). The nature, methods, and goals of personality assessment continue to be vigorously debated. Little agreement exists as to what personality assessment should be; still less, about its scientific status.

One component of personality assessment that has received relatively little critical attention is interpretation (Ramzy, 1976). Interpretation is the process a psychologist employs to give meaning to data about an individual. Interpretation includes (1) analyzing the data and translating it, via hypothesis and inference, into descriptive terminology, (2) testing and validating hypotheses, and (3) formulating those conclusions that have survived intensive logical scrutiny into an organized, composite picture of the individual.

In psychology, interpretation is an integral part of the clinical scene. Any clinician worth his salt interprets as s/he prepares personality profiles of patients and clients. Academic "personologists," or specialists in personality, also interpret when they prepare detailed case studies about the lives of individuals. Interpretation enables the researcher, as well as the therapist, to plumb the depths of the individual's psyche in an attempt to understand human nature.

Interpretation relies on the disciplined application of the assessor's intellectual skill. When not done accurately, interpretation produces false positives if data is faulty; it produces false negatives if methodology is at fault. When done correctly, it produces what is intended: the accurate description of latent and manifest personality processes and characteristics.

Despite its importance to the psychologist, interpretation has "low visibility" in personality assessment literature. The reason why interpretation is seldom critically examined is unclear. Perhaps it is because the interpretation process is taken for granted that it is seldom made explicit in personality assessment and has largely avoided academic scrutiny. Psychologists may also be less than eager to examine one another's interpretations, since the quality of a colleague's interpretations can be taken as a direct reflection of his skill in logic. Such investigations could prove embarrassing in a profession which rightly assumes that competence in rigorous thinking is a minimum requirement for professional standing. Rather than interpretation, what is commonly studied in personality assessment are issues that are legal and ethical (Bersoff, 1975), empirical (Kamin, 1974), conceptual (Bersoff, 1971, 1973; Ebel, 1974), and sociopolitical (Williams, 1971).[1]

In this Chapter we look at the role interpretation plays in personality assessment. The first section of the Chapter, "An In-Depth Look at the Individual," discusses the importance of interpretation methodology to the study of personality. The following three sections examine the relationship between interpretation and several major components of personality assessment: case studies, clinical method, psychological testing, and psychological reports.

AN IN-DEPTH LOOK AT THE INDIVIDUAL

Many psychologists spend substantial portions of their careers studying individual people intensively. "Personality assessment" is the name of one particular approach to studying the individual, one which has in-depth *description* of the individual as its goal. Personality assessment seeks to describe the person in terms that make clear the uniqueness of his personality.

What then is "personality?" Personality is a difficult term to define. Many authors have attempted definitions but none is accepted as a standard for psychology. For the time being we shall borrow Robert Holt's approach to personality (Janis, Mahl, Kagan, and Holt, 1969, p. 577). Holt sees personality as a weaving together of traits, or predispositions to behave in certain ways, and *patterns* of traits. The idea of a *unique* personality comes from both the outstand-

---

[1] Sloves, Docherty, and Schneider (1979, p. 29).

ing characteristics a person manifests and from the different strengths and weaknesses s/he shows when s/he is compared with other people on many different criteria. A person will be found to have a unique "pattern of deeds, feelings, and thoughts" when enough information is gathered about him (p. 577).

Because personality encompasses both actions *and* thoughts and feelings, the subject matter for personality assessment is both objective and subjective. It is objective when overt behaviors of a person are observed and reported upon by trained impartial observers whose findings can be substantiated by other impartial observers. It is subjective when the individual's own experience of himself and his life are examined. Unfortunately, however, the dual nature of personality raises great problems for the psychologist because the subjective aspect of personality is not amenable to scientific study. Consequently, to accomplish the goal of in-depth description, personality assessors use methodologies that make some compromises with science in order to retain subjective phenomena as subject matter. Let us digress briefly to see why this is so.

Psychology ideally is the study of the human "psyche," or the scientific study of the human emotional and mental apparatuses, the mind and soul, so to speak. In practice, psychologists have found they cannot readily carry out this endeavor. The closer they approach direct contact with a person's inner apparatus, as with, for example, psychotherapy, introspection, and psychoanalysis, the less scientific their methods; the more scientific rigor they employ, such as in experimental, comparative, and physiological psychology, the less they make direct contact with a real human psyche, and the more its functioning must be inferred from overt behavior and operationalized measures. To be more scientific and have less access to the psyche or to be less scientific and have direct contact with the psyche is the dilemma facing psychology.

In personality assessment this dilemma is generally dealt with by sacrificing some degree of scientific rigor and retaining direct contact with the psyche. This is particularly true for psychologists who conduct personality assessments in order to understand a *unique individual*, his *experience* of the world, and the *organization* of his inner life. Psychologists who conduct personality assessments generally believe the individual's experience of life, his personal thoughts and feelings, for example, are worthy subject matter for assessment and constitute important information for determining the makeup of the individual's personality. They are apt to relegate scientific methods to a secondary position if their ability to better understand this aspect of a person is at stake. For example, the psychologist will try to look at his client's problems through the client's eyes in order to better perceive them, and will seek explanations from the patient so that problems can be stated in the patient's own words and understood in the context of the patient's life experience. The psychologist will present his client with novel stimuli to see how he reasons and reacts in unusual circumstances, and also to elicit feelings or beliefs that might interfere with his satisfaction with life.

The personality assessor also assumes that the client's experience can be understood rationally and logically when sufficient information about the client is available and organized and analyzed systematically. Our digression has brought us back to the topic of methodology in personality assessment. We see that the assessor cannot use scientific methodology when s/he studies subjective aspects of personality. Instead, the methodology the assessor depends on is tight logic and reason. This understanding of the crucial role logic and reason play in assessment will help us understand the importance of the interpretation process to personality assessment. Interpretation *is* the process of systematically applying logic and reason as a methodology for understanding the individual. Without it, personality assessment would be all guesswork and intuition. The next three sections of Chapter 1, "Case Studies and the Clinical Method," "Psychological Tests," and "Psychological Reports," describe the role of interpretation in personality assessment in more detail.

CASE STUDIES AND THE CLINICAL METHOD

Psychologists who seek to describe the unique individual using personality assessment frequently employ the case study. "Case study" is the name given to research design when n = 1 (see, for example, Chassan, 1979; Dukes, 1965; White, 1975a, 1975b). The case study has a history in psychology dating back to the last century with such noted studies as Ebbinghaus' (1885) investigation of memory, Bryan and Harter's (1899) pioneer study of learning, and Stratton's (1897) famous account of the confusion caused by wearing inverting lenses. Noted cases in the study of personality where n = 1 included Prince's account (1905) of Miss Beauchamp's multiple personalities, and the case of Anna O. (Breuer and Freud, 1895) which helped launch psychoanalysis. Case studes continue to make important contributions to the psychology literature (Dukes, 1965) with studies of personality accounting for about 30 percent of the case study literature (Dukes, 1965).

Case studies have both advantages and disadvantages as a form of research design. The case study is advantageous when (1) inter-subject variability is low, that is, when there is not much difference from one subject to the next with regard to the variables under study; (2) when only rare opportunities are available to study the phenomenon in question, as in the case of a rare disease or condition; and (3) when it is thought that a certain relationship exists universally, but an exception is found (Dukes, 1965). We can thus see that the case study is ideally suited for exploring the uniqueness of an individual and describing his total personality.

Unfortunately, although the case study is a typical way to study the individual personality, it is not strictly scientific or experimental. Campbell and Stanley (1963) have pointed out that in real experiments an independent variable is manipulated by the experimenter and *changes* in dependent variables monitored. The only changes that can be monitored using case study design are historical, and these are not particularly relevant to personality assessment. For example, in case studies that examine historical change, a person may be observed over a period of time and measures of certain characteristics taken at intervals. Then statistical analysis is employed to document changes in the features that were measured. However, in personality assessment, *description* of the personality as it is, not the documentation of change, is the purpose of the case study. For example, in a typical personality assessment, all the data about an individual may be acquired in only one or two meetings between the subject and the assessor; no independent variables are manipulated in controlled situations and no dependent variables are monitored over time. Hence an experimental research design is inapplicable, except for validation purposes. The personality assessor generally does try to infer which personality characteristics are stable and which are transient, from his knowledge of theory and empirical literature on traits and patterns. Yet, it is only rarely that s/he has the opportunity to retest the individual at a later date to verify these assertions or to get feedback from the client or other professionals who deal with him down the road. Thus the assessor only has the rigor of his methodology to rely on and justify his conclusions.

What then are the methodological safeguards that make personality assessment in the form of a case study a respectable undertaking for psychologists? Traditionally the answer lay in the clinical method. "Clinical method," by definition, is the study of one person by a trained professional who examines another person directly and uses his mind to draw conclusions about the other.

The clinical method is amenable to both description of personality and to the study of inner personality structures. We have already discussed how inner structures like the mind and emotions are not amenable to examination by strictly scientific methods. In the clinical method, inner structures are inferred from data available to the clinician. Moreover, a broader spectrum of data is used than might be availed of with scientific methods. For example, not only are psychological test scores, objective measures, and a clinician's observations of the person possible sources of data. In addition, the clinician's *experiences* of the client also constitute potential data that can be analyzed and compared with the clinician's backlog of experience of other clients. Statistical analysis is also used, not to document change, as was the case with historical case studies, but to compare an individual's performance on tests with relevant group norms so that attributes and abilities being measured can be described in meaningful contexts.

It is not only the range of data used but also its analysis which distinguishes clinical method from more scientific approaches. Here we encounter "interpretation" with a somewhat different meaning from how we have used it so far. It is the name given to the method of analyzing data and drawing conclusions used in the clinical method (nothing new here), however, in the clinical method it includes not only rational processes but also a strong component of intuition and empathy. In the clinical method, the clinician may use both logic and intuition at all stages of interpretation to draw conclusions from data available about a person. Provided sufficient amounts of data about a client, for example the data in a battery of psychological tests, a clinician can fairly confidently construct a picture of the client's personality. Unfortunately, however, the clinical method has been severely criticized for the prevalence of intuition in its interpretation methodology. In the 1960s and 1970s, a number of noted graduate departments of psychology at major American universities went so far as to drop clinical psychology from their offerings due to its lack of methodological rigor. The low reliability and poor validity of many conclusions drawn by clinicians using the clinical method supported this stance.

Where then does this leave us in our attempt to describe a useful interpretation methodology for personality assessment that is based on rationality? Science is not amenable to studying the inner life of the person; the clinical method provides a set of assumptions that allow personality to be studied, yet its ground rules permit the use of nonlogic which is apt to lead to invalid conclusions. What we need is a selective approach to interpretation.* This will be our task in Chapters 3 and 4, where clinical method is discussed in detail as well as interpretation's relationship to scientific method. There we explore the extent to which interpretation based on the assumptions of clinical method can be used rationally without recourse to intuition. For the time being, however, let us continue to explore the role of interpretation in personality assessment in order to acquire more grounding in our subject matter.

PSYCHOLOGICAL TESTS

Data for case studies can be gathered in a variety of ways. Holt (Janis, Mahl, Kagan, and Holt, 1969, p. 666) has compiled a comprehensive list of methods of collecting data for personality assessment:

(1) Application forms, face sheets, objective records
(2) Interviews
(3) Autobiographies and other personal documents like letters and diaries
(4) Self-descriptive inventories and questionnaires
(5) Projective techniques
(6) Physical and physiological measures and other biological approaches
(7) Judgments by others (behavioral observation, sociometric,

---

*Based on the best of clinical method and on those scientific standards that are compatible with personality description.

and peer ratings)
(8) Objective and situational tests
(9) Tests of intelligence and other abilities
(10) Sociological and anthropological techniques for studying a person's background and culture.

Holt demonstrated the use of data derived from all ten of these methods in his informative case study about "Morris" (Janis, Mahl, Kagan, and Holt, 1969, p. 663-772). He and his colleague, Robert F. Bales, gathered extensive data about Morris during 1940 when Holt and Bales were graduate students at Harvard. Morris, an intelligent, articulate young man, generously gave his full cooperation to the study. Holt later conducted a lengthy and detailed follow-up study of Morris in 1966. The voluminous data gathered for the study spanned twenty-six years and provided Holt with material for one of the most comprehensive personality assessments ever reported in the literature.

Most case studies of personality do not enjoy the wealth of data and length of exposure to their subject that Holt and Bales had. Instead, due to time, financial, and other considerations, personality assessors often depend on various psychological tests that have been developed over the years in laboratory and field settings. Tests allow a sampling of personality data to be gotten from a subject in as little as one to four hours. A battery of psychological tests, objective and projective, are typically employed together with observations of the subject's behavior during test administration (Allison, 1968). Occasionally, this may be supplemented with a verbal history solicited from the client, or with comments of other professionals contained in the client's record. This is the type of data we will limit our discussion of interpretation to, with particular emphasis on psychological tests.

World War II and the post-war era saw a great rise in the use of psychological tests. By 1959 a national sample of clinical psychologists reported spending almost half of their professional time in activities involving testing (Lubin and Lubin, 1972). Since that peak there has been a decline in and criticism of test usage (Korchin and Schuldberg, 1981), such that by 1969, the percentage of time clinicians spent involved with tests was virtually cut in half (Lubin and Lubin, 1972).

Despite its decline in the 1960s, more recent research indicates that testing remains vital for many psychologists. For example, in their survey of 500 psychologists belonging to the American Psychological Association's Clinical Division, Wade and Baker (1977) found that 83 percent used psychological tests for some purpose. In the same study, 75 percent of the psychologists surveyed thought that young clinicians should become familiar with both objective and projective tests. Moreover, in a survey of employers running ads for clinicians in the 1971-1972 APA Employer Bulletin, Levy and Fox (1975) found that 91 percent of the 334 employers surveyed expected their job applicants to have testing skills, and 84 percent wanted clinicians employed by them to have skill in projective techniques.

So testing is still alive and well despite the vicissitudes of time. How does interpretation come to bear on it? Both objective and projective test data are generally given meaning through interpretation. Interpretation is used by the tester to place test data in a context and to infer information regarding various psychological variables that are being assessed. Every high school student is told that his raw scores on intelligence, ability, and other tests have little meaning in and of themselves. Only when they are viewed in comparison with scores of other people and in comparison with one's own effort, other skills and attributes do they begin to make sense. This is the essence of what the personality assessor does when s/he interprets personality test data. After raw scores are tabulated, scaled when necessary, and compared with norms or other referent material, interpretation enters the scene. With it the assessor reasons his way to conclusions about the personality. Thus, interpretation is inseparable from testing because it *is* the process of reasoning that gives test results meaning.

Interpretations made by psychologists based on test data often carry considerable weight in their clients' lives. They are influential in courts of law, mental institutions, medical facilities, schools, and personnel offices. The psychologist's interpretations can directly effect how a treatment team will view a patient and what therapeutic interventions are recommended. They bear on employment decisions, school placement programs, and military recruiting. Thus interpretations made on the basis of test data can have major consequences for the client and lasting effects on his life. For these reasons, responsible interpretation is of paramount importance to psychological testing.

Due to the important social, legal, educational, and medical functions psychological testing serves, it has received increasing, and often critical, attention from the press and public interest groups. Controversy over the proper use of personality testing led to congressional hearings in the mid-1960s. This was the culmination of debates questioning the appropriateness of using personality tests for selecting personnel for employment, particularly in government jobs (Haney, 1981). This dispute, together with public concern over the use of intelligence tests, ability tests, and other standardized tests, has brought psychological testing increasing scrutiny from the legal system (Bersoff, 1981), in addition to monitoring by professional associations and government agencies (Novick, 1981). Because of the strong influence testing (and more specifically, the interpretations based on the tests) have in our society, testing and interpretation are subject to legal controls and professional and ethical standards. The reader is referred to the special issue of the *American Psychologist* (October 1981) on "Testing" for a thorough review of current issues regarding testing and to the *American Psychologist* (June 1981) for a statement of APA's ethical principles and guidelines. In addition, ethical standards that are particularly relevant to interpretation are discussed in Chapter 2 of this book.

PSYCHOLOGICAL REPORTS

The psychological report is the tangible product of the interpretation process in personality assessment. It is used by the assessor to communicate his findings to colleagues and other personnel. Copies are often filed in the client's medical or other permanent records. Psychological reports are frequently prepared in response to a referral question about the client. The nature of the referral question determines the type of psychological report that is prepared.

Psychological reports have been divided into two types: the purely descriptive, and those that are diagnostic and predictive (London and Exner, 1978). Most psychological reports, however, are mixtures of both types. In diagnostic and predictive reports, a short taxonomic description may be rendered for purposes of classifying the salient problems and symptoms that trouble the client. Predictions about future behavior in response to specific stress situations are often included also. Diagnoses made by the assessor generally are based on nosological schemes, such as the categories in the American Psychiatric Association's *Diagnostic and Statistical Manual of Mental Disorders* (DSM-III) (1980), and require specialized skill in psychodiagnostics, a topic not covered in this text.

Psychological reports that focus on description do not depend on nosologies for classifying the individual. Nosologies may be employed as a means to expand the clinician's descriptive vocabulary but not for drawing diagnostic conclusions. Instead of classifying and predicting, the descriptive psychological report is used to describe the uniqueness and totality of the individuality as much as possible (Fowler and Epting, 1976; Klopfer, 1960; Stones, 1978). This kind of report takes the form of an elaborate picture of a person, viewed from many angles, and painted with broad brush strokes. It is used to give the reader a "feel" for the person and provide broad outlines about how the person deals with himself and his surroundings (see, Cronbach, 1960, p. 600-608). Ideally, this is the kind of report prepared in a personality assessment. Using interpretation in order to prepare this kind of psychological report is the focus of this text.

Some early research on clinical thinking by McArthur (1954) hints that the mental steps required for preparing a personality *description* may actually have to be done before accurate prediction and diagnosis can take place. In his study, McArthur asked psychologists to make predictions about several college students from ten-year old case files.* He also had follow-up information about these people, but the psychologists did not. Then McArthur asked each psychologist how s/he had arrived at his formulations. He found that some psychologists were quite accurate in their predictions and others not. He noted that:

(1) Psychologists who judged accurately tended to gradually build a *conceptualization* of the person in the record after viewing the entire record;

(2) Good predictions were made from this construct, not from any single datum;

(3) The accurate psychologists did not base their predictions on any single test or theory. Instead, they felt free to draw each

---

* containing school records, tests, interviews, etc. compiled while each subject was an undergraduate student at Harvard.

conclusion from a variety of results on different tests using diverse theories.

In contrast, the least successful psychologists did not first build a general picture of the subject and did not take an eclectic approach. Instead, for example, they applied rules derived from previous cases or from a psychological theory.

McArthur's observations suggest that to accurately predict from case study material, a psychologist may be well advised to first prepare a composite personality description. Once s/he has this general picture of the client, s/he can then predict from it future behaviors and outcomes for the client. *Therefore, learning to prepare descriptions of personality could be a necessary step before accurate clinical prediction takes place, even though such description is not sought in the referral question or contained in diagnostic or predictive psychological reports.*

What role does interpretation play in preparing a descriptive psychological report, which from this point onward we shall also call a "personality report?" Let us briefly look at the major tasks that must be carried out in a personality assessment to see the relationship between interpretation and the personality report. To conduct a personality assessment, a psychologist typically will:

(1) Select appropriate tests and measures.
(2) Administer the tests and measures in keeping with adequate professional knowledge about test usage in general, and those tests being used, in particular.
(3) Score raw data in keeping with adequate professional knowledge of scoring in general, and the tests in use, in particular.
(4) Analyze the raw data when appropriate in search of patterns and inferences.[2]
(5) Analyze the scored data independently for each test in search of patterns and inferences.[3]
(6) Cross-validate inferences by comparing findings from one test with those from other tests.
(7) Formulate all findings into consistent patterns that hold no logical contradictions. (The patient under study may seem to

---

[2,3] See "Responsibilities of Users of Standardized Tests" (1978) for a list of clarifications regarding analysis of raw data and scored data and the need for independent treatment of test scores.

be illogical, but the assessor's treatment of data about him should not be).

(8) Present findings in a cogent, cohesive, and coherent psychological report.

Mental preparation of the personality report begins with task #4 above and continues through task #7. These tasks, #4 to 7, comprise the process of interpretation. During these steps the psychologist must analyze, infer, cross-validate, deduce, and formulate, all of which are tacit mental processes seldom made explicit in the report. Interpretation culminates in the formulation of the personality picture, when all information from the assessment must be brought together in a logical and meaningful way. This picture is then selectively committed to paper in the psychological report, task #8.

Errors in interpretation or weaknesses in the skills of the psychologist in *any* of the eight tasks that are carried out in a personality assessment can affect the validity of the final report that is communicated to co-workers. Fortunately, considerable literature is available to help students of personality assessment master four of these tasks. Areas with ample instructive literature available are listed below together with sample references:

— Employment of psychological tests in general; their merits and limitations, e.g. Aiken, 1978; Anastasi, 1982; Cronbach, 1976
— Test selection, e.g. Andrulis, 1977; Buros, 1974; Prunkl, 1979
— Test administration and systems for scoring tests, e.g. Bender, 1938; Hathaway and McKinley, 1967; Murray, 1943; Wechsler, 1955, 1958
— Preparation of psychological reports, e.g. Bromley, 1977; Hollis and Donn, 1979; Huber, 1961; Klopfer, 1960; Mack, 1978; Tallent, 1976

Unfortunately, tasks #4 to 7, those which we called the interpretative process, have little literature published about them. Chapter 2, "Review of Literature on Interpretation," documents this fact and discusses its ramifications for personality assessment.

CHAPTER 2

REVIEW OF LITERATURE
ON PSYCHOLOGICAL INTERPRETATION

WHAT literature is there on psychological interpretation? In the last chapter we claimed that the psychology literature does not contain a clear description of how to interpret. It does contain, however, ample material about various aspects of interpretation. In this chapter we briefly describe eight major types of literature that are available on interpretation and point out deficiencies in this literature with regard to its treatment of interpretation methodology. Then we examine in greater depth the three kinds of interpretation literature that have the most bearing on *how to* interpret.

TYPES OF LITERATURE ABOUT INTERPRETATION

A number of authors deal with interpretation in their books and articles but do not attempt any discussion of how to interpret. Instead, an author may, for example, present interpretive hypotheses that can be associated with different clinical findings or test scores, but not attempt to explain how to move beyond the hypothesis stage. As a second example, an author may present a case study in which both test data and interpretive conclusions drawn from it are shown to the reader along with lengthy discussions about these interpretations. However, the thinking process used to derive the interpretations is not made explicit; the justification for the interpretations is the expert opinion of the author and not a logically compelling presentation of interpretation methodology.

Other psychology literature makes reference to interpretation methodology, makes comments that imply such a methodology, or assertions that have implications for interpretation methodology. However, no literature was found by the author that:

(1) Describes the process of interpretation explicitly;
(2) Presents comprehensive methodological principles to guide

the process of interpretation for nonstandardized tests;

(3) Discusses how to select among possible interpretative hypotheses; or

(4) Articulates and demonstrates the logical and mental processes involved in testing hypotheses and formulating interpretative conclusions.

As a way to give the reader an overview of the interpretation literature, eight general types of literature about interpretation are described below. The eight categories are not meant to be exhaustive or mutually exclusive. For example, some literature overlaps several categories. The eight divisions, however, do give us a way to discuss this rather unwieldy literature.

I. A sizeable body of literature catalogues interpretative hypotheses that are associated with different test responses and scores. For example, Ogden's handbook, *Psychodiagnostics and Personality Assessment* (1967), provides useful lists of possible hypotheses to associate with test results on the TAT, Draw-A-Person, Bender-Gestalt, and Rorschach. The hypotheses he lists are drawn from a broad range of empirical literature. Gilbert's more recent volume, *Interpreting Psychological Test Data v. 1* (1978), catalogues interpretative hypotheses associated with test responses drawn from a small number of classical texts on the Bender-Gestalt, Human Figure Drawing, WAIS, and Rorschach. Golden, in his volume *Clinical Interpretation of Objective Psychological Tests* (1979), does the same for a number of standardized tests. This literature does not generally go beyond the hypothesis stage.

II. In a second kind of literature about interpretation, only one test is discussed; clinical applications of the test are described as well as interpretive hypotheses that can be associated with different test responses. Often empirical studies about the test and about working hypotheses are included, but no effort is made to present a general picture of the interpretation process, and the methodology that is included tends to be *ad hoc*. Books of this sort include Gilberstadt and Duker (1965) on the MMPI, Hutt (1969) on the Bender-Gestalt, and Zimmerman and Woo-Sam's volume on the WAIS (1973).

III. A third kind of literature presents interpretive findings about a person in case study form. Often this includes lengthy discussions of the data and the interpretive conclusions. At times these discussions give the reader some insight into the mental processes the author used to interpret the data, but no effort is made to present an overview of interpretation methodology. Examples of such case studies are Fowler and Epting's "The Person in Personality Research: An Alternate Lifestyle Case Study (1976) and Freud's noted study of Dora entitled "Fragment of an Analysis of a Case of Hysteria" (1953). Several textbooks on personality assessment include instructive case study material, such as the case of Morris in Janis, Mahl, Kagan, and Holt (1969) and Pervin and Levenson (1975). These texts are discussed in some detail in the third section of this chapter.

Four books about interpretation also fit this category of literature. They are Allison (1968), Holt (v.1, 1978; v.2, 1978), and Levy (1963). Holt provides two excellent blind interpretations of cases. Each case presents his notes stating his primary references and assorted thoughts. The cases, however, do not draw substantially on empirical literature and do not pursue validation and testing of hypotheses systematically. Allison's volume gives an interpretation of a battery of psychological tests on a person test-by-test. As a useful safeguard, each test is interpreted independently by a different assessor before all their findings are compared. While it is an instructive reference for the student, the weakness in the volume is that each interpretation is stated as fact, not as an hypothesis to test against data and compare with alternate hypotheses. In addition, reference is not made to relevant research literature. Instead, interpretations are solely drawn from psychoanalytic theory. Levy's volume, while one of the most useful available on psychological interpretation, is no longer in print. However, it too, like the other references described in this section, does not systematize the type of thinking used in interpreting data, nor does it attempt to develop guidelines or principles of interpretation.

IV. Books and articles about writing psychological reports sometimes comment on interpretation and constitute a fourth type of literature. Texts about psychological reports generally tell what should be done to write high quality reports, e.g. Klopfer, 1960; Huber, 1961, and lately tend to have how-to-do-it formats, e.g. Hollis and Donn, 1979; Mack, 1978; Tallent, 1976. They discuss such things as mechanical preparation, criteria for good reports, the contents and organization of reports, writing style, and language usage. They also contain samples and models of finished reports. Articles on psychological reports tend to comment on or present research findings related to improving the quality of reports and examining how well the reports are received by readers (e.g. Appelbaum, 1970; Carr, 1968; Korner, 1962; Mayman, 1959; Tallent, 1956, 1958; Tallent and Reiss, 1959a, b, c). With regard to interpretation, psychological report literature calls for responsible interpreting and discusses the degree to which sources of inference should be documented in reports. It does not, however, describe or demonstrate the thinking used to analyze and interpret data and this is not its intention. In addition, case studies presented in this literature focus on the finished report, and tend to be limited to small samples of test data, with brief, if any, explicit portrayal of the methodology used to derive conclusions for the report.

V. A great body of psychoanalytic literature has been published over the years. Although we list it here as a fifth kind of literature that deals with interpretation, psychoanalytic publications do not fit neatly into one category. They include, for example, many case studies, e.g. Freud on Dora, 1905, cited above, as well as discussions about different aspects of interpretation, e.g. Schafer, 1954, and psychoanalytically oriented texts on individual tests, e.g. Klopfer, Ainsworth, Klopfer, and Holt, 1954, on the Rorschach. With regard to providing a description of how to interpret, psychoanalytic literature does not fare well. As was mentioned in the Introduction, Ramzy (1974, 1976) has reviewed psychoanalytic literature about interpretation methodology and has found it to lack a clear description of methodology or guidelines for conducting interpretation and using inference.

There are three final types of psychological literature that deal with interpretation:

VI. Reference works on professional standards for interpretation, such as the codes of ethics of professional societies like the American Psychological Association and the American Personnel and Guidance Association;

VII. Personality assessment textbooks geared to psychology students. These textbooks generally mention the topic of interpretation but it often receives only cursory treatment. Moreover, personality assessment textbooks tend not to distinguish interpretation methodology from interpretative hypotheses and interpretive conclusions;

VIII. Literature that discusses various aspects of interpretation, but not how to interpret *per se*. Several major reference works for clinicians fit this category. For example, Woody's edited volume, *Encyclopedia of Clinical Assessment* (1980), and Barnett's *Nondiscriminatory Multifactored Assessment: A Sourcebook* (1982) are guides to extant literature on clinical assessment and comment on current methodology and emerging practices. They do not, however, provide instruction about or describe the overall process of interpretation.

Although none of these three bodies of literature describes the interpretation process explicitly, each provides some information that has useful implications for understanding the process of interpretation. Therefore, each is discussed in the remainder of this chapter in separate sections entitled: "Standards for Psychological Interpretation," "Personality Assessment Textbooks," and "Other Literature about Psychological Interpretation," respectively.

STANDARDS FOR PSYCHOLOGICAL INTERPRETATION

The codes of ethics of several major professional associations in which personality assessors frequently hold membership contain passages that are relevant to interpretation as it is used in personality assessment. Ethical principles from two associations assessors are most likely to belong to, the American Psychological Association (APA) and the American Personnel and Guidance Association (APGA), are quoted below and then discussed.

APA's Policies

The most recent revision of standards for professional practice was published by the American Psychological Association in June 1981. Entitled "Ethical Principles of Psychologists," it updates an earlier version entitled "Ethical Standards for Psychologists" (1977, revised 1979). Of the ten principles listed, Principle 8 deals with assessment. It is reprinted below in its entirety (1981, p. 633-638).

Principle 8
ASSESSMENT TECHNIQUES

In the development, publication, and utilization of psychological assessment techniques, psychologists make every effort to promote the welfare and best interests of the client. They guard against the misuse of assessment results. They respect the clients' right to know the results, the interpretations made, and the bases for their conclusions and recommendations. Psychologists make every effort to maintain the security of tests and other assessment techniques within limits of legal mandates. They strive to ensure the appropriate use of assessment techniques by others.

a. In using assessment techniques, psychologists respect the right of clients to have full explanations of the nature and purpose of the techniques in language the clients can understand, unless an explicit exception to this right has been agreed upon in advance. When the explanations are to be provided by others, psychologists establish procedures for ensuring the adequacy of these explanations.

b. Psychologists responsible for the development and standardization of psychological tests and other assessment techniques utilize established scientific procedures and observe the relevant APA standards.

c. In reporting assessment results, psychologists indicate any reservations that exist regarding validity and reliability because of the circumstances of the assessment or the inappropriateness of the norms for the person tested. Psychologists strive to ensure that the results of assessments and their interpretations are not misused by others.

d. Psychologists recognize that assessment results may become obsolete. They make every effort to avoid and prevent the misuse of obsolete measures.

e. Psychologists offering scoring interpretation and services are able to produce appropriate evidence for the validity of the programs and procedures used in arriving at interpretations. The public offering of an automated interpretation service is considered a professional-to-professional consultation. Psychologists make every effort to avoid misuse of assessment reports.

f. Psychologists do not encourage or promote the use of psychological assessment techniques by inappropriately trained or otherwise unqualified persons through teaching, sponsorship, or supervision.

More elaborate standards regarding interpretation are found in APA's *Standards for Educational and Psychological Tests* (1974).[1] Section J, regarding interpretation of test scores, is reprinted below, excluding APA explanatory "Comments" that accompany each standard in the original (1974, p. 68-73).

[1] The A.P.A., in conjunction with the American Educational Research Association and the National Council on Measurement in Education, is currently rewriting the Standards; the revision will not be formally adopted or published until late 1983 or 1984.

J. Interpretation of Scores

Standards in this section refer to the interpretation of a test score by the test user and to reports of interpretations. Reports may be made to the person tested, to his agent, or to other affected people: Teachers, parents, supervisors, and various administrators and executives.

J1. A test score should be interpreted as an estimate of performance under a given set of circumstances. It should not be interpreted as some absolute characteristic of the examinee or as something permanent and generalizable to all other circumstances. Essential

J1.1. A test user should consider the total context of testing in interpreting an obtained score before making any decisions (including the decision to accept the score.) Essential

J2. Test scores should ordinarily be reported only to people who are qualified to interpret them. If scores are reported, they should be accompanied by explanations sufficient for the recipient to interpret them correctly. Desirable

J2.1. An individual tested (or his agent or guardian) has the right to know his score and the interpretations made. In some instances, even scores on individual items should be made known. Desirable

J2.2 A system of reporting test results should provide interpretations. Essential

J2.2.1. Scores should ordinarily be interpreted in light of their confidence intervals rather than as specific values alone. Very Desirable

J.2.3. In general, test users should avoid the use of descriptive labels (e.g. retarded) applied to individuals when interpreting test scores. Desirable

J3. The test user should recognize that estimates of reliability do not indicate criterion-related validity. Essential

J4. A test user should examine carefully the rationale and validity of computer-based interpretations of test scores. Essential

J5. In norm-referenced interpretations, a test user should interpret an obtained score with reference to sets of norms appropriate for the individual tested and for the intended use. Essential

J5.1. It is usually better to interpret scores with reference to a specified norms group in terms of percentile ranks or standard scores than to use terms like IQ or grade equivalents that may falsely imply a fully representative national norms group. Essential

J5.2. Test users should avoid the use of terms such as IQ, IQ equivalent, or grade equivalent where other terms provide more meaningful interpretations of a score. Essential

J5.3. A test user should examine differences between characteristics of a person tested and those of the population on whom the test was developed or norms developed. His responsibility includes deciding whether the differences are so great that the test should not be used for that person. Essential

J5.3.1. If no standardized approach to the desired measurement or differences are so great that the test should not be used for that person. Essential

J5.3.1 If no standardized approach to the desired measurement or assessment is available that is appropriate for a given individual, (e.g., a child of Spanish-speaking migrant workers), the test user should employ a broad-based approach to assessment using as many methods as are available to him. Very Desirable

J5.4. Local normative data or expectancy tables should ordinarily be developed, if possible, when administrative decisions are based on test scores. Very Desirable

J5.5 Ordinarily, normative interpretations of ability-test scores should not be made for scores in the chance range. Essential

J6. Any content-referenced interpretation should clearly indicate the domain to which one can generalize. Essential

J7. The test user should consider alternate interpretations of a given test score. Essential

J7.1. When cutting scores are established as guides for decision, the test user should retain some degree of discretion over their use. Desirable

J7.2 A person tested should have more than one kind of opportunity to qualify for a favorable decision. Desirable

J7.3. A procedure for reporting test results should include checks on accuracy and make provision for retesting. Desirable

J8. The test user should be able to interpret test performance relative to other measures. Very Desirable

J8.1. A test user should be able to use and interpret data regarding the statistical significance between scores. Very Desirable

J9. A test user should develop procedures for systematically eliminating from data files test-score information that has, because of the lapse of time, become obsolete. Essential

Standards for Educational and Psychological Tests also provides detailed standards for the construction and publication of tests, manuals, and reports; for reports of reliability and validity; and for the selection, administration, and scoring of tests. While all these standards are important to the responsible personality assessor, standards regarding the qualifications of the assessor are particularly relevant to interpretation and are printed below, again deleting the "Comments" that follow some of the standards in the original (1974, p. 57-68).

G. Qualifications and Concerns of Users

G1. A test user should have a general knowledge of measurement principles and the limitations of test interpretations. Essential

G1.1. A test user should know his own qualifications and how well they match the qualifications required for the use of specific tests. Essential

G2. A test user should know and understand literature relevant to the tests he uses and the testing problems with which he deals. Very Desirable

G3. One who has the responsibility for decisions about individuals or policies that are based on test results should have an understanding of psychological or educational measurement and of validation and other test research. Essential

G3.1. The principal test users within an organization should make every effort to be sure that all those in the organization who are charged with responsibilities related to test use and interpretation (e.g., test administrators) have received training appropriate to those responsibilities. Essential

G3.1.1. A test user should have sufficient technical knowledge to be prepared to evaluate claims made in a test manual. Very Desirable

G3.2. Anyone administering a test for decision-making purposes should be competent to administer that test or class of tests. If not qualified, he should seek the necessary training regardless of his educational attainments. Essential

G4. Test users should seek to avoid bias in test selection, administration, and interpretation; they should try to avoid even the appearance of discriminatory practice. Essential

G5. Institutional test users should establish procedures for periodic internal review of test use. Essential

APA's standards that bear on interpretation do not convey as much detail about methodology as the portion of APGA's policy statement "Responsibilities of Users of Standardized Tests" (1978), that deals with interpretation. It is presented next.

APGA's Policies

Like APA's standards, APGA's policies do not describe the actual mental processes involved in ethically interpreting test data. They do, however, provide standards against which the thinking used in interpretation can be measured. The section of APGA's "Responsibilities for Users of Standardized Tests" (1978, p. 7-8) which deals with interpretation is printed below.

TEST INTERPRETATION

Test interpretation encompasses all the ways we assign value to the scores.

A test can be described as a systematic set or series of standard observations of performances that all fall in some particular domain. Typically each observation yields a rating of the performance (such as right or wrong and pass or fail), then these ratings are counted and this count becomes the basis of the scores. Such scores are usually much more stable than the result of any single performance. This score reliability creates the possibility of validity greater than can be obtained from unsystematic or nonaggregated observations.

The proper interpretation of test scores starts with understanding these fundamental characteristics of tests. Given this, the interpretation of scores from a test entails knowledge about (1) administration and scoring procedures; (2) scores, norms, and related technical features; (3) reliability; and (4) validity.

Adequate test interpretation requires knowledge and skill in each of these areas. Some of this information can be mastered only by studying the manual and other materials of the test; no one should undertake the interpretation of scores on any test without such study.

Administration and Scoring:

Standard procedures for administering and scoring the test limit the possible meanings of scores. Departures from standard conditions and procedures modify and often invalidate the criteria for score interpretation.

1. The principles in the section on administration and scoring need to be understood by those engaged in interpretation.

2. Ascertain the circumstances peculiar to the particular administration and scoring of the test.

A. Examine all reports from administrators, proctors and scorers concerning irregularities or conditions, such as excessive anxiety, which may have affected performance.

B. Weigh the possible effects on test scores of examiner-examinee differences in ethnic and cultural background, attitudes and values in light of research on these matters. Recognize that such effects are probably larger in individual testing situations.

C. Look for administrators' reports of examinee behavior that indicate the responses were made on some basis other than that intended — as when a student being tested for knowledge of addition-number-facts adds by making tallies and then counting them.

3. Consider differences among clients in their reaction to instructions about guessing and scoring.

4. Recognize or judge the effect of scorer biases and judgment when subjective elements enter into scoring.

Scores, norms and related technical features:

The result of scoring a test is usually a number (or a set of numbers) called a raw score. Raw scores taken by themselves are not usually interpretable. Some additional steps must be taken.

The procedures either translate the numbers directly into descriptions of their meaning (e.g., pass or fail) or into other numbers called derived scores (e.g., standard scores) whose meaning stems from the test norms.

To interpret test scores, these procedures and the resulting descriptions or derived scores need to be thoroughly understood. Anything less than full understanding is likely to produce at least some, and probably many, serious errors in interpretation. The following are imperatives for interpreting tests:

1. Examine the test manuals, handbooks, users' guides and technical reports to determine what descriptions or derived are produced and what unique characteristics each may have.

2. Recognize that direct score interpretations such as mastery and non-mastery in criterion-referenced tests depend on arbitrary rules or standards.

A. Report number or percent of items right in addition to the indicated interpretation whenever it will help others understand the quality of the examinee's test performance.

B. Recognize that the difficulty of a fixed standard, such as 80 percent right, will vary widely from objective to objective. Such scores are not comparable in the normative sense.

C. Recognize that when each score is classified as pass fail, mastery-nonmastery or the like, that each element is being given equal weight.

3. Use the derived scores that fit the needs of the current use of the test.

A. Use percentile ranks for direct comparison of individuals to the norm or reference group.

B. Use standard scores or equal unit scaled scores whenever means and variances are calculated or other arithmetic operations are being used.

4. Recognize that only those derived scores that are based on the same norm group can be compared.

5. Consider the effect of any differences between the tests in what they measure when one test or form is equated with another, as well as the errors stemming from the equating itself.

Give greater credence to growth or change shown by the same test (including level and form) than to equated measures except where practice effects or feedback have destroyed the validity of a second use.

6. Evaluate the appropriateness of the norm groups available as based for interpreting the scores of clients.

A. Use the norms for the group to which the client belongs.

B. Consider using local norms and derived scores based on these local norms whenever possible.

7. Acquire knowledge of specific psychological or educational concepts and theories before interpreting the scores of tests based on such knowledge.

Reliability:

Reliability is a prerequisite to validity. Generally, the greater the number of items the greater the reliability of the test. The degree to which a score or a set of scores may vary because of measurement error is a central factor in interpretation.

1. Use the standard error of measurement to obtain a rough estimate of the probable variation in scores due to unreliability.

2. Use the reliability coefficient to estimate the proportion of score variance that is not due to error.

3. Consider the sources of variance attributable to error in the particular reliability indexes reported in relationship to the uses being made of the scores.

4. Assess reported reliabilities in light of the many extraneous factors that may have artificially raised or lowered these estimates, such as test speededness, sample homogeneity or heterogeneity, restrictions in range and the like.

5. Distinguish indexes of rater reliability (i.e., of objectivity) from test reliability.

Validity:

Proper test interpretation requires knowledge of the validity evidence available for the test as used. Its validity for other uses is not relevant. The purpose of testing dictates how a test is used. Technically proper use for ill-understood purposes may constitute misuse. The nature of the validity evidence required for a test is a function of its use.

Prediction — developing expectancies: The relationship of the test scores to an independently developed criterion measure is the basis for predictive validity.

1. Consider both the reliability and the relevance of the criterion measures used.

2. Use cross validation data to judge the validity of predictions.

3. Question the meaning of an apparently valid predictor that lacks both construct and content validity. Assess the role of underlying and concomitant variables.

4. Consider the validity of a given measure in the context of all the predictors used or available. Does the measure make an independent contribution to the prediction over and above that provided by other measures?

5. Consider the pitfalls of labeling, stereotyping and prejudging people. The self-fulfilling prophecies that may result are often undesirable.

Placement/selection: Predictive validity is the usual basis for valid placement. Consider the evidence of validity for each alternative (i.e., each placement) when inferring the meaning of scores.

1. Obtain adequate information abut the programs or institutions in which the client may be placed in order to judge the consequences of such placement.

2. Estimate the probability of favorable outcomes for each possible placement (e.g., both selection and rejection) before judging the import of the scores.

3. Consider the possibility that outcomes favorable from an institutional point of view may differ from those that are favorable from the examinees' point of view.

4. Examine the possibility that the clients' group membership (race, sex, etc.) may alter the reported validity relationships.

5. Use all the available evidence about the individual to infer the validi-

ty of the score for that individual. Each single piece of information about an individual (e.g., test score, teacher report, or counselor opinion) improves the probability that proper judgments and decisions can be made.

A. Test scores should be considered in context; they do not have absolute meaning.

B. Single test scores should not be the sole basis for placement or selection.

Description/diagnosis: Distinguish between those descriptions and diagnoses using psychological constructs that can be validated only indirectly and those for which content specifications suffice.

1. Identify clearly the domain specified by those asserting content validity. Assess the adequacy of the content sampling procedures used in writing and selecting items.

2. Identify the dimensions of the construct being measured when multiple scores from a battery or inventory are used for description.

A. Examine the content validity and/or the construct validity of each score separately.

B. Consider the relative importance of the various subtests, parts, objectives or elements yielding separate scores and judge the weight they each should be given in interpretation.

C. Recognize that when scores are summed or averaged their weight is a function of their variances.

D. Recognize that when each score is classified as pass-fail, mastery-nonmastery or the like, each element is being given equal weight.

3. Examine the completeness of the description provided, recognizing that no set of test scores completely describes a human being.

Growth — Studies of change: Valid assessment of growth or change requires both a test having descriptive validity and a procedure for establishing that the scores obtained differ from those that might arise when no change has occurred.

1. Report as possibilities all the interpretations the study or evaluation design permits. Point out those interpretations that are precluded by the design used.

A. When standard procedures such as the RMC models (see Tallmadge, GK. and Horst, D.P., A procedural guide for validating achievement gains in educational projects; Mountain View, Calif: RMC Research Corp., Dec. 1975) for measuring growth in achievement are employed, use the descriptions of strengths and weaknesses provided.

B. Look for naturally occurring control groups not part of design whenever possible.

2. Consider the strengths and weaknesses of the particular tests used with respect to this use.

Consider the possibility of floor or ceiling effects, the content changes level to level, the adequacy of articulation in multilevel tests, the comparability of alternate forms, the adequacy of the score-equating across forms, and the comparability of timing of the testing to that of the norm-ing.

3. Recognize the unreliability of individual score differences as measures of change.

4. Recognize the limitations of scoring scales such as grade equivalents that may not have the comparable meaning they appear to have at different levels of the scale.

5. Recognize the need for equal interval scales when trying to assess the amount of change.

Discussion

Several organizations have written standards for psychological interpretation. In addition to the APA and APGA, there are the American Education Research Association, the National Council on Measurement in Education, and others. All call for the interpreter to be knowledgeable of all topics relevant to his task. Topics include the following:

test theory
test selection
test administration
scoring
empirical studies about phenomena being discussed
statistical analysis of data
reliability and validity
nondiscriminatory practice and cross-cultural limitations of assessment

The sample APA and APGA policy statements printed above speak for themselves in this regard.

The standards are less clear about what constitutes ethical interpretation methodology. Although they clearly state that interpretation is necessary for test results to be communicated ethically, e.g. APA standard J2.2., and tell us that interpretation must be carried out sensibly and with full cognizance of test theory, construction, and technical analysis, the standards do not tell us how to interpret; this, of course, is not their purpose. Instead, they set forth minimum criteria that must be included in interpretation and assume that the sharply honed mind of the interpreter will carry out the rest responsibly in light of the fine training and the supervised assessment experience s/he has had.

If you fear that your training has been wanting in some respects, do not despair. Before you can master interpretation, it is wise to have the general outlines of what it is you are trying to learn. Once you discern these, it is easier to frame questions to fill in the contents, and many psychologists and teachers will be happy to respond to your clearly stated questions or direct you to appropriate sources if they do not have the answers themselves.

With regard to assessing personality, it is notable that both the APA and APGA codes imply that using assessment to describe personality has lost some professional stature in recent years. Both APA's and APGA's standards emphasize the use of *standardized, quantitative* measures, which are not conducive to describing personality. This psychometric emphasis is not surprising in light of the increasing use of psychometric tests compared with more clinical measures like the TAT and Human Figure Drawing (Korchin and Schuldberg, 1981, p. 1148), and may reflect a suspicion of more clinical methods due to their subjective nature, poor showing on reliability and validity measures, and dependence on clinical judgment. The implication is that both subjective measures (i.e. measures lacking established norms, expectancy tables, or criterion values) and subjective subject matter (e.g. personality and the inner experience of a person) are at the borderline of respectability for professionals.

This hesitancy to address clinical endeavors is understandable because they are so dependent on the individual clinician's thinking and not on objective criteria. It would be most difficult to describe ethical standards regulating the individual's thought processes when using clinical methods except for general statements regarding competency and integrity [cf., APA's Principle #8 (1981) and standards G1-G5 (1974)].

In personality assessment the assessor, not a test, is at the center of the assessment process (Korchin and Schuldberg, 1981, p. 1148). In the words of Korchin and Schuldberg (1981, p. 1148),

> The clinician has to organize and conceptualize the questions to be answered, the techniques to use, and finally integrate diverse findings into a coherent whole. At all points, clinical judgment and inferences are required, and the value of the assessment findings ultimately depends heavily on the skill and knowledge of the interpreting clinician.

This orientation contrasts most sharply with procedures that remove interpretation entirely from the clinician, as in the case of multitrait inventories that are processed by computers that produce printouts that interpret the data for the psychologist. Often the use of psychometric measures is not taken to this extreme, however, and even with automated scoring services the clinician may need to play a significant role in giving test results meaning.

The codes of ethics seem to assume that abilities, performance skills, behaviors, and other objective attributes or situation dependent variables that are subject to quantification are being sought in assessment. Interpretation of this kind of data is dependent upon quantitative comparisons. This is a safe stance for the professional organizations to take, especially in view of the many legal questions that are being raised in courts, school systems, and medical institutions about the validity of psychological findings. While the codes do not prohibit the assessment of personality, the study of inner structures, descriptive statements about the "whole" person, or use of the clinical method, they do imply that these undertakings may not meet the ethical standards since they are not aptly done with solely quantitative measures.

Where does this leave the personality assessor who is attempting to describe a unique person? It leaves him in search of a conceptually valid methodology which can stand up to logical scrutiny and can produce better results than sole reliance on the clinical method. Once logical criteria for sound interpretation of personality data are established, it will be more fitting for professional societies to comment upon them and develop standards for conducting personality assessments in their regulative principles. Here we return to the point of departure for this book: the need for a description of interpretation methodology used in personality assessment. To carry out personality assessment ethically, a rational, logical interpretation methodology is absolutely mandatory or the results of personality assessment cannot hope to comply with professional standards or even enter their province.

PERSONALITY ASSESSMENT TEXTBOOKS

Texts on personality assessment are reviewed below to determine the coverage the topic of interpretation methodology receives in this literature. Textbooks on personality assessment are the principle training material available at present to students of assessment.

Their portrayal of the role of interpretation in personality assessment reflects the treatment interpretation receives in personality assessment literature in general and in all likelihood influences the approach to interpretation budding psychologists take.

Eleven personality assessment textbooks are currently in print and available for purchase and classroom use:

> Holt, R.R. *Assessing Personality* (1971), originally published as Part Four of *Personality: Dynamics, Development and Assessment* Janis, I.L., Mahl, G.F., Kagan, J., and Holt, R.R., (1969)
>
> Horst, P. *Personality: Measurements of Dimensions* (1968)
>
> Kelly, E.L. *Assessment of Human Characteristics* (1967)
>
> Lanyon, R.I., and Goodstein, L.O. *Personality Assessment* (1971)
>
> Malony, M.P., and Ward, M.P. *Personality Assessment: A Conceptual Approach* (1976)
>
> Mischel W. *Personality Assessment* (1968)
>
> Pervin, L.A., and Levenson, H. *Personality: Theory, Assessment and Research* (1975)
>
> Shertzer, B., and Linden, J.D. *Fundamentals of Individual Appraisal: Assessment Techniques for Counselors* (1979)
>
> Sundberg, N. *Assessment of Persons* (1977)
>
> Vernon, P.E. *Personality Assessment: A Critical Survey* (1979)[4]
>
> Wiggins, J.S. *Personality and Prediction: Principles of Personality Assessment* (1973)

These books, with the exception of Vernon (1979),[5] were surveyed with the help of the questionnaire in Appendix A. Questions for the survey sample some of the key ingredients of the criteria listed in the Introduction and look at the extent to which the line of reasoning used to interpret data is explicitly (1) described, and (2) demonstrated in each text. Several of the questions are open-ended so that the coverage that interpretation received in the texts could be viewed without preconceptualization before it was tallied and abbreviated in Table I which follows.

[4,5] This volume is not yet published although it is listed in *Subject Guide to Books in Print 1979-1980 v. 2* (1979). A 1964 edition not in print was examined but not included here. The titles of Cattell (1969), Daily (1971), Eysenck and Eysenck (1969), and London and Exner (1978) sound as though they are personality assessment textbooks, but they were not included in our list; London and Exner (1978) is an edited collection, and the other three serve to present their authors' personality theories and are not suitable as general texts for teaching personality assessment.

Table I summarizes the coverage of relevant interpretation material in the texts. The rating each text received on the chart was done in a liberal manner rather than conservatively. For example, a topic in the questionnaire could be covered very briefly in a text, say in one paragraph or less, for the text to receive a "yes" score for presence of the material. The same terminology used in the questionnaire was not sought in the texts. Thus a synonym or expression implying the same ideas as the questionnaire was scored "yes," for presence of the material in the text. Table I contains some notes in addition to clearcut "yeses" and "nos" to clarify the type of coverage a text provides and to denote gray areas.

RESULTS. Virtually all the texts at least mention the need to analyze and interpret data, though often their portrayals of how to interpret are done in several pages or less. Some texts teach that interpretation and data analysis are carried out by particular methods, such as, factor analysis or computers. Such texts tend not to mention the mental processes used to interpret data but rely on plugging it into specific technologies, e.g. Horst, 1968; Wiggins, 1973.

The majority of texts mention the need for hypothesis building and testing, but most of these minimize the topics, implying that they are not necessary to teach. Moreover, most of these texts do not present concepts about interpretation or discuss how scientific thinking and logical standards can be applied to psychological interpretation. For example, Malony and Ward (1976) make an outstanding effort to describe the use of inference for generating interpretative hypotheses; however, they do not deal much with testing and reformulating hypotheses, nor do they discuss the ways in which scientific methods could aid in these tasks. Their work is characteristic of a genre of psychological literature which grew up in the 1950s and 1960s and saw inference as *the* tool for interpreting. This literature, typified by Sarbin, Taft, and Bailey's often-cited book *Clinical Inference and Cognitive Theory* (1960), centered around clinical judgment literature. It took inference as far as it could go as a methodology for interpretation but underestimated the importance of hypothesis testing and cross-validation. Consequently, this literature got stuck at the hypothesis generation stage (although it did not call it this; hypotheses were called "interpretations," "conclusions," "predictions," etc.), and it has been relatively unproductive in the past decade.

TABLE I

SURVEY OF PERSONALITY ASSESSMENT TEXTBOOKS CURRENTLY IN PRINT: SUMMARY CHART

	Holt (1968)	Janis et al. (1969) [Holt, 1971]	Kelly (1967)	Lanyon and Goodstein (1971)	Maloney and Ward (1976)	Mischel (1968)	Pervin (1975)	Shertzer and Linden (1979)	Sundberg (1977)	Wiggins (1973)
Type Of Book	empirical psychometric; not gen. text	broad coverage text	paperback intro. text	general text	general text	behavioral; emph. interaction between person & situation	text	text for counselors emph. decisions, not pert. assess.	undergrad. text	emph. prediction & diagnosis; use of expt. data & stat. technology
Discusses How To Analyze & Interpret Raw Data	yes	yes - briefly	yes - briefly	yes	yes	yes	yes	yes	no	little
Models Or Methods Used For Analysis & Interpretation	technology, computers, factor an., etc.	projective & some psychometric; says methods depend on your pt. of view	rational, factor analysis, empirical	theoretical empirical	disciplined inquiry; sci. method	situational; varies with the theory; anti-clinical judgment	depends on theory used	objective tests; no project. tests used	NA	automated interp.; varies with theory; empirical
Discusses Scientific Mode Of Thinking For Analysis & Interpretation Of Raw Data	not explicitly	yes - briefly	yes	yes	yes	not explicitly	yes - much	not explicitly	not explicitly	no
Discusses the following:										
Generating Hypotheses	no	yes - briefly	no - limited to logic for making inferences	yes	yes	yes - indirectly	yes	yes - partially & indirectly	yes - indirectly	yes - but assumes only 1 hyp. is needed
Testing Hypotheses	no	yes - briefly	no	yes	yes	yes - indirectly	yes	yes - partially & indirectly	assumed	yes - but uses only 1 hyp. to fit data
Relevance Of Test Literature	yes	yes - briefly	yes	yes	yes	yes - indirectly	yes - little	yes	yes - indirectly	yes
Relevance Of Other Research Lit.	yes	yes - briefly	yes	yes	yes	yes - indirectly	no - treats each test separately w/ test theory	yes	yes - indirectly	yes
Testing Alternate Hypotheses	no	no	no	no	implied		yes	not explicit	yes - indirectly	no
Demonstrates How To Apply Scientific Mode Of Thinking In A Case Study Or Studies	no	yes	no	yes - some very brief examples	yes	no	yes	no	no	no
Demonstrates the following:										
Generating Hypotheses	no	yes	no	yes	yes	no	yes	no	no	no
Testing Hypotheses	no	yes	no	yes	yes	no	yes	no	no	no
Relevance Of Test Literature	no	yes	no	yes	yes	no	little - test lit. only	no	little	yes
Relevance Of Other Research Lit.	no	yes	no	no	no	no	no	no	little	yes
Testing Alternate Hypotheses	no	yes	no	no	no	no	no	no	no	no

TABLE I (continued)

	Horst (1968)	Janis et al. (1969) [Holt, 1971]	Kelly (1967)	Lanyon and Goodstein (1971)	Mahoney and Ward (1976)	Mischel (1968)	Pervin (1975)	Shertzer and Linden (1979)	Sundberg (1977)	Wiggins (1973)
Provides Sample Assessment Reports That Incorporate The Above	no	yes	no	no	no	no	no	no	sample reports are given but do not demonstrate above	no
Provides Case Studies Or Samples From Case Studies Showing Sources Of Each Interpretation Made (e.g. lore, hunch, experience, test lit., other research lit., theory)	no	yes – sources of some interps. are given	no	yes – little	yes	yes – some	no	no	no	no
Provides An Extended Case Study In Personality Assessment Using Typical Battery of Tests	no	yes	no	no	no	no	yes	no	no	no
Demonstrates the following: Interpretation Of Raw Data For Each Test	no	yes	no	no	no	no	yes	no	no	no
Assessment Report for Each Test	no	no	no	no	no	no	no	no	no	no
Grand Summary Assessment Report Synthesizing Results Of All Tests	no	yes	no	no	no	no	no	no	no	no
Is Student Likely To Develop Skills In Interpretation For Personality Assessment From This Book?	no – only in use of computer technology, etc.	yes – but not rigorous systematic use of sci. thinking.	a little only; re: logic used for making inferences	yes – somewhat in area of hypothesis-building	little	no – book does not emphasize assess. of total person, but traits, etc.	yes – an intro.	no – book does not treat assess. of total person, but objective tests for eval., etc.	no	no

About half the texts demonstrate at least one aspect of interpretation methodology in a case study. Only one text (Holt, 1971) demonstrates interpretative thinking in a case study in detail. Also about half the texts give primary sources in the data for some of their interpretative hypotheses.

When it comes to demonstrating the use of rigorous interpretation methodology on data from a battery of psychological tests, the kind of material personality assessors typically deal with in the field, no text gives thorough coverage. Holt (1971) is again the most thorough; however, he does not demonstrate enough of his methodology. For example, he does not explore null and alternate hypotheses routinely to safeguard against first impressions, and the thinking he makes explicit is not rigorous and systematic throughout the case study (although being the fine interpreter Holt is, his unstated thinking is probably excellent and his interpretative conclusions accurate). Also, his raw material is drawn from an exhaustive long-term study of an individual and is not limited to the battery and interview more typical of clinical field settings. His case is nonetheless highly instructive in its own right.

SUMMARY: Textbooks on personality assessment tend to discuss the importance of interpretation if only cursorily. They describe it in general terms and give examples of interpretation. Most texts do not demonstrate the actual thinking used in the analysis and interpretation of raw and scored data or the translation of working hypotheses into interpretive conclusions for the psychological report. Those books that do give demonstrations of interpretation do not emphasize and portray the use of rigorous thinking, and do not make clear the extent to which scientific methods can supplement more subjective clinical methods.

OTHER LITERATURE
ABOUT PSYCHOLOGICAL INTERPRETATION

The final category of literature about interpretation is the number of books and articles that deal with various aspects of interpretation, ranging from common fallacies in clinical inference (Sarbin, Taft, and Bailey, 1960) to criteria for judging Rorschach interpretations (Schafer 1954) and assumptions underlying interpretative hypotheses used with the TAT (Lindzey, 1952). Although none of them tell *how to* interpret, some of these works provide useful ideas for helping to construct a description of interpretation methodology. Several particularly significant references are discussed in this section. Others are mentioned in the next three chapters where relevant.

Harrower (1964), Levy (1963), and Sarbin, Taft, and Bailey (1960) have written three unusually detailed books about interpretation. Their titles are given below and reflect how interpretation is approached in the psychology literature through various avenues.

Harrower, M. *Appraising Personality: An Introduction to Projective Techniques*, 1952, 1964.

Levy, L.H. *Psychological Interpretation*, 1963.

Sarbin, T.R., Taft, R., and Bailey, D.E. *Clinical Inference and Cognitive Theory*, 1960.

All three date from the 1960s, a time when the intricacies of clinical thinking were holding sway and scholars were attempting to describe how clinicians think and interpret data. A quick skimming of these works demonstrates how scant the theoretical underpinnings of these efforts were. The assumption at the time seemed to be that clinicians were doing something important and that if their thinking could be committed to paper, or at least some cues that tagged critical junctures in their thinking, then the problem of statistical versus clinical prediction would be solved.

Back in the 1950s Meehl had drawn the attention of many psychologists to the issue of the questionable validity of clinical thinking with his now famous article, "Clinical versus Statistical Prediction" (1954). In this article he questioned the usefulness of clinical methods of analysis and interpretation compared with statistical approaches to combining data and drawing conclusions. His purpose was not to malign clinical thinking. In fact, in a later article, "What Can the Clinician Do Well?" (1959), he went so far as to ask psychologists not to misconstrue his meaning in the earlier article and described six circumstances, listed in Chapter 3 of this book, where he believed clinical method was advantageous over more empirical or scientific methods.. However, the logic of Meehl's pro-clinical argument did not dominate the literature, and clinical thinking continued to be probed and found wanting in many respects.

The three books introduced above are all efforts to put clinical thinking in a meaningful context and retain it as a useful methodology in psychology. None seeks to provide a theory about what rigorous clinical thinking *should* consist of. Instead, each seems to place a tacit faith in clinical thinking *per se*. This author seeks a working model or set of constructs about an ideal form of interpretative thinking that the personality assessor can use to compare, improve, and develop his own thinking. It is doubtful that clinical thinking *per se*, in its unrefined state, has been worthy of the extensive attention it has received. Rather it would be encouraging to see more literature devoted to improving the thinking skills of psychologists.

Harrower (1964) has written one of the few volumes with this end in mind. Her volume *Appraising Personality* is an introduction to clinical thinking written with the novice in mind. Harrower shows, in a number of vignettes that illustrate important circumstances in which the psychologist must use his own judgment to draw conclusions, how high quality clinical thinking is done. She points out its thoroughness, logical rigor, and similarity to detective work. However, her volume limits the application of clinical thinking to projective techniques, and for this reason it may have received less than its fair share of attention as projective methods have declined in popularity.

A second relatively unappreciated work is Levy's *Psychological Interpretation* (1963). This volume is the only extensive exploration of the theoretical and practical aspects of interpretation in the literature. It takes the form of a discussion of issues in interpretation, then gives clinical examples and applications. However, while it focuses directly on the interpretation process, it does not discuss the critical importance of logical systematic thinking and testing to interpretation and instead remains in the clinical thinking camp. Also, like other literature that tries to demonstrate interpretation for the reader, it does not carry out its demonstration on a large volume of data, such as that generated by a battery of psychological tests. Despite its limitations, Levy's volume is a valuable reference on interpretation. Unfortunately, it is no longer in print.

"Clinical" Inference

Sarbin, Taft, and Bailey (1960) made one of the most valiant attempts in the literature to formulate clinical thinking, as it is done by clinicians, into a logical process. Their approach was based on the then newly popular cognitive approach to psychology. Consequently, they sought a system of cognitive regularities used by all clinicians in their thinking. The result was that they tried to subsume clinical thinking under clinical inference and claimed that both the rational and intuitive aspects of clinical method could be translated into the language of inference. To make this translation work, unfortunately, the authors had to resort to defining "inference" differently from how it is used in logic or in the dictionary. To this end they coined the term "clinical inference" to mean assigning an individual to a group whose members share common characteristics and, from which membership, attributes ascribed to the group can be inferred to fit the new member.

This is not what inference usually means; on the contrary, inference generally means using inductive or deductive logic to make assertions about something. Deductive inference occurs when assertions are deducted from other statements, i.e. going from the general to the specific; inductive inference occurs when an assertion is made based on "n" samples (in other words, it is the act of making generalizations from a number of observations). Like this definition, Sarbin, Taft, and Bailey's definition of "clinical" inference contains both an inductive aspect (assigning the individual to a group) and a deductive aspect (deducing other attributes of the individual from attributes the group has). Moreover, their two-step process goes a long way in helping to conceptualize the thinking involved in making predictions about someone. However, it holds some major flaws.

First, assigning an individual to a group is only one kind of inductive inference used in assessment. Rather than only labeling, diagnosing, or making other classifications, personality assessors also typically use inductive inference to make general descriptive statements about an individual that do not relate to classificatory schemes. Recall our earlier discussion in Chapter 1 of McArthur's (1954) observations about the thinking used by psychologists he studied who made *accurate* judgments about a number of Harvard students: first the psychologists gradually built a mental conceptualization of the client based on a case file about him; then they deduced predictions about his behavior from this picture. This sounds a lot like Sarbin, Taft, and Bailey's process. The difference is that for Sarbin, Taft, and Bailey, first the individual is *categorized*, then predictions are made. In contrast, McArthur observed that in examples of accurate clinical judgment, first a *conceptualization* of the individual is made; then predictions are made. Thus a fallacy in the clinical inference model is that inductive inference, as it is used in clinical judgment, consists simply of deciding which groups an individual belongs to. Instead, it looks like a conceptualization of the unique individual occurs in the thinking of the accurate clinician before s/he makes predictions that fit the individual. The formation of this conceptualization is, of course, the goal of personality assessment when it is carried out as a descriptive discipline and involves many more mental steps than simply assigning the individual to a number of categories.

Here a second problem with Sarbin, Taft, and Bailey's model becomes apparent: they claim that "clinical" inference is sufficient to describe the thinking used to make interpretative conclusions. (If it is sufficient to describe what some clinicians do, that is probably unfortunate for the client!) Inductive inference *is* used to generate hypotheses and to relate data to hypotheses, and deductive inference *is* used to make predictions about a person from general statements about him. However, inference — clinical or otherwise — is not adequate in itself to describe the logical steps that intervene between hypothesis generation and prediction based on the final picture of the client. In between these two steps are many logical processes involved in interpretation, for example, hypothesis testing, cross-validation, and the search for logical consistency among hypotheses. All of this must be taken into account in a description of interpretation methodology.

In 1968 Goldberg (1968) asked in his aptly named article, "Simple Models or Simple Processes?" if clinical thinking was not being oversimplified when it was viewed simply as a process of inference. He also looked at the other side of the coin and wondered if the poor validity of many clinical judgments was not possibly due to oversimplified thinking on the part of the clinicians. He knew that really good judgment always involves more than simply making hypotheses or drawing deductive conclusions from them. Good judgment in any field has to include hypothesis testing, feedback, retesting, reformulation, etc., or the logical operations used in scientific research. In the remaining three chapters of Section I we will follow Goldberg's advice and look to scientific method and logic for insights into interpretation methodology. We will also continue looking at clinical methods, since they form the foundation of personality assessment, but we shall do so cautiously, knowing that clinical methods produce a host of pitfalls for the personality assessor if used uncritically.

CHAPTER 3

THE CLINICAL CONTEXT
OF INTERPRETATION

THE personality assessor makes certain assumptions regarding the study of the inner person which preclude full use of scientific methods. These assumptions are called "clinical" because they had their origin in the clinic, where psychologists first worked directly with individual patients and had to come up with quick, practical recommendations for solutions to pressing personal problems. There was neither the time, nor the resources, for controlled experimentation or correlational studies in the clinic. It was noted that methods that seemed to work drew on a set of assumptions about how to approach understanding individuals in general. In this chapter the clinical point of view is discussed in detail. In the first section, we look at the outstanding features of clinical method and compare it with more standardized procedures. In the second section, we discuss "judgments," or the results of clinical method, and try to find out why some judges are able to apply the clinical method with much better results than others. Throughout the entire chapter, our aim is to clarify the extent to which personality assessment methodology must rely on clinical assumptions and methods.

CLINICAL METHOD

Clinical method is the framework within which interpretation is embedded when it is used for case studies in personality assessment. Clinical method provides a context with which to understand interpretation and a vocabulary and set of assumptions regarding the way interpretation is dealt with in assessment. It is discussed in detail in this section.

Clinical method is the process by which one human can use his mind as a tool to fathom the depths of another person. This is the nature and heart of clinical assessment. The term "clinical-personological" method has been used by some writers, such as, Fowler and Epting (1976), who reject the term "clinical" for having come to connote "helping" and the employment of a medical model of humans. In the medical model, a person is viewed as ill and under treatment; frequently drugs are employed to treat symptoms and manage the illness. Fowler and Epting (1976), Stones (1978), and others prefer the term "clinical-personological" because they claim it connotes a more humanistic orientation than the word "clinical" does, where mental problems can mean positive growth and not only illness. In discussions I have seen which use the term "clinical-personological," I have been struck by the lack of difference between the clinical approach and the clinical-personological approach. Both involve a clinician who is attempting to understand a unique, "whole" person. Over the years the theoretical framework the clinician uses to view his client has been changing from viewing the client's problems solely as an indication of illness or maladaption to viewing them as an opportunity for growth and change. I see no need here to coin a new phrase in place of the word "clinical" to denote changes in the personality theories that underlie treatment. "Clinical method" remains the name of the process used when the psychologist uses his mind as the chief tool to fathom another person.

The clinical method has the following basic features which have been described aptly by Garfield in his excellent article, "The Clinical Method in Personality Assessment" (1963):

(1) Clinical method relies heavily on the observations of the clinician. Whatever s/he sees or experiences constitutes potential data.

(2) The clinician's own personality is fundamental to the operation: his skills in logic and inference; his sensitivity to others; his past experiences, motivation, and strategies for dealing with his surroundings; his vocabulary. All of these become tools for understanding another person.

(3) Clinical method is a more flexible pursuit than more traditional empirical methods. Flexibility is drawn on when the clinician structures a conversation or an interview with a patient. S/he may structure the conversation as s/he warrants. Flexibility is also available in relating to patients actively or passively, quietly or verbosely, and in terms of what information is gathered and how. A problem with some literature critical of the clinical method is that it criticizes clinicians as a group and does not take into account imprudent use of this flexibility by some professionals.

(4) The clinical method focuses on the individual case as pur-

ported, for example, in Murray's seminal work *Explorations in Personality* (1938). The case study, already discussed in Chapter 1, has been a part of psychology for many years (see, for example, Weiss, 1958; White, 1975).

(5) The clinical method employs a "wholistic" view of man. This is not a recent concept, as some new humanists might contend, but an old idea in psychology dating back to Allport (1937). Many techniques that rely on interpretation to study personality take this point of view (such as, psychotherapy, transactional psychology, and psychoanalysis.)

(6) The clinical method is interested in the inner life of a person. This is the antithesis to what is appropriate subject matter when scientific methods are being used, because inner experience is beyond direct observation by the human senses of the observer, with or without the aid of instruments that expand the range of sensitivity of the senses (Lastrucci, 1963). Inner structures, mind, emotion, etc. are subjective phenomena in that they are directly experienced only by the client and can only be inferred by the clinician from behavior samples.

(7) The clinical method, regardless of the theoretical orientation of the individual clinician, places its major emphasis on understanding the individual. It does not care if two people share the same trait nearly as much as it cares about the extent to which the two people are really, in fact, shades different from each other with regard to that trait.

Clinical Method and Psychometry

Meehl (1954, 1959) has distinguished between two general types of data, psychometric and nonpsychometric. The clinical method can make use of both kinds of data; in addition, results on a given test, such as the WAIS, can be viewed as psychometric data when the clinician uses scaled scores and group norms, and as nonpsychometric data, as when the clinician looks at patterns of verbal responses. The methods of combining data have also been divided into two main classes: they are called the formalized and the judgmental by Meehl (1954, 1959) and the psychometric and the clinical by Sarbin, Taft, and Bailey (1960).

In the study of personality, data obtained from a given test or technique can be analyzed in a formal or psychometric manner, or in a nonstandardized or clinical manner. How does the clinical differ from the psychometric? Sarbin, Taft, and Bailey (1960) have answered this question with the following four points:

(1) In the clinical method the patient is observed in different situations and his behavior sampled. An understanding of the sampled behavior is derived from the clinical judgment of the clinician. Thus, the cognitive activity of the clinician is an important topic in understanding clinical method. The psychometric method does not lean so heavily on individual judgment. Instead, it employs standard procedures and norms for analysis.

(2) In the clinical method inferences are drawn from the data at hand. In the psychometric method, most inferences to be employed were perceived when the test was constructed, or have been amended as a result of empirical research.

(3) In the clinical method it is assumed that the clinician has a theoretical framework to guide his observations and formulations. The psychometric approach can be described as a purer form of empiricism.

(4) Using the clinical method, the clinician relies on his own experience with techniques. This experience comes from formal training, knowledge of research literature, professional experience. It can also come from his own life experiences and learning about human nature from studies of his own psyche using introspection and psychotherapy. One source of poor quality in findings by clinicians can be faulty inference and interpretation. Another source, however, can be the clinician's lack of understanding of himself, since his view of others is limited by his knowledge of himself.

Shapiro (1957) has argued that to use nonpsychometric data as a source of inferences about personality factors is akin to using "an unvalidated and unstandardized psychological test." The term "unstandardized" is worth further comment here to help develop the point being made by Shapiro. The vocabulary of science is not yet uniform. Some terms are used in different ways by different writers, and even by the same writer. Thus, Shapiro and others use the word "standardized" in different ways. On the one hand the term refers to data that have been made normative with means, averages, and variance measures, or standards, against which an individual's standing can be compared with that of others. On the other hand, "standardized" can mean that which is measured against experience. In other words, standards can be acquired by the person doing the measuring over the course of his gaining familiarity with people who fit the group s/he is studying. In the latter case, the standards are clinical because they derive from the personal experience of a professionally trained observer.

These "clinical" standards may be used by the clinician in varying ways. One clinician may use his experience with a projective technique to help him judge depression levels; another may use it to measure intelligence. In the clinical method, neither is wrong to limit the technique as long as his judgments are based on ample experience with the novel application. Varying a technique to fit the task at hand is not uncommon among clinicians and can be the forerunner for later validation studies to make the novel use of the technique, a formalized, well-documented procedure. However, this practice can also produce grossly unwarranted results if tests are used in an *ad hoc* fashion and personal standards are not developed during the course of lengthy clinical experience. It is this practice in particular that Shapiro warned against.

Some psychologists like London and Exner (1978) and typified by Cattell (1957, 1946 in 1969), an early leader in the use of psychometric data and its formalized treatment, advocate taking psychometry to the extreme and using it only, and no subjective techniques, for studying personality. Psychometric methods do produce precise, valuable pieces of the total personality puzzle, and personality assessors usually include some objective tests in their batteries to get quantitative information about the relative standing of the client on various traits and other dimensions compared with other individuals. Such quantitative information is indispensable to accurate assessment of the individual because without a certain amount of comparison with others, assessors could not make accurate judgments about the individual's relative standing on matters such as intelligence factors, vocabulary, and number skills.

The reason psychometric methods are not adequate by themselves for carrying out personality assessment is that they are limited to measuring that which is objective and quantitative. This produces information that tends to be relatively static, discrete, and incomplete compared with the broad dynamic descriptive statements sought by personality assessors. Dynamic interactions and patterns constitute personality description, not objective statements about the strength of preconceived variables and specific traits. This kind of personality information is best gotten with nonpsychometric methods and with tests that elicit open-ended responses that the client (and the assessor) must structure himself, e.g. the Rorschach and TAT. The lack of formalized procedures and preconceived notions about an individual is the major advantage of clinical method over psychometry.

An increasingly quantitative emphasis in psychology has cast doubt on the value of the clinical method of psychology. Yet, many of the most important ideas, concepts, and theories about human personality in use today have come directly from employing the clinical method. Without it, the means to understand one individual human, Mr. Joe Smith, by a professional psychologist would be almost nonexistent. Instead, the person could disappear from psychology and his heart rate, limbic system, words, gestures, movements and traits would remain, each part studied by separate specialists and reported upon in separate journals. Carlson (1971) noted with alarm, in her study of 226 articles in major journals of personality psychology, the lack of *persons* in the literature. In the apt title to her article she asks, "Where is the Person in Personality Research?" The answer is, the person is with psychologists who employ clinical methods.

CLINICAL JUDGMENT

"Clinical judgment" has a two-fold meaning. It can mean the final *product* of clinical thinking and denote a conclusion, interpretation, or judgment. It can also mean the *process* of clinical thinking, that is, the tacit methodology the clinician uses to produce judgments. The word "clinical judgment" is used in the literature to mean either of these and, sometimes, both simultaneously. At times syntax distinguishes one meaning from the other in a publication, sometimes not.

Beyond what we have said about clinical method, clinical judgment as a thinking process is difficult to describe because it encompasses the wide range of activities that the clinician engages in while mentally processing information in pursuit of accurate judgments about a person. Pure clinical judgment is not about criterion-related measures. There are no independent measures besides the mind of the clinician that are employed for drawing conclusions about the client from information available about him. More important, clinical judgment makes ample use of intuition and speculation to let the clinician divine characteristics befitting the subject. Although intuition and insight are valid topics of inquiry, they are not yet firmly enough established or understood to be a part of scientific psychological methodology: although they are invaluable for hypothesis generation and brain-storming, they are not suitable methodology on which to base psychological conclusions. Using intuition and speculation to produce judgments is, however, permitted when using the *process* of clinical judgment.

Consequently, the *product* of this process, that is clinical judgments with the first meaning we gave, are neither more nor less than opinions or decisions made by the clinician. As the name "judgment" clearly implies, they do not lay claim to the status of proven fact and cannot be dealt with on the same grounds as more scientifically derived conclusions.

You might be wondering then, What good are judgments? or What good is a clinician's judgment? Meehl (1959) answered these questions by describing a number of circumstances where he claims clinical judgment can be more useful than psychometric procedures. Meehl, the man who launched the clinical versus statistical controversy, ironically was one of the most vocal in pointing out the importance of retaining clinical judgment in psychology. In his essay, "What Does the Clinician Do Well?", he listed six factors that make clinical judgment valuable. These factors are paraphrased below and include this author's comments regarding their applicability to personality assessment.

(1) When the task at hand is not amenable to being described in the form of an exhaustive set of categories or prespecified criterion dimensions, an open-ended situation exists in which "the very content of the prediction has to be produced by the predictor" (p. 596). Hoffman (1960) was one of the first psychologists to attempt to describe clinical judgment using mathematical models. He noted that mathematical models cannot produce information that can be assessed experimentally in situations that are unstructured. Mathematical models can be applied when data and outcome are conceptualized in

some kind of quantitative form, minimally in binary terms, like "greater than" and "less than." But some types of personality description cannot be put into even binary form.

(2) Sometimes the psychologist can use mental constructs for scanning and classifying data that exemplify laws of human nature, which have not yet been verbalized in the scientific community. This situation might occur in the case of a very unusual person who is presented for personality assessment. To the extent that each person is unique, it would apply to each one.

(3) Sometimes a situation can arise where unusual sets of events produce the need for clinical judgment because psychometric technologies have not yet encountered these events or built descriptive codes about them into their systems. This could again apply to the case of studying unique persons in the context of their own life situations, i.e. personality assessment.

(4) When there is a need to build new, as yet unstated hypotheses, or when new concepts are necessary, human judgment is necessary. Again, this could be necessary for describing the rare person and also for finding the right words to describe what is unique about an individual.

(5) Sometimes a decision is required so fast that there is no time to use psychometric technologies, and clinical judgment is called for. This is not likely to happen in personality assessment, since by nature it is relatively time consuming for the clinician to acquire data and then analyze it, and since it is not oriented toward a decision, goal, or prediction, but toward description *per se*. If anything, personality assessment done by clinicians could be criticized for being *too* time consuming.

(6) Sometimes using clinical thinking and insightful processes, the clinician can make subtle distinctions or fine discriminations which psychometric technologies would not have noted. Again, this can be the case in personality assessment when the clinician attempts to accurately describe an individual and verbalize his uniqueness and complexity.

Much literature has been written about "judgment" and "clinical judgments," ranging from how clinical judgments vary with such things as the patient's mood (Haccoun and Lavigueur, 1979), sex (Lowery and Higgins, 1979), or attractiveness (O'Leary et al., 1979), to judging personality from nonverbal behaviors (Glasser, 1979), to the relative merits of the clinician versus the computer (Leli, 1979). In the Introduction to this volume, we also reviewed significant bodies of literature on the validity of judgments and efforts to simulate clinical judgment. Chapters 1 and 2 looked at clinical thinking and clinical inference, which are tightly interwoven with clinical judgment.

In all this literature there is a common thread: we see that clinical processes, clinical judgments, if you will, are mental processes that are ultimately idiosyncratic to the clinician. Because of the great variability and leeway allowed in clinical thinking, its resultant judgments have been found repeatedly to be unreliable and of questionable validity. Add to this the fact that clinical methods do not require sound logic in their methodologies or the employment of such safeguards as hypothesis testing, reformulation, cross-validation, and retesting of hypotheses, and we see that clinical judgments hold little if any conceptual validity by virtue of the methods used to attain them.

Yet, some clinical judgments are accurate. Moreover, studies indicate such accuracy is not random but seems to be characteristic of certain judges. Who are they? Perhaps if we know more about them, it will help us understand how they produce accurate judgments, and thus add useful information to our task of finding out how clinical processes can be useful to interpretation methodology.

Good Judges

Clinical methods have been compared with other approaches to the study of the human psyche by writers such as Hall and Lindzey (1957), Meehl (1954), and Sarbin, Taft, and Bailey (1960), to name just a few. In such comparisons, the clinical method often fares poorly.[1] This poor showing is puzzling, however, since sometimes the method gives excellent results. For example, in his now classic study, Lindzey (1965) demonstrated that two experienced clinical psychologists could outperform "objective" processing of the same data. Several earlier studies had shown that judgments made by *some* individual clinicians are highly reliable and accurate. For example,

---

[1] See reviews by Holt (in Janis, Mahl, Kagan, and Holt, 1969), Meehl (1965), and Sawyer (1966).

Holtzman and Sells (1954) studied the ability of clinical psychologists to make predictions about aviation cadets using certain kinds of test data. They found that as a group clinicians' predictions were no better than chance. But there existed considerable variability among individuals. With twenty judgments to make, some clinicians performed much worse than chance and got as few as four right. Other clinicians performed much better than chance and got as many as fourteen right. Chambers and Hamlin (1957) got a similar type of finding in their study of individual differences in clinical judgment among clinical psychologists. Given five judgments to make, two of the twenty judges studied got all wrong; five of the twenty got all right.

Who are these good judges? Unfortunately, psychologists who are good judges have received relatively little attention in the psychology literature. Instead, research has focused on building mathematical models to simulate the judgments made by clinicians in general, regardless of their proclivity to accuracy, e.g. Hoffman, 1960; Hammond, Hursh, and Todd, 1964. It is known that good judges of others, whether they are psychologists or not, are likely to be more intelligent than poor judges, and tend to be superior on artistic or aesthetic sensitivity. They also tend to be popular with others, though not highly sociable, and are perceived by others as complex or not easy-to-judge-persons. Good judgment is found to increase with age until about age thirty to forty and does not depend on the age of the judge (Kelly, 1967, p. 65-68) but is affected by sex role (Whitley, 1979) in trained professionals. It is also known that for accuracy in judgments it helps to be like the person you are studying (Allport, 1961). Perhaps this increases the chances of a judge knowing concepts that can explain a person.

From some of the early studies of clinical judgment we can get some clues about how good judges think. We have already discussed McArthur's (1954) observation that psychologists he studied who made the most accurate judgments about an individual worked from a conceptualization of the person which grew gradually as they surveyed the person's case file. This conceptualization then served as a dynamic model of the person from which to predict and draw conclusions. The conceptualization itself was a general picture of the client's personality, and the elements that went into it seemed to be attained inductively, McArthur noted, (p. 209), rather than being deduced from bits of data and existing psychological theory. No cluster of data or sudden flash of insight or idea gave the accurate judge his picture of the personality; instead, it seemed to emerge bit by bit from amalgamating and pondering all the data. This is worthwhile to note for the personality assessor who might wish there were a quick and easy way to draw up a personality description.

In another early empirical study, Koester (1951) looked at the thinking of ten counselors by having them verbalize all their thoughts while reading through case folders for three clients. After recording and classifying these responses, he concluded that each counselor was consistent in the way s/he responded to the data from one case to the next. In other words, it looks as though each clinician had her/his own style of thinking about a case. It may be the soundness of her/his thinking process determined the accuracy of her/his judgments and made her/him a relatively accurate judge from client to client, or a relatively inaccurate one. The diligent student of personality assessment should thus take care in the habits s/he acquires when s/he thinks through case studies, since these habits are not only apt to become lasting, but also may determine his chances of becoming a good judge.

In a final early study, Parker (1958) also tried to study how clinicians think. He had ten counselors from a university counseling service verbalize their thoughts while they read case folders, predicted clients' behaviors and feelings, and listened to an interview of the client. He found that the counselors did not have a linear method of thinking but seemed to engage in giving meaning to data, synthesizing, hypothesizing, and evaluating hypotheses continuously and in an interrelated fashion and without any particular order throughout the period their thinking was monitored. Parker also found that counselors who did more testing of their hypotheses were no better predictors than those who did less testing. However, there is a problem in terminology here since Parker did not consider "hypotheses" to be the inferences drawn from the data. Instead they were many logical steps down the road and were made up of initial "interpretations" of data and "syntheses" of interpretations and data. The problem here is with Parker's coding system and logic: No attempt was made in Parker's study to examine the validity of the logic used by the counselors in forming their initial inferences and "interpretations." Therefore, increased testing by counselors of what Parker calls their hypotheses may not have affected the accuracy of predictions because a number of logical errors may have already occurred by the time they were tested. Perhaps an examination of the cross-checking and testing that went on at *early* stages of the counselors' thinking would have been more strongly associated with the accuracy of prediction.

Unfortunately, other studies of clinical thinking seem to run into as many methodological problems in research design (if not more) as Parker. A basic problem seems to be the lack of concepts and terminology for what is done in the course of clinical thinking. What one researcher calls "hypotheses," another calls "inferences," and another "interpretations." Scorers used in the studies to distinguish which type of clinical thought is being made by the clinicians consequently have few or inadequate guidelines about what scoring terminology means. This probably accounts for the fairly low reliability in ratings made across scorers, such as is noticeable in Parker's study.

Conclusions

In the clinical method, interpretation largely relies on the sensitivity, perceptiveness, and cognitive abilities of the individual clinician (Sarbin, Taft, and Bailey, 1960), not upon systematic methodology. The results are sets of "warranted assertions," to use Dewey's (1938) term, whose validity depends upon the soundness of the clinician's judgment. Since clinical method does not contain logical standards for employing clinical judgment, there are no built-in methodological steps against which to check one's thinking in the clinical method.

In contrast to the clinical method, assertions determined using scientific methodology depend upon the degree of rigor employed in attaining them. This is the major area in which science contributes to interpretation methodology: It demands that methodology be explicit, rigorous, and include a hypothesis testing component. The scientific aspects of interpretation methodology are explored in the two remaining chapters of Section I.

CHAPTER 4

INTERPRETATION
AND SCIENTIFIC METHODOLOGY

INTRODUCTORY STATEMENT

IN earlier chapters of this volume we have discussed how the subject matter of personality assessment, that is, the "inner" person or the psyche, is not generally considered appropriate subject matter for scientific study. Lastrucci (1963, p. 12), for one, in his survey of general reference works about science, found that a consensus of authorities do not consider subjective phenomena to be proper subject matter for science. Summarizing his findings, he writes, "science is applicable to any behavior or event that has objectively demonstrable attributes or consequences. . . . if an event is presumed to be inherently subjective, e.g. an idea, a feeling, an inspiration, or dream, then it is not amenable to scientific analysis. . . unless its presence can be demonstrated by objective phenomena."

In Chapter 1 we discussed how some fields of psychology make aspects of the psyche more amenable to scientific analysis by operationally defining subjective phenomena. For example, "inner contentment" could be operationalized in terms of the presence of smiling, the absence of unusually aggressive behavior, and self-reports of inner peace corroborated by positive peer evaluations. However, operationalized definitions can be a far cry from the phenomenon intended: Our operationalized definition of inner contentment may be like real inner contentment in name only, since real contentment may derive from one's relationship with God or loved ones and be an *inner* state not directly related to observable behavior. The point is that by operationalizing subjective phenomena, one may lose a good deal of the phenomenon one is attempting to study. In Chapter 1 we also discussed how some psychologists attempt to retain subjective phenomena *per se* as their subject matter and consequently give up a certain degree of scientific rigor. Psychotherapy, psychoanalysis, and personality assessment are all examples of fields of inquiry in which the subjective psyche is examined as directly as possible.

In Chapter 3 we saw how clinical methods arose in response to the need for a set of assumptions, or postulates, for working with the psyche. These postulates allowed psychologists to have a common set of beliefs underlying their approach to the psyche. Unfortunately, we saw that the clinical method is wanting in many respects, and frequently produces questionable or invalid results.

Where does this leave us if we wish to pursue the study of the psyche directly and minimize the degree to which we operationalize it? We cannot expect the study of personality will ever become purely scientific: To the extent we seek to describe the individual personality, the unique, "whole" person, our investigations must stay somewhat outside the realm of pure science since we are investigating in part the very things science abhors: internal states of being, subjective experience, and unreplicable and unverifiable events!

It leaves us in search of a better methodology than clinical methods offer, yet one not as restrictive as the purely psychometric and operationalized approaches. In other words, we want the best of both worlds: those clinical assumptions which allow us to study subjective subject matter, and that scientific methodology which is compatible with this endeavor.

We have already discussed how clinical assumptions help make the subject matter of personality assessment amenable to examination. To what extent can scientific methodology be employed in this examination? Answering this question is the task of this chapter.

NONSCIENCE AND PSEUDOSCIENCE

It would be inaccurate to state that interpretation methodology used by personality assessors is scientific. It is more accurate to state that many assessors are striving to make their methods for arriving at interpretive conclusions more scientific. The intention of this book is, in part, to help assessors take some steps in that direction.

Interpretation methodology as it stands today is not scientific because it does not meet the criteria of science. To help clarify the methodological demands of science, let us first understand what science is *not*. Lastrucci (1963, p. 17-24) lists three characteristics of "nonscience:"

(1) Ascertaining "truth" based on habit;

(2) Ascertaining "truth" based on what one's reference group

claims is true;

(3) Ascertaining "truth" based on what an ideology claims is true.

What he calls "pseudo-science" is subtler to discern (1963, p. 17-24):

(1) It is usually subjective, not objective, relying on unique personal interpretations by a particular practitioner;
(2) It is illogical, in violating one or more of the rules of inference, definition, argument, proof, etc.
(3) It is unsystematic and lacking in internal consistency;
(4) It is "closed" and not open to new facts;
(5) It has low reliability;
(6) Its predictions do not fare better than chance.

A personality assessor does not *have* to deal in nonscience when s/he interprets, but s/he does when s/he interprets personality data to mean "such and such" without a justification for the assertion other than the fact that,

(1) S/he habitually makes this association;
(2) Other clinicians (such as supervisor or coworkers) claim the association is true; or
(3) A certain ideology (or personality theory) says it is true.

Here are examples of justifications that would make the assertion less "pseudoscientific":

(1) The association is documented in empirical literatures which have used independent criteria to validate the association.
(2) Expert practitioners independently examining the data conclude the same association is present.
(3) The association does not present any logical contradictions when it is viewed in the context of all the information available about the subject.
(4) The association was arrived at by employing sound logic.
(5) Test data from other personality tests that are examined independently suggest the same association.
(6) When new information that becomes available about the subject at a future time is examined logically, findings support the presence of the association or indicate changes in it over time.
(7) When the assessor puts the data away for a month and returns to look at it again when s/he is in a much different mood from

the first time s/he examined the data, s/he draws the same conclusion.

(8) Future behaviors of the subject are understandable in terms of the association posited better than any other explanations.

Even if only one of these eight justifications were not true, the assessor would be using pseudoscientific methodology. The personality assessor may not examine all eight types of justification for every interpretive conclusions s/he draws. However, s/he should (a) be prepared to defend his/her interpretations on these grounds, (b) include as many of the eight as possible when drawing each interpretative conclusion; and (c) be prepared to change or reexamine the interpretations if any of these eight justifications are sought and not found.

A sensitive assessor may feel it is natural for him to use empathy or intuition to interpret data, but these gifts must be used only at the stage of posing interpretative hypotheses to be tested using more scientific methodology. Empathy and intuition cannot replace the eight justifications borrowed from science which serve as methodological aids to check that an interpretive conclusion is sound.

THE GOAL OF SCIENCE

What is it that we are seeking when we interpret? Is it not at least a hint of the "truth" about someone? The search for "truth" has characterized science for centuries. However, the meaning of "truth" has changed significantly in recent centuries. In his historical account of the scientific method, Blake (1960) describes how in past history the "truth" that was sought through scientific inquiry was conceptualized differently from the way it is viewed in this century. In the past, "facts" and "truth" were thought of as concrete absolutes. For example, Leonardo da Vinci (1452-1519) sought a science of Nature, which held complete certitude without any recourse to probability or relative truths. It is for *this* reason he followed rules of observation, hypothesis, experiment, description, and comparison, believing they would produce knowledge of irrefutable truth.

Other great thinkers like Francis Bacon, Descartes, and Hobbes also viewed science as a venture into absolute truth, which included nothing merely tentative, hypothetical, or problematic. Their conception of science was that of a divine mode of inquiry into absolute truths about nature. For this reason, they were not at odds with Church doctrine which also viewed the refined human intellect as capable of discerning real truths.

It was Copernicus who was one of the first great rationalists of this millenium to conceptualize truth differently and thus come into conflict with Church teaching. He contended that no astronomer could ever know true causes (in his case, of celestial movements) only God could. To him the human mind was limited to inventing mathematical fictions, or hypotheses, which would permit calculation of the observed motions. The hypotheses need not be true or even probable. They just need to fit the data.

His stance implied that any fiction could be introduced by science provided the calculations fit. This viewpoint was fought by followers of religious scripture who upheld the Church view that the human mind *could* encounter and comprehend absolute truth.

The final breach with absolute truth was carried out by men such as Isaac Newton and his contemporary, Christian Huygens. They completely abandoned the possibility of science uncovering any absolute certainty or finality.

Nowadays science is something of a discipline of consensus (Goldstein and Goldstein, 1978). It is not adequate for one person to carry out scientific procedures to establish fact. For scientific findings to be accepted as scientific "truths," it is necessary that a number of persons in the scholarly community bear witness to the findings, validating and replicating them.

With regard to the role of science in the interpretation process, the above discussion suggests some obvious limitations. Interpretation is generally carried out by a single assessor: there is no community of scholars to replicate his findings or confirm them. Even though clinical data is frequently recorded and available to other professionals in the client's record, it is rare in practical field settings that a second personality assessor's opinion is sought. Time and labor costs are just two reasons for this. Consequently, we can see that interpretative conclusions are not even in the ball park of contemporary science to the extent that it requires corroboration of findings by other experts.

In the manner in which it is currently carried out, personality assessment often resembles the science of pre-schism thinkers like da Vinci and Bacon more than it resembles contemporary "science."

Not only is a consensus frequently lacking in most personality assessment, in addition, the nature of the interpretive conclusions that are sought resemble early quests for real truth more than they resemble Copernicus' or Newton's search for hypotheses that fit the data (but are not expected to describe the true nature of the phenomenon studied.) Personality assessors are not looking for models that fit the data about their subject as much as they are seeking descriptions of their clients that are true!

This goal of personality assessment is reflected in clinical assumptions that assert that there *is* a unique, whole person whose inner life or soul contains stable, idiosyncratic features and patterns called his personality which are amenable to description. There is a sense here that the personality is the core of the person; a hint that there is an enduring, perhaps eternal, absolute nature unique to each person, which, however, often becomes distorted during life on earth. Although the personality assessor may feel s/he is ill-equipped to document the existence of the personality, s/he acts with a faith akin to that of Church theologians, believing that the human mind is capable of encountering, discerning, and comprehending the truth about another person.

Personality assessors do not, however, dwell on the absolute nature of truth. They are happy to describe the personality they see before them in whatever terms seem to fit best. The point is, though, that in personality assessment, there is an underriding approach to science that sees scientific inquiry as capable of producing real truths about a person.

The Attributes of Scientific Methodology

So far in this chapter we have discussed how interpretation methodology can avoid being non- or pseudoscientific, and how its goal is to use scientific methodology to produce accurate findings about a person, not simply to create a fictitious model that fits the data. To what extent can the interpretation process involve methodology that is actually scientific? To answer this question, we need to know what "science" is.

Lastrucci (1963) in seeking a definition of science examined scores of standard books about science. While he did not find a clear, comprehensive definition of "science," he did find a consensus among authoritative writers about the essential attributes of science. He found that a consensus of authorities describe "science" as a "method of analysis of phenomena, devised to permit the accumulation of reliable knowledge" (1963, p. 6). Moreover, the defining attributes of science as a method of analysis are that it is *systematic, self-critical, logical*, and *objective*.

Science is *systematic* in that it involves the orderly organization of problems and methods, internal consistency, and a systematic form of analysis. Science is *self-critical* in that it contains in its methods tools for its own analysis. Self-criticism is an attitude evidenced by skepticism toward ideas—even well-established ones and "pet theories"—,retesting of facts seemingly already proven, and objective verification by third parties. Science is not static; what is true today may be found false tomorrow. Thus the scientist is a doubter of everything s/he knows.

Science is *logical* in that it is guided by accepted rules of reasoning standardized by reputable logicians. It assumes competence in crucial aspects of logic, like rules of definition, forms of deductive inference, and theories of probability. Lastly, science is *objective* in that it is devoid of personal whim or bias. Impersonal procedures safeguard this. Science is centered around the publicly demonstrable qualities of phenomena. It is available to interested, competent persons, regardless of their ascribed characteristics. It is factual, not conjectural; truth, however fleeting, is ascertained by demonstration and evidence for proof. Authority in science derives from the accumulation of publicly ascertainable evidence and does not depend on dogma, the position of persons, or authorized sources.

This ideal picture of science may not fit all of what is called "science" today because it sets high standards of inquiry and conduct. Many psychologists have had first-hand experience in situations where the power, persuasive skill, or status of persons affected the degree of influence their "scientific" findings had. But even allowing for a certain amount of leeway in the degree to which we apply these ideal criteria of science, interpretation methodology is a long way from being legitimately called "scientific." With regard to being *systematic*, interpretation methodology is not so when an assessor handles scored data, analysis of data, hypothesis testing, and the formulation of findings in an *ad hoc* fashion, varying his procedures and emphases according to whim or intuition. Interpretation becomes more systematic, and consequently more scientific, when the assessor is consciously aware of the order in which s/he handles his data and hypotheses, and has a sound rationale for his particular manner of proceeding. S/he may vary his procedures depending upon the situation, client, referral question, and knowledge of factors at issue. This is akin to "flexibility" in clinical jargon, but differs from the clinical method by virtue of the orderly approach that the assessor brings to interpretation, and the internal consistency of the ratonales behind his procedures. These factors enable him to use the interpretive process in keeping with the spirit of scientific inquiry.

Assessors are often not *self-critical* in their use of interpretation. While nonclinicians are often critical of the field of personality assessment and its interpretative methodologies, clinicians sometimes seem more prone to defend their practices than establish them. For example, literature on the validity and reliability of clinical findings tends to be either strongly anti- or strongly pro-clinical methodology. Einhorn and Hogarth (1978) have discussed this phenomenon in terms of the surprising degree of confidence people have in their fallible judgment. For example, Oskamp (1965) found that self-confidence in clinicians regarding their judgments increased as a function of the amount of information available to them but without an increase in judgmental accuracy. To the extent that assessors do not include self-criticism in their interpretation methodology, by monitoring, testing, evaluating, and viewing with skepticism their interpretive conclusions, they decrease their scientific rigor.

Despite the importance of testing to establishing their assertions, some assessors state their interpretive hypotheses in forms that are untestable. For example, if an hypothesis is generated using intuition, there may be little data that relates to it, so the hypothesis cannot be tested against other test data. Alternatively, the hypothesis may be about a topic which has not received attention in the empirical literature, thus leaving the assessor no empirical literature against which to test his claim. These examples are just two of the dangers posed by intuitive hypothesis generation in interpretation.

Not all interpretive hypotheses are untestable, of course. Although an assessor may not be experienced in making testable assertions, numerous reports exist on the validation of specialized techniques which have been developed to increase the self-critical component of interpretation methodology (see, for example, Ainsworth,

1954; Garfield, 1957; Schafer, 1954; and Watson, 1951). Minimally, all assertions made during the course of interpreting should take a form in which they can be tested against other available data.

We have seen that interpretation methodology can vary in its resemblance to scientific methodology. It is unlike science when the assessor is not systematic in the way s/he handles data and thinks through his interpretations, accepting some hypotheses too readily and discarding data inconsistent with these hypotheses. Moreover, the assessor's personality may interfere with his ability to be self-critical of his methods and findings, and may make him less sensitive to some data (Garfield, 1963, p. 490). Interpretation methodology bears more resemblance to science when the assessor learns to distinguish arguments and opinions from facts; formulates assertions into terms that are testable against other data and empirical literature, and treatable using logic and inference; and strives for detachment, precision, and logical consistency, while at the same time being open to conflicting evidence and ideas.

In the next section of this chapter we explore ways in which the personality assessor can increase the degree of *objectivity* of this interpretive methodology by using (a) statistical concepts and methods of analyzing data, and (b) impersonal procedures and measures. We will not discuss the *logical* aspect of interpretation methodology until Chapter 5, where we examine a number of mental operations the assessor can use to increase the scientific rigor of interpretation.

STATISTICS AND MEASUREMENT

The use of statistics and measurement in personality assessment makes it possible for the assessor to draw interpretive conclusions of greater precision and a higher likelihood of accuracy than their non-use would allow. Statistics and measurement increase the *objectivity* of the assessor because they serve as impersonal instruments with which to gather data and describe and analyze it. For these reasons, a substantial knowledge of statistical concepts, statistical analysis, and psychological measurement is necessary for the personality assessor. Without such expertise, interpretation methodology would rest on a weak infrastructure of conjecture and good guesses. In this section we explore the nature of statistics and psychological measurement in some depth. Then, in the fourth and final section of this chapter, we clarify the importance of statistics and measurement to interpretation methodology and point out the types of statistical expertise the personality assessor must have in order to interpret well.

The term "statistics" pertains to "facts or data of a numerical kind, assembled, classified, and tabulated so as to present significant information about a subject...[and, to]...the science of assembling, classifying, tabulating, and analyzing such facts or data" (Guralnik, 1982, p. 1391). The thrust of statistics is clearly to bring quantification to subject matter. Thus statistics make it possible for personality assessors to quantify phenomena and apply analytical methods which bring a precision to personality assessment which would otherwise be lacking. Quantification and numerical comparisons are basic to any scientific endeavor because they permit observations and statements of greater accuracy and greater universal meaning to be made than is possible using non-numerical language.

"Measurement" is closely akin to statistics because it involves assigning numerals to objects or events according to given rules (Lorge, 1967.) Measures are not limited to strict *ratios* or *intervals*; they can also involve measures used to count equal members, called *nominal* measures; and relative measures, such as statements like "greater than" and "less than," which are called *ordinal* measures. For each of these types of measurement, different statistics are applicable. Stevens (1946) has summarized these relationships in his classic article, "On the Theory of Scales of Measurement." Table II below, which is adapted from Stevens (1946) and Lorge (1967), states these basic relationships.

Although other writers have sometimes amended Steven's basic picture, it provides a succinct overview of the relationship between measurement and statistics. From Table II one can see that statistics provides measurement with mathematically descriptive terminologies which simultaneously serve as methods of analysis for empirical phenomena.

When statistics are used in psychology, they can be viewed as forms of psychological measurement. Let us digress briefly to demonstrate the validity of this assertion.

Lorge (1967) stated in his seminal article, "The Fundamental Nature of Measurement," that "measures" include the processes of, the results of, the instruments for, and the units used in measuring.

TABLE II

SCALES OF MEASUREMENT

Scale	Basic Empirical Operations	Permissible Statistics	Typical Examples
Nominal	Determination of equality	Number of cases Mode Contingency correlation	"Numbering" of football play-ers Assignment of type or model number to cars
Ordinal	Determination of greater or less	Median Percentiles	Hardness of min-erals Pleasantness of odors Quality of silk
Interval	Determination of equality of in-tervals or dif-ferences	Mean Standard deviation Rank-order corre-lation Product-moment correlation	Temperature, e.g. Fahrenheit Calendar dates Standard scores on tests
Ratio	Determination of equality of ratios	Coefficient of variation Logarithmic transformations	Length, weight, force, etc. Pitch scale Loudness scale

From *Problems in Human Assessment* edited by Douglas N. Jackson and Samuel Messick. Copyright® 1967 by McGraw-Hill, Inc. Used with the permission of the McGraw-Hill Book Company.

He wrote that "measure" can not only mean "the act or the process of determining the extent, duration, and dimensions of a thing, but...[also]...the instruments by which the process is done; the units in which the instruments are graduated; and the results of the act itself" (p. 43). With this broad sense of the meaning of "measure" in mind, one can see that the possibilities for "psychological measurement," or those particular measures that are employed in the field of psychology, are vast: psychological measures include not only the thousands of *psychological tests* that are surveyed in such reference works as Buros (1970, 1974, 1978), but also the *methods* for determining the presence (or degree) of discrete psychological factors that are reported in much of the empirical literature of psychology and constitute the measuring devices used to carry out countless experimental and correlational studies in psychology.

One must bear in mind also that the term "psychological measure" does not only refer to an instrument or process; it can also refer to the very units of calibration and the results of measuring. Therefore, the statistics used to sample populations, describe and analyze data, and test the strength of relationships are themselves psychological measurements. Moreover, to the extent it is done scientifically, psychology is dependent upon psychological measures since virtually no conclusions can be drawn that have any scientific basis unless measures are made to justify the statements empirically.

Mathematics in Psychology

The use of mathematics in psychology has a long history, dating back to the eighteenth century and perhaps as far back as Aristotle (Miller, 1964). What is called "mathematical psychology" is not exactly a field of psychology, but more a style of (or strategy for) investigating psychology problems that makes use of mathematical models, among them statistics.

In mathematical psychology, psychologists basically attempt to make models of some aspect of psychology using more abstract mathematical systems. This involves isolating an empirical phenomenon, selecting a particular formal system, and then establishing a correspondence between the two—macroscopic measurement, so to speak. Many different models may be used to do this: geometric, algebraic, and probabilistic systems. Models may be stated as computer programs, systems of equations, or in axiomatic form.

Psychological relationships have been put into mathematical form by such noted psychologists as Spearman, in the course of measuring "intelligence;" Thurstone, in studying attitude; Hull, in attempting to elucidate the basic principles of learning; and Lewin, in describing social learning. Recently, information theory, game theory, statistical decision theory, and computer science have all been used in representations of psychological phenomena and simulation efforts.

Although a person may not be well-versed in these mathematical specialties, s/he is apt to encounter them in some personality assessment research literature. For example, in the Introduction we saw that even such a subjective phenomenon as clinical judgment has received extensive mathematical attention in the course of efforts by psychologists to simulate it and better understand the outcome of clinical thinking, e.g. Hoffman, 1960; Hammond, Hursch, and Todd, 1964.

Consequently, although personality assessors may not be mathematically oriented psychologists, minimally they should be familiar with the basic mathematical models that are particularly popular in personality research, such as, systems of regression and models of linear functions, and with the basic mathematical concepts used in psychology to sample, describe, and analyze data, and test the strength of relationships. Statistics underly both sets of endeavors, and for this reason it is a required course of study for professional psychologists, whether their work is clinical, applied, or research oriented.

THE IMPORTANCE OF STATISTICS AND MEASUREMENT TO INTERPRETATION METHODOLOGY

Even though personality assessment can never be totally scientific, a wide variety of statistical concepts, statistical methods of analysis of data, and psychological measures are employed in it in order to increase its precision and objectivity and make personality assessment more scientific. Statistics and measurement are intricately tied to personality assessment, and therefore to interpretation, and provide the assessor with impersonal procedures for describing and analyzing data. Even the simplest psychological measures have implicit statistical underpinnings. Moreover, the relationship between measurement and statistics is so fundamental that the ethical standards of the American Psychological Association and the American Personnel and Guidance Association both state explicitly that persons who employ psychological measures must have adequate knowledge of the statistical assumptions and procedures involved in psychological measurement, regardless of the setting or purpose for which the measures are applied.[1] Clearly, then, the personality assessor should have substantial expertise in statistics and measurement since both constitute the scientific means at his disposal for organizing the collection of data, and more important to interpretation, for describing and analyzing data.

Knowledge of statistical methods and concepts is indispensible to the proper application of psychological tests in personality assessment. Statistics are used in *test construction* (for example, in choosing sample population, selecting test items, doing item-analysis, and establishing group norms and the applicability of test scores to various populations); for *scoring data* (e.g. using parametric statistics to assign normalized scores and nonparametric statistics to assign meaningful scores to data in classes where a normal distribution of population cannot be assumed) for *analyzing scores* (e.g. by comparing an individual's scores with appropriate group scores using normalized distributions, standard deviation, frequency tables, etc.); for studying the *reliability* of measures (e.g. by looking at stability over time, homogeneity of test items, and inter-scorer reliability); for *validating* measures;[2] for *reexamining* psychological measures in order to keep them up-to-date and relevant to their intended uses; and to study the *empirical ramifications* of particular psychological measures.

Knowledge of statistics is also necessary in order to understand the *rationale* underlying much of the research about psychological tests. It was stated earlier that statistics give psychology the means to quantify. This is particularly important to the basic strategy used in testing: Psychologists know they can never hope to measure all people for all phenomena; therefore, they take samples and draw inferences from the sample about a larger population using probability theory to estimate how likely their assertions are to be correct. An assessor would need to understand statistics and concomitant probability theory to understand the construction of psychometric tests, and also to understand the statistical strengths and weaknesses of different tests that can be used to collect assessment data. Only with such knowledge can an assessor judge the soundness of his findings

---

[1] See, for example, "APGA Ethical Standards, 1974" (1976); "Ethical Principles of Psychologists" (1981); National Education Association (1971); and "Responsibilities of Users of Standardized Tests" (1978).

[2] Validity is a complex subject. See, for example, APA's *Standards for Educational and Psychological Tests* (1974).

that are based on test data and scores, and properly utilize test methods and practices in his own practice.

Statistics are also used in personality assessment to refine existing measures to give them more meaning, to remove bias, and to add to the discriminating power of measures. In addition, after all is said and done, it still is often unclear what a test is really measuring. For example, generalizations about age differences, sex differences, and racial differences that are based on test performance can be conflicting and unfair because one does not know just what abilities a test is sampling. Some psychologists have devoted considerable portions of their careers trying to get at the actual dimensions being tapped by psychological measures by developing intricate correlational and matrix techniques to "factor out" the basic ingredients and cluster them into discrete and meaningful groups. Knowledge of the technically complex statistics involved in *factor analysis* is necessary to understand this important research, its findings, and psychological tests whose construction is based on this methodology.

Statistics themselves frequently *are* the psychological measures being applied in personality assessment. A major use of statistics is to summarize or describe the characteristics of a set of large quantities of data clearly and conveniently. The term *descriptive statistics* is given to this large endeavor. Descriptive statistics uses a number of different methods to describe data: for example, frequency *distributions and graphs* are used to simplify and describe data, as well as *measures of central tendency*, or numbers that describe where the general location of a distribution of scores falls, e.g. the mean. A third kind of descriptive statistic is *measures of variability*, where a single number can be used to describe how spread out a set of scores is. In addition, scores may be transformed into percentiles or normalized scores so that new scores replace each original score and make meaningful comparison among scores in a group possible. All of these kinds of descriptive statistics are commonly used in analyzing data during interpretation and constitute psychological measures themselves. The assessor uses them to compare the client's performance meaning relative to a larger group of people. The assessor with no knowledge, or an inadequate knowledge, of such statistics would have little understanding of this broad category of psychological measures and their importance to interpretation.

Descriptive statistics are often juxtaposed with *inferential statistics* or the use of statistics to draw conclusions about a general population from a sample, because all of the cases can not be measured individually. Here numerical quantities (called *parameters*) are inferred about a general population from numerical quantities (called *statistics*) based on samples. Inferences about a general population might take the form of a *point estimate* (computed from a single sample); an *interval estimate* (or a likely interval which includes the population mean); or a probability statement about the odds of obtaining certain kinds of sample results under certain population conditions. All of these types of statistical concepts and statements both assist psychological measurement and, at times, are the chief measures. They must be understood by any person who tries to generalize from one or several people to a larger group.

Although inferential statistics is not directly used for drawing interpretive conclusions about a client, it is frequently employed in the empirical literature the interpreter draws on to buttress his interpretations. For example, if extroversion is known to be characteristic of 90 percent of the people who score in the top 10 percent on a given test, the assessor who uses that test can use this information to better guess the odds of his client being extroverted if s/he scores in the ninety-second percentile. But it must be remembered that generalizations that apply to the group do not necessarily have validity for the individual, see, e.g. Piotrowski, 1982. The assessor must have a clear understanding of the limitations involved in applying findings that are true for groups to individuals.[3]

Knowledge of statistical concepts is also needed by assessors in order to understand the empirical personality literature and other research literature frequently drawn on during the interpretation process to help generate hypotheses and validate them. Empirical literature can take the form of *correlational* and *experimental* studies (Cronbach, 1957). For both types of studies, the psychological measures that are used rely on statistical concepts and statistical analysis. In correlational studies, statistical methods are used, for example, to quantify data and results, to estimate the probability of the correctness of conclusions, and to infer the applicability of sam-

---

[3] This limitation is, of course, part of the *raison d'être* of interpretation methodology: it allows good guesses to be made about an individual under study using information from inferential statistics to help establish the *subjective* probability that the guesses are accurate.

ple findings to general populations. In experimental studies statistics are used to quantify data and calibrate instruments, to estimate the probability of correctness of results, and to estimate the applicability of findings to general populations; it is also used to quantify changes being made by the experimenter in creating different experimental conditions, and to monitor and document resultant effects on dependent variables. Consequently, a lack of understanding of statistics would leave the reader unable to follow much psychology literature relevant to personality.

With all of these applications of statistics to psychological measurement, and in view of the critical importance of psychological measurement to personality assessment, the lack of knowledge of statistics would be devastating to personality assessors. Tests and measures typically employed in assessment could not be well understood, nor properly selected, used, studied, or criticized by such individuals. Nor could data derived using the measures be properly interpreted. Such assessors would not have the necessary mental concepts to "think" critically with many measures typically used in personality assessment, could not manipulate them knowledgeably in specific contexts, and would be unable to make responsible judgments about the usefulness or results of psychological measurement.

CHAPTER 5

THE COMPONENTS OF INTERPRETATION

INTRODUCTORY STATEMENT

I N Chapter 1 we listed eight general tasks that are involved in a personality assessment, and four of which constitute the interpretation process. We will review these four steps here, and then refer to them in the discussions presented in this chapter.

The General Steps of Interpretation

Interpretation begins with an analysis of raw and scored data. Ideally each test has been scored separately and the analysis of the data for each test is being done independently. The analysis involved in interpretation includes searching for patterns in the data, searching for relationships among scores and verbal responses, and inferring hypotheses to explain these patterns and scores and the verbal and nonverbal responses of the clients. This analysis is best carried out separately for raw and scored data so that the assessor is not confused by the different kinds of information provided by these two types of data. The first two steps of interpretation summarize these operations:

(1) Analyze the raw data when appropriate in search of patterns and inferences.
(2) Analyze the scored data independently for each test in search of patterns and inferences.

Next, each inference is examined in a variety of ways. First, it is stated in language that makes it a testable hypothesis; then alternate hypotheses are generated to explain the same phenomena addressed by the hypothesis. Finally, each of these hypotheses is checked in terms of its fit with all the data to see what, if any, adjustments have to be made in the hypothesis and to see if any of the alternate hypotheses might explain the data better. In addition, each hypothesis is reviewed in terms of the support it receives from the empirical literature and personality theories the assessor is familiar with. This

73

review may produce further modifications in the hypotheses which must again be checked for their fit with the data, or new hypotheses to examine. This process of stating hypotheses, testing them against the data, and cross-validating them against each other, empirical literature, personality theory, and the assessor's personal knowledge and accumulation of clinical experience continues until a set of hypotheses remain which seem to best fit the data. *It is important to remember that the presence of contradictory inferences and hypotheses is not bad in itself; it can indicate the need to generate some overriding hypotheses that can explain the presence of seemingly contradictory states in the client.* All of these operations are summarized in the third and fourth steps below:

(3) Cross-validate inferences by comparing findings from one test with those from other tests.

(4) Formulate all findings into consistent patterns that hold no logical inconsistencies with all available information.

I would like to be the first to say that these four steps are gross oversimplifications and do not in any way capture the complexity of thinking involved in interpretation. They are presented here only as a form of outline to help organize our discussion of interpretation, and to serve as roadmarks in this chapter's presentation of information about the logical concepts and mental operations that can be called "components" of interpretation.

Our presentation of these components proceeds in the following fashion: first, a number of logical principles important to interpretation are described and their role in interpretation pointed out. Secondly, there is a discussion of several sets of mental operations the assessor uses to process the data, make use of all available information, and draw conclusions about the client. Finally, a framework for describing the thinking used by the assessor to cover the entire interpretative process of drawing interpretive conclusions from the data is proposed. Each of these three endeavors constitutes a separate section of this chapter entitled, respectively, "Logical Principles," "The Mental Operations of Interpretation," and "A Scheme of the Interpretation Process."

LOGICAL PRINCIPLES

Interpretation is guided by logical principles, whether it is being used in personality assessment, or in the course of research and scientific experimentation. Several basic principles that have already been mentioned in previous parts of this book are discussed in some detail below.

The Logical Treatment of Hypotheses

Interpretation is dependent upon the logical treatment of hypotheses (Lastrucci, 1963 p. 225). An "hypothesis" is a plausible speculation about a set of data that seem to be related. It is tentative and not yet proven. Hypotheses used in personality assessment can be taken from personality theory, research literature, clinical lore, and volumes that list hypotheses to associate with raw and scored data (such as those reviewed in Chapter 2). Hypotheses can also be generated by the personality assessor who uses inductive logic to group data together and relate it in meaningful ways that take into account his knowledge and experience. Finally, hypotheses can be generated empathetically or intuitively.[1] However, we have already discussed some of the problems inherent in over-reliance on intuition in assessment.

During the course of a personality assessment, the assessor typically puts forward many hundreds of possible explanations, or interpretive hypotheses, for clusters of data ranging from the very small, e.g. several related responses on one test, to the very large, e.g. similar patterns across tests. This *hypothesis generation* occurs repeatedly throughout steps 1 and 2 of interpretation. In addition, logical inconsistencies uncovered in steps 3 and 4 will frequently put the assessor back into steps 1 and 2 in search of better hypotheses.

Whatever hypotheses are generated by the assessor set limits on the interpretative conclusions that can finally be drawn about the client. The larger their scope, the larger the scope of the description of the client; the more complex or detailed, the more complex or detailed the client's personality picture; the more interesting, the more interesting the person's personality appears. So the assessor's hypotheses set the style of interpretation, so to speak. Carelessly worded or poorly thought out hypotheses can be difficult to test or worse still, produce misleading conclusions about the subject. Similarly, if hypotheses are inferred in a logically unsound manner,

---

[1] See Glossary for the distinction between these two terms.

drawn from poor quality empirical literature, or not rigorously cross-validated against the data, the interpretive conclusions based on them will be unwarranted. All such cases of the inaccurate use of logic should be guarded against in interpretation with regard to the generation of and treatment of hypotheses.

Logicians elaborate two main classes of principles to establish the validity of hypotheses:

(1) PRINCIPLES OF ENUMERATION, whereby an inductive hypothesis is accepted if it has not been refuted and has been confirmed on "n" occasions; and

(2) PRINCIPLES OF ELIMINATION, which suggest that an hypothesis be considered valid if it has not been refuted but alternate hypotheses have been refuted.

Both of these logical principles are used in steps 3 and 4 of interpretation, although assessors may not know them by these names.

Inference

Interpretation involves elaborate forms of inference. To "infer" means to derive conclusions in logic by reasoning from evidence and known fact. Thus inference is the key that makes interpretation, and consequently personality assessment, possible. The application of inferential logic permits the assessor to track characteristics of a person from traces left behind, like footprints, on the paths of life. Each trace represents potential information about characteristics and behavior patterns of the person, which the diligent assessor may be able to decode using inference.[2]

Both inductive and deductive inference are employed in interpretation. *Inductive inference* is that which looks at a number of samples, or a body of evidence or known facts, and infers from them a general principle. *Deductive inference* starts with a general principle, such as a postulate from personality theory, and then deduces from it other information. A fallacy in the general principle leads to inaccurate deductive inferences even if the deductive reasoning is sound. Thus, induction and deduction are distinct logical tasks. Yet, together they are the logical processes that link together test design and hypotheses with interpretive methodology.

---

[2] Sigmund Freud has been credited with originating this use of the concept "trace."

Minimally an assessor's inferences should have better than chance probability of being right; otherwise the assessor would do just as well to flip a coin to determine the presence, or degree, of different features of personality and would not need to bother spending many hours interpreting data.

Two types of outcomes are possible when interpreting personality data: accurate conclusions and inaccurate conclusions. If the data are accurate, then faulty inference or deductions from it are the cause of inaccurate interpretive conclusions. In the case of inaccurate data, faulty inference and deductions from it can also produce inaccurate interpretive conclusions. Moreover, if faultless inference and deduction are applied to inaccurate data, inaccurate interpretative conclusions result. But they are the result of poorly comprehended experience and not unsound logic. Only accurate data combined with accurate inductive and deductive inference produces interpretive results befitting scientific inquiry. These four combinations are summarized in Table III below:

TABLE III

ACCURATE INTERPRETATION DEPENDS
UPON ACCURATE DATA AND ACCURATE INFERENCE

DATA

		accurate	*inaccurate*
	accurate	accurate interpretation	
INFERENCE			
	inaccurate		

Meehl (1954) has pointed out the value of quantification and statistical analysis in providing measures of the probability of inferences being correct. Unfortunately, hypotheses based on the assessor's own "empathic perceptions," to borrow Meehl's terminology, have not been tested for reliability and validity at all. The assessor has no estimates or frequency counts of the number of times his guesses have been correct in comparison with independent measures. For this reason, empathic perceptions are best avoided as a source of hypotheses unless there is additional evidence in support of an intuition-based hypothesis from research literature or theory.

Stones (1978) summarizes three types of inferences that are encountered in the literature characteristic of personality assessment. In the first type, inference is employed in order to delineate the individual's position on various dimensions describing the degree to which a given trait is present. In the second type, inference is used to delineate symptom complexes, or clusters of personality characteristics that function in a negative fashion. The third type of inference produces assertions about how traits of a person observed interact with his environment in ways that give rise to adaptive or maladaptive behavior. In addition, for our purposes in this book, we can point out the use of inference to generate hypotheses, to draw conclusions in the course of evaluating hypotheses, and to select those hypotheses from among all considered that best describe the dynamics of the personality in question.

These uses of inference in personality assessment serve interpretive methodology across steps 1, 2, and 3. They do not, however, take us as far as step 4, where all findings are formulated into a composite picture of the individual. Important logical principles that are involved in this task are discussed next.

The Personality Formulation
As Theory Construction or a Gigantic Hypothesis

In personality assessment, the final formulation of the personality is the sum total of all those conclusions, or those hypotheses, that have withstood logical tests of their validity and have been qualified and "fine-tuned" to the highest degree of accuracy the assessor can attain. Yet, simply adding together all of the conclusions and hypotheses that have survived testing does not in itself produce a formulation of personality. The formulation is an *integrated* picture of the psychological workings of the "whole person" that arises in the mind of the assessor as s/he ponders many inferences and much supplementary information. It takes the form of a composite, meaningful, internally consistent picture of the client, which is organized systematically, and from which deductions or predictions about the client can be made. How does this integrated picture of the client's personality arise in the mind of the assessor? This is a question about step 4 of interpretation, or formulating.

Formulating a picture of a personality is like building a theory. All of the logical rules involved in theory building also apply to formulating. This is also like generating a gigantic and complex enough hypothesis that (a) subsumes all the apparent personality relationships that have been verified to some degree about the client, and (b) provides general principles about the personality that explain its observed operation. Thus the logical principles that apply to hypotheses and the use of inference also apply to formulating. Yet, these are very abstract and general statements about formulating and do not help us understand the practicalities involved in generating a personality formulation. We need a more detailed breakdown of the mental steps involved in formulating.

Some readers may think that formulations derive from higher planes of consciousness or occur as a flash of insight in the mind of the assessor, accompanied by cries of "Eureka." They would receive support in their opinion from earlier writers like Reichenbach (1951) who claimed that (p. 231), "the act of discovery escapes logical analysis: there are no logical rules in terms of which a discovery machine...could be engineered." This viewpoint, however, is being challenged. Complex computer programs have been designed which do in effect "discover." Moreover, recent writers, like Loeser (1978), are considering whether creative insight can be attained by means of logical operations and are attempting to articulate these steps and their interrelationships.

On the other hand, if the insight required to produce a formulation does derive from some plane of higher consciousness, the question arises whether that higher consciousness itself is logical. Since the refined intellects of Western civilization's most able thinkers, like Einstein and Newton, produced some of the most sophisticated examples of logic in our human record, it is not unlikely that the purest forms of intellect are logical in nature. This is not a new idea, but an old one dating back to ancient scripture, e.g. *Srimad Bhagavatam*,

1978.

Here we will view formulating as a logical process and attempt to describe its mental operations in the next section. In doing so we will find out, not surprisingly, that formulating is closely interwoven with the mental operations used to carry out steps 1, 2, and 3 of interpretation.

THE MENTAL OPERATIONS OF INTERPRETATION

The mental operations used in interpretation are common to all disciplines that require rigorous thinking. However, certain aspects of *rigorous thinking* are relied upon more than others when interpreting. By "mental operations" we mean those processes used to mentally represent and process information. They include such things as perception, memory, reasoning, problem-solving, and decision-making (Sternberg, 1981). We will not attempt to discusss all forms of mental operations here, but only those that are particularly salient in the interpretation process. We will also take special care to denote those operations that assist in the formulation stage of interpretation.

What is "rigorous thinking" and how can it help our understanding of interpretation methodology? The concept of "rigor" in thinking derives from the rationalist tradition which, together with the empiric tradition, has marked the classical sciences from their earliest development (Bazhenov and Samorodnitskī, 1976). Rigorous thinking involves striving for exactness or accuracy and is manifested in forms of thinking that are logical, objective, systematic, and self-critical. These four forms of thinking are, you recall, the four attributes of science described in Chapter 4. It is no coincidence that the four describe rigorous thinking as well as science, since rigorous thinking *is* characteristic of the sciences. It is used in non-experimental endeavors also, e.g. literary criticism and history, and represents the mental tools with which scholars hone their concepts and ideas to as fine an edge as possible.

Recent research in cognitive psychology has brought renewed attention to the mental operations involved in processing information (Sternberg, 1981). Among those information processing operations that are most important to interpreting are critical thinking, problem-solving, and decision-making. Each of these is discussed in a separate subsection below. In addition a discussion of logical thinking is provided as a prologue to these three topics, since it is basic to all.

Logical Thinking

Logical thinking is the act of correct reasoning, which takes into account relationships among propositions in terms of implications, contradictions, inconsistencies, conversion, and cause and effect (Guralnik, 1982, p. 832.) It is the system of principles underlying any science (Guralnik, 1982, p. 832) and is treated in detail in many fine texts on the subject, e.g. Dewey, 1938. In the previous section of this chapter we discussed several principles of logic particularly important to interpretation. These and the use of sound logical thinking in general form the infrastructure of the interpretation process.

The accuracy of logical thinking depends on the mental activity of the individual thinker. In his doctoral research R.W. Holt (1978) demonstrated that the use of logic by clinicians could be studied. He examined information and decision-making processes regarding causal attribution, and studied their usage in situations of varying inferential difficulty. Holt was able to make measurements about the amount of information chosen by a subject by recording the average latency of selection, the accuracy of choices, and the confidence level in selections; he meanwhile varied inferential difficulty by varying the minimum amount of information about a pattern of events needed to infer causality. He also varied the quantity of information about background events surrounding the pattern of events under study. Holt found that these background events had a significant impact on the thinking of the clinicians. Although logically unrelated to the logical task at hand, they could confuse subjects and cause the unwary to make unsound inferences.

These same difficulties in logical thinking that Holt documented are encountered when interpreting. Background data may confuse the assessor who needs to focus on limited information for each inference made. Likewise, the degree of good judgment an assessor uses in selecting specific data from all the test data and scores available to him about which to make inferences will directly affect the quality of the final picture of the client. Similarly, the assessor's degree of confidence in his choice of data and his inferred judgments from this data will shape the sharpness and conviction with which s/he formulates the "whole" picture s/he writes about his clients' personality.

Ideally, interpretation would be conducted in a rarified air of pure intellect, unlimited relevant data, and timelessness. In practice, however, time presses, relevant data is lacking, and the intellect of the assessor is preoccupied with the petty concerns of everyday life: when to pay the bills, who to visit Friday night, where to get a babysitter, why his supervisor seems upset. Periodically the intellect turns to the logical task at hand; more frequently it may amble across the mind's varied terrain.

The great intellect, and the intellect the assessor might strive to emulate, would be that one with logic, orderliness, strong memory, and focused attention. Concentration and strength of mind are mental disciplines studied as such in the East and striven for using various meditation practices. In the West, the mind is not so often looked upon as a tool requiring strengthening, discipline, and exercise; more often than not Western minds can be undisciplined, scampering about. It is possible that a useful approach to disciplined thinking would be to train the mind using those practices of the East and West that teach how to focus the intellect on a task over a period of time.

Critical Thinking

Critical thinking is "the ability to logically assess whether statements are proposed correctly" (Garett, 1978, abstract). Critical thinking involves using logic to validate assertions. In the process of interpretation, critical thinking becomes the logical tool for validating inferences and is important to hypothesis testing in all four stages of interpretation.

Using critical thinking, inferences are tested by:[3]

(1) Looking for contradictions in the implications of inferences that are interrelated with one another;

(2) Looking for contradictions between an inference and all data relevant to it;

---

[3] Adapted from Lastrucci, 1963, p. 223-242.

(3) Checking for the influence of unknown variables not elicited during the course of gathering data;

(4) Stating the limitations in the application of a given inference;

(5) Checking each implication for exceptions to the rule;

(6) Looking for contradictions within and across groups of data;

(7) Denoting causation clearly when possible.

While a substantial amount of research has been conducted in the area of critical thinking as a basic component of abstract thinking, little research exists that relates critical thinking to personality or individual differences in the ability of judges (Garett, 1978). Wiggins (1973) reviews literature on critical thinking and found clear evidence of logical fallacy and the ability to recognize fallacy among clinicians. Other researchers have recently begun to wonder if ability in critical thinking relates to such variables as intelligence, reasoning ability, and introversion-extroversion (Garett, 1978).

Problem Solving

Personality assessment has been viewed as a process of problem solving (Sloves, Docherty, and Schneider, 1979). Problem solving bears on rigorous thinking and is used when interpreting. A sizeable body of literature exists on problem solving and is reviewed by Bourne, Ekstrand, and Dominowski (1971, p. 81-118). Problem solving is often used synonymously with the term "goal-directed" thinking. As any problem solver knows, solving problems can be extremely complicated and intricate. However, most psychological research to date studies simplified forms of problem solving, so little is known about the intricacies of the complex type of thinking involved in tasks like personality assessment.

To characterize the set of solutions for any but the simplest tasks, it is necessary to take into account, according to Bourne, Ekstrand and Dominowski (1971):

(1) The subject's knowledge relevant to the task;

(2) How the knowledge is organized;

(3) How the utilization of the knowledge will vary with different solutions strategies.

These same three items give us a list of categories for studying the assessor's approach to interpretation. Each assessor can be viewed as a problem solver about to tackle a mass of information about a person in order to find a solution or picture that will fit all the data together neatly, like putting together a picture puzzle.

The skill of the assessor in piecing together this puzzle will depend upon his knowledge of puzzle assembly, so to speak, how that knowledge is organized into steps for him to carry out, and how the use of his prior knowledge about the puzzle will change depending upon the procedures actually carried out in piecing the puzzle together.

The assessor comes to the task of interpretation (the jumbled puzzle needing analysis according to our steps 1 and 2 of interpretation), with a body of knowledge derived from his training, experience, self-knowledge, etc. S/he may use this knowledge in an organized fashion and choose, for example, to separate pieces of the picture by color, putting bits of sky in one pile, grass in another, and so on. This subdividing will increase the chance of finding links between pieces compared with the chance if s/he haphazardly chooses random pieces from the pile and tries to fit them together.

If s/he has an eye for shapes, s/he may organize pieces according to fine differences in curvature or angles. The point is that s/he brings prior knowledge to bear on the puzzle to facilitate the linkage of the pieces. Similarly, the assessor's prior knowledge can be used to cluster bits of data and scores into groups with an increased likelihood of being associated. S/he thereby simultaneously reduces the sheer number of isolated bits of data and introduces concepts into the assessment.

These concepts will most likely derive from personality theories and any tests being used. However, they can come from research literature or the assessor's general vocabulary. The advantage of using concepts from one personality theory, and not mixing many theories and other unrelated concepts together, is that one theory has built-in relationships among its concepts that make it simpler to relate the clusters of data bearing these concepts. When an assessor mixes together concepts from many different sources, it becomes harder to put the total picture of the person together at the formulation stage of interpretation. It could involve, for example, the need to bring about a *rapprochement* between Freud and Skinner and existentialism. Many assessors, calling themselves "eclectic," do mix together concepts from many different theories, and in earlier chapters we advocated eclecticism ourselves. It must be noted, however, that while this approach gives assessors a bigger descriptive vocabulary to use in interpretation, it can make an internally consistent formulation difficult to achieve.

An assessor may employ different solution strategies as s/he interprets. At one extreme, some assessors may have a series of steps that they are aware of explicitly that they use from start to finish of the assessment. At the other extreme, some may weave without a pattern, so to speak. To carry this metaphor a step further, it takes a master weaver to produce a finely woven cloth without using a pattern. Beginners might produce pretty messy, unfinished pieces. In this sense, the master assessor may weave his personality assessment without an explicit pattern of steps for interpretation once s/he has become so expert at interpretation that the logical steps are so rapidly done they are not all conscious to him. But for the beginner, for whom the use of logic and inference with large sets of data are not second nature, it is wiser to have explicit steps to follow. One set of steps is given in the final section of this chapter which follows shortly.

Decision Making

Personality assessment also employs the mental processes involved in decision making. Making decisions rationally, according to Shaklee (1979, p. 329), involves:

(1) Identifying and classifying large quantities of information;
(2) Retrieving information from memory;
(3) Weighing information in terms of reliability and validity for each dimension of interest;
(4) Evaluating alternatives according to several criteria like feasibility, desirability, and long– versus short-term consequences;
(5) Deciding upon a course of action.

The first three operations above are carried out by the assessor during the first two stages of interpretation. (The last two operations of decision making are employed in assessment cases which require formulating a psychological report that diagnoses and makes recommendations for treatment, prognosis, etc., but not in cases of pure personality description.) The assessor must first mentally organize a large body of data about an individual. To this data s/he adds information from her/his own memory about tests, relevant research, comparable cases s/he has dealt with in the past, theoretical issues, etc. All the information in the total pool bearing on the case that the assessor draws on must be weighted according to saliency, reliability, validity, and dimensions of interest.

The assessor diverges from the operations of decision making after step three above and must use another set of operations to complete steps 3 and 4 of interpretation. These are broken down into four steps by Garfield (1963):

(1) Formulating hypotheses about the client;
(2) Testing these assertions against data from one test and across tests, to determine intra-test and inter-test validity of the assertions;
(3) Steps (1) and (2) are repeated until a set of "warranted assertions" remain which have survived the scrutinous search for logical inconsistencies;
(4) These warranted assertions are integrated into a formulation about the client.

If all the information fits together meaningfully and logically and explains the client's behavior, the assessor may begin to feel a sense of closure and success in piecing together the pieces of the puzzle into a picture of the client that can be communicated to others. However, assessors must guard against oversimplification in interpreting. Slovic, Fischhoff, and Lichtenstein (1977), in their studies of decision making, found that not only are judgments compromised by faulty logic, but that judgments of reality are bounded by simplification: the simpler the view of reality a perceiver brings to the task at hand, the greater his risk of error: for example, assessors may join camps of one theoretical school of thought or another. To the extent they hold firm to one theory of personality, their ease in explaining the client under study is increased, but their accuracy is decreased.

In applying this finding to the interpretive process, we can note that *any* theory is an oversimplification of reality. If an assessor subscribes to one theory, it limits the wealth of constructs that would allow him to use a broader vocabulary and make finer discriminations about the human psyche. Simon (1957) coined the term "bounded rationality" to convey the idea that a human typically constructs a simplified model of the world and behaves rationally with respect to it. Although the mind of any person cannot be completely rational at all times, it would seem self-evident that a human usually has some rational context for what s/he is doing and how s/he is living. The type of "bounded rationality" an assessor brings to the person under study would seem to be most likely to capture the flavor of the individual if it can include some of the broadest and more meaningful constructs the person under study uses to organize his life, rather than if the assessor limits himself to imposing only those constructs allowable in his favorable personality theory.[4]

A SCHEME OF THE INTERPRETATION PROCESS

Interpretation methodology can be bounded by faulty logic, invalid inferences, and poor decision strategies. Poor use of problem-solving strategies and the lack of adequate concepts can also produce suboptimal results in interpretation. A major task lies ahead for personality assessment: to delineate strategies that are being used by personality assessors to interpret data, distinguish those which are sound from those that are faulty, and promulgate the sound ones.

One set of strategy steps are described below. They are an amalgamation of the concepts covered in this chapter. Because they represent my own formulation regarding the process of interpretation, they will necessarily impose my "bounded rationality" upon the reader. If your approach to interpretation is more detailed, please add your steps to these. My pattern of steps can also be amended to include other logical steps, or a different ordering of steps. The purpose of this summary of steps is to provide a framework for studying and teaching interpretation methodology, or to help organize one's own approach to interpretation.

When processing a battery of tests for a personality assessment, some assessors may analyze and interpret one test at a time. Others may prefer to look at all test results at once. The latter, however, is a harder task, hinders the independent treatment of test scores, and increases the likelihood of error because of the great increase in the quantity of information being dealt with at one time. Therefore, it is

---

[4]Compare George Kelly's (1955) Personal Construct Theory.

recommended that battery results be analyzed and interpreted one test at a time, with frequent reference to other test results for cross-validation of hypotheses at the hypothesis testing stages of interpretation and beyond.

The following summary of steps in interpretation starts at the point where all test data has been assembled, read, and scored. The four starting principles for analyzing data are:

(1) Review all scored and unscored data from the battery administered;

(2) Look at results test by test, grouping intratest data into meaningful clusters drawn from test literature and theory. Include meaningful sequences of data and notable patterns of data;

(3) Group intratest data into meaningful clusters drawn from the assessor's cognitive schemes. Include meaningful sequences of data and notable patterns of data;

(4) Sort clustered items into subcategories.

Then hypotheses are formed by:

(1) Relating subcategories of data to one another using inference. Here possible hypotheses are derived from personality theory, research literature, test literature, clinical experience. Brainstorming or intuition may be used here with great caution;

(2) Testing hypotheses against intratest data;

(3) Double-checking hypotheses across tests to see if they are supported by data from other tests;

(4) Reformulating old hypotheses and formulating new ones as data are reviewed again and again;

(5) Forming, stating, and testing at least one alternate hypothesis or the null hypothesis for each hypothesis generated. For each hypothesis generated, alternates should be proposed routinely to relate the same phenomena. This is an important mental discipline which serves as a check-point to catch and remove the assessor's biases and "pet theories" from his inferences.

Substantiated hypotheses, or inferences, are tested again by:[5]

(1) Looking for meaningful implications of the hypotheses that are logically unsound when interrelated with one another;

---

[5] Adapted from Lastrucci (1963), p. 223-242.

(2) Seeing that each hypothesis is logically related to all relevant test data;

(3) Being aware of the possible influence of unknown variables not elicited or tapped in testing and positing their influence. This is a source of additional alternate hypotheses that may prove more likely inferences than the first ones. As competing hypotheses are tested against more and more data, one may prove capable of explaining more data than the others;

(4) Qualifying hypotheses being generated in terms of situation specificity, time parameters, latency, threshold of manifestation, and so on;

(5) Checking each implication for negative causes, exceptions to the rule, etc.

(6) Looking for meaningful differences within classes of phenomena as well as across groups;

(7) Denoting causation clearly.

Final inferences that have survived this testing and retesting are formulated into statements that form a picture of the client by:

(1) Repeating the above steps for hypothesis formation and hypothesis testing in order to generate the personality formulation and test it, but in this case, validated hypotheses are the primary data for the formulation. Here the assessor must be aware of model dependence upon personality theory, research literature, test theory, and so on. In his formulation, the assessor should be prepared to specify models borrowed from the empirical and other reference literature.

Summary of Operations

The eighteen operations we have described above are stated in condensed form below:

(1) Review all data;

(2) Group intratest data into meaningful clusters in keeping with test theory and test construction;

(3) Sort clustered items into subcategories;

(4) Relate subcategories of data to one another using inference;

(5) Test hypotheses as necessary;

(6) Reformulate hypotheses as necessary;

(7) State the null hypothesis and alternate hypotheses for each standing hypothesis;

(8) Test null and alternate hypotheses against the data. See whether the original hypothesis or the alternates explain more data with logical consistency;

(9) Reformulate hypotheses again and again seeking logical consistency and an increasing scope of explained data;

(10) Look for implications of inferences which are logically unsound when interrelated with other inferences;

(11) Check that each inference is logically related to all relevant test data;

(12) Attend to the possible influence of unknown variables;

(13) Qualify inferences as necessary;

(14) Check each inference for negative causes and exceptions to the rule;

(15) Check for meaningful differences within classes of phenomena as well as across groups;

(16) Denote causation clearly;

(17) Formulate descriptive statements from hypotheses that are logically consistent;

(18) Formulate an organized, composite personality picture by repeating steps 1-17, using validated hypotheses as data to construct an overriding theory (or gigantic hypothesis) to describe the client's personality.

SECTION II

Interpretation Demonstrated: A Case Study

INTRODUCTION TO SECTION II

We have spent the first part of this book trying to describe how to think clearly when interpreting data for the purpose of constructing descriptive statements about personality. Now let us apply the interpretation process described in Section I to data about a real person, Mrs. R. This is the task of the second half of the book, where we take a set of test reponses that Mrs. R gave on a battery of psychological tests the author administered to her and think through the process of translating this data into interpretive conclusions about Mrs. R's personality.

CHAPTER 6

INTRODUCTION TO THE CASE STUDY

S ECTION II of this volume presents a descriptive case study
which demonstrates the interpretation process discussed in Section I. Methodology for the case study, where n = 1, is adapted from
Chassan (1979) and Holtzman (1963). The case study is based on
test data for a Mrs. R, who is introduced to the reader in the first
section of this chapter. The organization of the case study, test selection, data collection, and methods of data analysis are described in
subsequent sections of the chapter under separate headings. The
final section of this chapter entitled, "Limitations to the Case Study,"
points out natural limitations to the case study that the reader should
be aware of. Some of these limitations are inherent in case study
methodology, others in the personality assessment undertaking.

THE SUBJECT FOR THE CASE STUDY

The subject for this case study is Mrs. R, who was a patient on
the psychiatric ward of a general hospital. She was tested by me during the course of my responsibilities on the ward as part of her "work
up" upon admission to the hospital. In keeping with APA's Principle
#5 regarding confidentiality in the *Ethical Principles of Psychologists*
1981, p. 635-636, the identity of Mrs. R is thoroughly disguised by
making enough changes in the background information about her
that she cannot be traced.

Mrs. R was referred for testing, having entered the hospital vol-
untarily, because, in her words, her job, home, and responsibilities
had become "too much." She also showed symptoms of a thyroid
condition according to her referring doctor.

At the first of two formal meetings I had with Mrs. R (one for
interview and testing; the second for testing only), it was difficult to
get information from her. Her thinking was spotty and run-on; her
mind wandered off tangentially into tales with unidentified people
and events. However, with frequent verbal reminders from me she
was able to stay with a topic and respond appropriately. She was

93

cooperative and made attempts to be friendly, but seemed dependent, self-deprecating, and depressed.

In the second meeting with me five days later she was much more coherent verbally and much less rambling in her discourse. She still behaved in a dependent manner frequently asking my permission or approval, spoke in a self-deprecating fashion, and softly mumbled her words so I often could not understand her and continually had to ask her to repeat what she had said. She smoked frequently, complained of thirst, and often mentioned food and hunger. Generally she seemed tired, sad, listless, and depressed.

A brief history of Mrs. R was obtained from a one-hour interview I had with her before administering the tests, supplemented by about 30 minutes of chatting on the ward on other occasions. This information is presented below.

History

Mrs. R is a thirty-three-year-old mother of three children. Of average height with short, dull brown hair, she is matronly and plain-looking with no outstanding physical features. She smokes frequently, handled food, drink, and cigarettes a lot in our meetings, and says she has an "obnoxious" appetite. Legally separated from her alcoholic husband, a fireman, for the past three and a half years, she has since become largely self-supporting. Since her husband has been living away from home she has worked as a waitress, computer key punch operator, claims agent, and presently is secretary to the man in charge of security at a large urban company.

This is Mrs. R's second marriage. Following an illegitimate pregnancy with her first child, which she kept although others advised against it, she entered a marriage of convenience with a man (not natural father) whom she describes as a homosexual who wanted a marriage for a cover to his activities. Although aware of the husband's reasons for wanting to marry before she married him, she says she was dissatisfied with the marriage and divorced him about a year later. She has been married to her second husband for eleven and a half years.

Mrs. R had two other children by her second marriage, a daughter, eight and a half, and a son, six. Her first child, a son now age fifteen and a half, remained with Mrs. R after the divorce but is now living with foster parents following trouble with the police, which Mrs. R claims was for "attention" since it occurred at the time her second marriage was collapsing. She says her second husband has never accepted this son and throws up the fact to him that he is illegitimate. Mrs. R says she in no way blames her son for his delinquency and for not wanting to return home.

She says that "something funny" happened after her third child was born: her husband started denying it was his child, friends began to disappear, and the husband started drinking. He paid attention only to the other two children so Mrs. R paid extra attention to this child. This pattern has continued to the present. Although they do not live together, the husband still visits the children, of which Mrs. R approves.

Mrs. R finished tenth grade. She had little interest in school until high school when her growing facility at art increased her interest in school. A high point in school was the possibility of a partial art scholarship. She mentioned this to her parents. They laughed, and she reports that soon afterward she left school, returning to night school, but never getting a high school diploma. She says she would like to have done art and missionary work.

Mrs. R was raised by her parents and "lots of other families" (foster) in Rochester. When living with her parents the family moved from one rooming house to the next because her father worked "on and off," gambled, and drank. Her mother often worked to support the family. She says she dislikes her parents because "they could have created a better life for their children." When asked to comment on her mother, she answered with her father, and later when the question was repeated merely said, "She never bothered me and I never bothered her." She describes her father as intelligent, a perfectionist, who was "very strict when he was interested" and "beat the daylights out of us."

She says she got the feeling her parents had not wanted children and reports that her mother told her that her father wanted marriage but not children. Mrs. R does not know "why she [mother] never left him" [father] because he even kicked the mother in the stomach once; Mrs. R concluded about her mother that "in her own way she loves us." Mrs. R has one sibling, a sister seven years older than herself whom she says "got stuck watching me," and about whom she says her parents were always concerned, although they lacked concern for Mrs. R ("You take care of yourself—we don't have to worry about you.") Mrs. R states she once had to pound on the front door half an hour to get in at night, although the parents would wait up for the other daughter to come home. Mrs. R says she now treats her own three children equally.

Mrs. R believes it is important for her children to be exposed to normal family conditions, if not in her own, then in other people's families. Although she dislikes her parents, now living nearby, she dutifully visits them but complains her parents keep asking for her sister, who Mrs. R reports dislikes them also, pays them no attention, and lives married with her family in Ohio. She also says her parents are resentful that she and her sister do not support them financially. In spite of her own feelings about them, Mrs. R "tries to create grandparents" for her children and wants her children to have good relations with, and draw their own opinions about, their father and her parents.

Just after the youngest child was born, Mrs. R says her husband began to say he wanted to put her in a mental institution and the children on the state dole so he would be free of his responsibilities. After an incident when Mrs. R overheard, and confirmed with her older son, that her husband had offered him (the older son) money to accompany him to have Mrs. R institutionalized, she called the police and brought him to court on a variety of charges, such as, neglect, assault, and battery (especially when drunk, he would cuff the older boy, and when Mrs. R would defend the child, the father would hit her instead.) At one point when the court asked her to decide if she wanted to give up her children or try to bring them up and support them herself with limited support from the father, she says she went to the beach to think about it and thought of suicide. She claims this is the only time she ever thought of killing herself. She finally decided to keep the family together as much as she could but would not allow the husband back "because he is so bad when he is drunk."

Immediately prior to admission to the hospital, Mrs. R had moved with her children from her home because she claimed someone had gone through the basement, and her recent subletters on the other side of the duplex where she lived had taken pictures at the company where she is employed as secretary to the security agent. Police reports seem to be negative, and Mrs. R was aware that the problem might rest with herself.

HOW THE CASE STUDY IS ORGANIZED

The case study is organized as follows:

Mrs. R's test results are presented one test at a time in Chapters 7 to 12, respectively, in the order:

WAIS
Bender-Gestalt
Draw-A-Person
TAT
Rorschach
MMPI

Each of these chapters opens with some general comments and a brief review of literature about the test being looked at in that chapter. Empirical literature about the validity and reliability of the test are particularly emphasized to provide an estimate of the degree of accuracy that can be associated with traditional hypotheses based strictly on the test scores and responses. This introductory discussion of each test also introduces the rationale behind the way Mrs. R's responses to each test are treated in the case study. For example, even where validity and reliability of some aspects, or the whole, of a test seemed low, traditional hypotheses together with other inferences could still be used as working hypotheses and kept in mind as possibilities awaiting support or negation from other sources.

Next, Mrs. R's raw and scored test results are reported in each chapter, verbatim. Notes regarding interpretation, hypothesis-building and hypothesis-testing follow, as well as some research findings from empirical studies that bear on some of the more salient features of Mrs. R's results. Because of the vast amount of information provided by the battery, only a relatively small number of aspects of test performance are followed in depth. They nonetheless represent the set of data focused on by the author with which to build the personality picture of the subject. Because hundreds (and for the Rorschach, thousands) of studies have been done on each of these psychological tests, I found it useful to use summaries of literature provided by several scholars who are cited along the way and by test reviews in the *Mental Measurements Yearbooks* (Buros, 1959, 1965, 1978).

The integration of test findings, or the final write-up, appears in Chapter 13, entitled "Summary Report and Recommendations." This final chapter of both the case study and the book summarizes what I thought I learned about Mrs. R from her test battery and test behavior. It is written in a form in keeping with professional standards for communications to psychologists and related mental health professionals.[1] The reader might prefer to skim this report before reading all the details that were considered in its making.

SELECTION OF TESTS FOR SECURING DATA

Six popular tests commonly used in personality assessment were used to secure data for the case study:

— *Wechsler Adult Intelligence Scale* (WAIS), a general intelligence test that explores various types of intellectual functioning;
— *Bender-Gestalt*, a visual motor test that is used to assess functioning of the brain;
— *Draw-A-Person*, a highly unstructured projective test;
— *Thematic Apperception Test* (TAT), a projective test with standardized picture stimuli used to reveal conscious and unconscious processes;
— *Rorschach*, the oldest and probably still the most widely used projective technique, which uses standard ink blot stimuli;
— *Minnesota Multiphasic Personality Inventory* (MMPI), a structured inventory free of subjective scoring, which has numerous subscales.

The rationales for using a battery of tests are threefold. First, an individual's performance is apt to vary from one test to another.[2] Secondly, with a battery different aspects and levels of functioning of a person are given a chance, theoretically, to manifest in the tests, thus exposing "blind spots."[3] Finally, using a battery allows the assessor to make use of research literature associating different combinations of test results with different subgroups of characteristics.[4]

The particular tests chosen for inclusion in our battery were se-

---

[1] See, for example, Hollis and Donn (1979), Huber (1961), Klopfer (1960), and Tallent, (1976).
[2] Harrower (1952, p. 48).
[3] Rapaport, Gill, and Schafer (1945-1946).
[4] Rapaport, Gill, and Schafer (1945-1946).

lected due to the variety of areas they tap, their diversity in methods of eliciting behavior samples, and the variety of theoretical origins they represent. Most important to our demonstration of interpretation, they are among the most frequently used psychological tests in the United States. According to Lubin, Wallis, and Paine (1971), these six are the most commonly used battery of psychological tests for adults. Sundberg (1961) found that the six most popular are these except for the MMPI. In place of the MMPI, his list of the top six includes the Stanford-Binet because of its usefulness with children and retarded people. (It is, however, less useful for studying personality.) A later study by Brown and McGuire (1976) confirms that our six remain in the top ten despite small shifts in rank order over the years. Moreover, Wade and Baker (1977) report that clinicians use these tests frequently because they are familiar and trusted for giving insight. Apparently, clinicians value them more than they value other more technically objective measures and feel they have no better alternatives when clinical decision making is called for.

ADMINISTRATION AND SCORING OF TESTS

Tests were administered by myself during two private sessions with Mrs. R held on the psychiatric ward. Raw data was scored by myself. Test administration was carried out in keeping with each test's respective test manual and related psychological literature, cited in the text. Raw data was scored using appropriate scoring systems and with reference to test manuals and test literature. Comparisons were made between Mrs. R's scores and selective samplings of other people by using test norms, distribution tables, and appropriate statistical analysis. Raw and scored data are displayed in the text in standard charts and formats. Chapters 7 to 12 describe test administration, scoring of raw data, test norms, and analytical procedures used, test by test and in detail.

DATA ANALYSIS

Scored data was analyzed and interpreted using methods described in Section I and standards drawn from the codes of ethics regarding assessment. The detailed description of the analysis and interpretation of raw and scored data forms the body of Chapters 7 to 12. It is appropriate here to make some general comments about data analysis.

Many of the inferences in the case study that are based on theory have been studied empirically with sample populations. I have tried to include empirical literature about some of the more salient theoretical inferences in the case study in an attempt to assess the likelihood of their being correct with regard to Mrs. R. Statistical inference is the most quantified of the modes of hypothesis generation discussed in Chapter 5, and it has been the easiest for which to find studies that help estimate the chances of such inferences being correct for Mrs. R. I have also tried to present some pertinent empirical findings about some of the more salient inferences drawn from cookbooks, norms, etc., that were useful in lending meaning to Mrs. R's test data.

In considering the value of empirical validity studies regarding inferences drawn from statistics and from theory, we are drawn into the heart of the controversy over clinical versus statistical (or actuarial) prediction. Do we mainly want to classify the subject into one or more of a variety of diagnostic or group categories, or do we mainly want to, in Meehl's words (1954, p. 4), "formulate some psychological hypotheses regarding the structure and dynamics of this particular individual?" Holt points out that in reality the psychological report does both; but it has already been pointed out that this case study's purpose is largely the latter aim, i.e. description not prediction. However, inferences which mainly serve to classify the individual into group membership, e.g. MMPI results, can also be very useful for hypothesis-building about an individual. Because even those inferences which stand firm in the light of empirical investigations (and thus have a relatively high probability of correctness) always stand *some* chance of being wrong for the individual in question, e.g. a problem of overgeneralization from sample to general population, it seems that the best strategy to follow is to treat all inferences, whatever their sources, as interpretive hypotheses initially.

Although the chance of any hypothesis being correct is increased by corroborating support from a variety of bits of data about Mrs. R and from the logical checks a hypothesis is ultimately subject to, the final test of any hypothesis being a fairly good one, such that it makes its way into the final personality report in Chapter 13, must be against my own clinical judgment as to the meaningfulness and importance of the hypothesis in relation to a general formulation of information about the personality of Mrs. R as a whole.

Unfortunately, the hypothesis-building model described here has some major weaknesses which should be noted. Corroborating information is most confidently used when it comes from several independent sources. Although I would like to think that the observations I make about each test in the battery are independent, they of course are not. I have examined each test separately, but cannot pretend to have done them "blind," or without some knowledge of Mrs. R's history and performance on other tests influencing my perceptions and interpretations. Besides the nonindependence of many of the observations, there is the problem that two or more wrong inferences do not make a right one: there is always the chance that several tests will each strongly suggest the same hypothesis which is ultimately wrong. This type of error is possible even though one would hope for an increased degree of confidence and validity with respect to final hypotheses that have been based on increasing amounts of supporting evidence. As a subjective measure of my personal degree of confidence in the final personality report of Mrs. R, I would place a bet with odds of 4:5 that my picture of her is accurate.

LIMITATIONS TO THE CASE STUDY

Several limitations to the case study are described in this section. Some are inherent in case study research design; others derive from the nature of personality assessment and the limitations of interpretation methodology.

(1) The ideal situation for conducting a personality assessment of an individual is one where there is a subject who is totally cooperative and articulate; where there is unlimited time on the parts of the assessor and the subject; and where the assessor has unlimited access to data about the subject drawn from many vantage points, e.g. personal documents like diaries, peer judgments, self-report, observations, testing, interview, other professionals, etc. Reality for psychologists is not like this, and this case study is no exception. It is based on the kind of data and clinical situation which is apt to be encountered by practicing psychologists. The subject is a disturbed person who has been referred to a psychiatric clinic for evaluation.

She is of average intelligence, and not unusually cooperative or articulate. She is also receiving medication which hampers the clarity of her responses and span of concentration.

The data secured on Mrs. R are limited to an hour long interview conducted by myself in which a verbal history was secured, and the results of a battery of psychological tests I administered to her. The total time I spent with Mrs. R in testing, interviewing, and brief chatting on the ward was approximately four hours. Although the case study is based on this limited amount of data, this limitation is typical of personality assessments carried out by psychologists in the field and is thus representative of the data a beginning assessor is apt to deal with. Moreover, studies suggest that increasing amounts of time and data do not necessarily increase the accuracy of the assessment (see Goldberg, 1968, for review).

(2) You will recall that one aim of this book is to make explicit the applicability of logical and scientific thinking processes to interpreting data from a test battery. Since it would be impossible to describe every thought that goes on in my head in perceiving data, giving it meaning, etc., the demonstration of interpretation methodology in the case study is limited to a portrayal of sufficient amounts of thinking to make it clear to the reader what mental processes are being carried out, with what degree of rigor, and with what complexity of thought in interrelating data, theory, and empirical literature.

(3) It has been reported that only two basic features are correlated with accurate impressions of another person: (a) being like the person; (b) having known the person intimately over a period of years. Since the latter is ruled out because I only knew Mrs. R during a span of two weeks, it may well be that the accuracy of my impressions will be right only to the extent that I am similar to her. This does not mean that I need to share the same features as she, however. I could, for example, have some degree of a feature, have experienced it in extreme situations in the past or vicariously. I could also have the same features but have them organized differently in my personality, or I could employ them differently than she in response to environmental demands.

(4) In 1948 Schafer (1948) cautioned psychologists about letting their own professional, technical, and personal problems and needs influence the test results of their clients. The importance of his warn-

ing was born out in studies which have tended to show that test results and their interpretation are likely to mirror the tester and not necessarily x-ray the patient.[5] To some extent we can only see that which we have some familiarity with. Hopefully I have a broad enough experience with life and a knowledge of others to have sufficient concepts to describe Mrs. R accurately. Hopefully I also have enough self-knowledge and honest insight into my weaknesses, fears, and defensive ploys to recognize where I could be liable to distort or project my own inner workings and thereby grossly distort my perceptions of Mrs. R when I interpret her data. I have found that when I feel strong emotions during an interpretation, either positive or negative, it can indicate an area of personal sensitivity for me where I must exercise extra caution in this regard and monitor my own dynamics so that I do not distort my view of the subject.

(5) Psychological tests, particularly the projectives or nonstandardized ones, tend to suffer from problems with reliability and validity. The projectives used in this case study are no exception. For example, in his discussion of the incremental validity of several of these tests (that is, how much *additional* information a test provides, as contrasted with its convergent and discriminant validity[6]), Sechrest (1967) describes several studies which are rather discouraging:

Winch and More (1956), using a multiple-correlation technique in attempting to determine the increment in information produced by TAT protocols over a semi-structured interview and case material, found no basis to conclude that the TAT contributed anything beyond what was given by case histories and interviews. It could be argued, however, that the TAT may be a more efficient use of time than interviews and case histories. However, in another study, also cited by Sechrest, Sines (1959) reported that although the Rorschach was found to yield better than chance predictions, not only did it seemingly not add to information obtained from interviews and a biographical data sheet, but it is reported to have produced a net decrement in predictive accuracy. Sechrest also cites Kostlan (1954) who found that judges made better than chance inferences about patient's behavior only from minimal data (age, occupation, education, marital status, and source of referral). When test results were

---

[5] See, for example, Sanders and Cleveland's study (1965) about the Rorschach, and Hammer and Piotrowski (1965) on the House-Tree-Person test.

[6] See Campbell and Fiske (1959).

used to make the same judgments, only the social history yielded more accurate inferences than those made from simple biographical facts.

Before throwing up your hands in dismay, however, recall the discussion in Chapter 3 of the failure to distinguish good judges from inaccurate ones in clinical studies. This failure to look at the judge applies to many studies of tests too. I know of no psychological or counselling body which qualifies its members based on the accuracy of their work. Personality assessors and test users become so based on their knowledge of testing and assessment, but their accuracy in using tests and assessment is not examined. This could at least partially account for many of the negative findings about assessment and projective tests.

To safeguard the accuracy of inferences we draw from projective tests in the case study, we will use projective test data only as material from which to infer working hypotheses. According to our interpretation methodology, these can be obtained from three sources: (1) my empathic perceptions (which implicitly draw on my training and experience as they manifest in my personality); (b) inference based on theory; and (c) statistical inference (such as, comparison of data with group norms and "cookbook" recipes.) For a specific inference based on any of these three modes of hypothesis generation there is associated probability that the inference is correct, as opposed to being wrong for Mrs. R. Our interpretation methodology hopefully will optimize the chance of accuracy.

(6) The global picture of a person which results from a personality assessment is difficult to evaluate: to the extent that personality assessment tries to describe the uniqueness of the individual and does not dwell on classification or prediction or diagnosis, the validity of the results is difficult to ascertain. The case study does not contain a component to evaluate the final personality report. Instead, its validity is dependent upon the care with which the report is constructed and the degree to which it is conceptually valid.

CHAPTER 7

WAIS

REVIEW OF LITERATURE

THE Wechsler Adult Intelligence Scale (WAIS), (Wechsler, 1955, 1958), is one of the most widely used tests of adult intelligence. It is designed to be a broad sampling of a wide range of abilities.[1] The WAIS tries to assess general intelligence as the composite of several separately measured intellectual functions. The test should ideally provide differential information about some specific abilities of the individual and convergent information about general abilities. However, besides the problem of the meaning of a general theory of "intelligence," as a test of intelligence the WAIS is limited to tapping only the limited number of skills which make up Wechsler's concept of "intelligence." Content and construct validity studies can nonetheless expand and clarify the range of intelligence to which it can be applied.

The WAIS IQ for an individual tends to stay constant despite the tendency of point scores to decline after about age thirty, because the WAIS IQ is based on standard deviation units from the mean per age group.[2] The WAIS standardization sample on which the norms

[1] A revised WAIS, the WAIS-R (1981) has been published by the Psychological Corporation this year. For ages sixteen to seventy-four, it is based on the same concept of intelligence as the 1955 WAIS, that is, that intelligence is a global entity that can be inferred from performance on a variety of tasks. The content of the WAIS-R is similar to the 1955 edition. About 12 percent of the question items are new and 8 percent are modified from the 1955 WAIS. Except for this revised content, the eleven tests of the WAIS-R remain the same as those comprising the WAIS 1955, although they are changed in their order of presentation to the examinee.

Norms for the WAIS-R were taken from the 1970 U.S. census and more recent population reports. The sample for the WAIS-R was 1,880 adults, controlled for age, sex, race, geographic region, occupation, and education, as was the 1955 sample.

[2] All in all the WAIS-R is not a radical change over the 1955 WAIS. Moreover, it has received very little use at the time of the writing of this volume. Therefore, the WAIS (1955) is deemed acceptable for use in this case study. For the sake of confidentiality, the test data on the subject of this study have been withheld from publication for several years as an additional safeguard to protect the identity of the subject. At the time of testing the subject, the 1955 WAIS was the test of choice. Because of the great similarity between the 1955 WAIS and the WAIS-R, the demonstration in this case study using the WAIS 1955 should be easily transferred and applicable to the WAIS-R.

for comparison of scores are based is two times the size of the sample used in developing its predecessor, the Wechsler-Bellevue. The great care taken in sampling, testing the sample, and deriving the norms seems to be one of the test's major assets, such that the WAIS often serves as the criterion itself for validating new measures of intelligence.[3]

Correlations of the WAIS with other intelligence tests range from .50 to .90, e.g. WAIS correlation with the Stanford-Binet is about .85. Correlations with other criteria, such as school success (about .64), selection of mental defectives, differentiation of occupational groups, and so on, are not always very strong (and should not be expected to be strong.) It seems that rather than external criteria of validity, acceptance of the WAIS has come to depend upon the content validity involved in (1) the care taken in construction of the test, and (2) on the test's underlying rationale as the best evidence that it is effective in measuring what it purports to measure.

As regards reliability, split-half internal consistency of the WAIS is .97, repeat reliability about .90. The reliability of individual subtests is lower but still good. The reliability of differences among subtests, however, is only fair and this fact has been used as a criticism of scatter analysis, that is, interpretation of the pattern of abilities as measured by different subtests. Note that the same criticism can be made of MMPI profile interpretation, whose different subtests are hardly more reliable than those of the WAIS and are about as highly intercorrelated. Wechsler (1958) asserts that the pattern of subtest scores of the WAIS may provide useful diagnostic indicators, but there is contradictory support of this contention from research accrued over the years (Guertin, reviewer in Buros, 1959). For example, Jones and McNemar (cited in Rapaport et al., 1968) have pointed out that difference scores (such as, Vocabulary scatter) are more unreliable than the subtests on which they are based, so that according to the calculations of Field (also cited in Rapaport et al., 1968), a WAIS subtest weighted score should differ from the

---

[3] The WAIS (1955) sample consists of a nation-wide stratified sample of 1700 male and female adults, plus 475 adults over age sixty, matched in proportion to the 1950 U.S. census for occupation, education, urban-rural residence, geographical region, age, sex, and race. This was certainly one of the most carefully selected samples I have seen in reviewing literature for this volume.

mean of all others by at least 5.75 for the difference to be significant at the .05 level.

Since none of Mrs. R's subtest scores differed by as much as 5.75 and only Digit Symbol and Picture Arrangement differed by as much as 5 scaled points, this raises the question of whether it would be meaningful to focus on the differences between her subtest scores as is required by scatter analysis. Another problem of scatter analysis involves factor analysis. Intrinsic to a test which purports to measure "intelligence" should be large general factors. For example, Cohen (cited in Rapaport et al., 1968) has found three major factorial structures in the WAIS which involve verbal, performance, and memory skills. However, he found relatively little factorial specificity of subtests, which raises the theoretical question of whether or not scatter represents much more than a loading on these three factors. Nonetheless, a pattern of such loading could possibly have diagnostic significance, and in support of scatter analysis in general, Rapaport et al. (1968) report they have found it to be diagnostically accurate in 30-40 percent of the cases in which it is employed. It appears that the scatter pattern of Mrs. R's scores should at least be worth looking into for some possible hypotheses about her.

Besides insight derived from comparison of Mrs. R's scores with Wechsler's norms, the WAIS has also been useful to me in this case study as a source of personality and intellectual functioning hypotheses based on inferences derived from her verbalization of answers, qualitative features of Mrs. R's approach to the tasks, and her behavior during the testing. Because of the lack of validation studies involving measures of precisely what each subtest is measuring,[4] it should be pointed out that many of the inferences which follow in the interpretation subsection of this chapter depend in the final analysis upon what the interpreter thinks the test is measuring.

---

[4]Actually, the literature contains many confirmations of the *rationales* for many of the subtests.

WAIS

RAW DATA AND SCORING

WAIS RECORD FORM
Wechsler Adult Intelligence Scale

Name _____

Birth Date _____ Age _____ Sex _____ Marital: S M D W
mo   day   yr.   CIRCLE ONE

Nat. _____ Color _____ Tested by _____

Place of Examination _____ Date _____

Occupation _____ Education _____

TABLE OF SCALED SCORE EQUIVALENTS*												
	RAW SCORE											
Scaled Score	Information	Comprehension	Arithmetic	Similarities	Digit Span	Vocabulary	Digit Symbol	Picture Completion	Block Design	Picture Arrangement	Object Assembly	Scaled Score
19	29	27-28		26	17	78-80	87-90			36	44	19
18	28	26		25		76-77	83-86	21		35	43	18
17	27	25	18	24		74-75	79-82		48	34	42	17
16	26	24	17	23	16	71-73	76-78	20	47	33	41	16
15	25	23	16	22	15	67-70	72-75		46	32	40	15
14	23-24	22	15	21	14	63-66	69-71	19	44-45			14
13	21-22	21	14	19-20		58-62	66-68	18	42-43	30	38-39	13
12	19-20	20	13	17-18	13	54-58	62-65	17	39-41	28-29	36-37	12
11	17-18	19		16	12	15-16	58-61	15-16	35-38	26-27	34-35	11
10	15-16	17-18	12	14	11	40-46	52-57	14	31-34	23-25	31-33	10
9	13-14	15-16	11	13	10	12-39	47-51	13	28-30	20-22	28-30	9
8	11-12	14		9-10		28-31	41-46	10-11	25-27	17-19	25-27	8
7	9-10	12-13	7-8	7	9	22-25	35-40	8-9	21-24	15-17	22-24	7
6	7-8	10-11	6	5-6	8	18-21	29-34	6-7	17-20	12-14	19-21	6
5	5-6	8-9	5	4		14-17	23-28	5	13-16	9-11	15-18	5
4	4	6-7	4	3	7	11-13	18-22	4	10-12	8	11-14	4
3	3	5	3	2		10	15-17	3	6-9	7	8-10	3
2	2	4	2	1	6	8	12		3-5	6	5-7	2
1	1	3	1		4-5	8	12	1	2	5	3-4	1
0	0	0-2	0	0		0-7	0-11	0	0	0	0-2	0

SUMMARY			
TEST	Raw Score	Scaled Score	
Information	17	11	(11)
Comprehension	19	11	(11)
Arithmetic	10	9	(9)
Similarities	13	10	(9)
Digit Span	12	11	(11)
Vocabulary	48	11	(11)
Verbal Score		63	
Digit Symbol	41	8	(8)
Picture Completion	12	9	(9)
Block Design	38	11	(11)
Picture Arrangement	31	13	(14)
Object Assembly	30	9	(9)
Performance Score		50	
Total Score		113	

VERBAL SCORE 63 IQ 102
PERFORMANCE SCORE 50 IQ 101
FULL SCALE SCORE 113 IQ 102

*Clinicians who wish to draw a "psychograph" on the above table may do so by connecting the subject's raw scores. The interpretation of any such profile, however, should take into account the reliabilities of the subtests and the lower reliabilities of differences between subtest scores.

I. INFORMATION	SCORE 1 or 0		SCORE 1 or 0		SCORE 1 or 0
1.	1	11. prob. 5'6-5'7	0	21. I'd say 48-52	0
2.		12. Rome?	1	22. beginning of life, of earth, this world began	1
3.	1	13. because they don't reflect the heat	1	23. up to 130°. 130.	0
4.	1	14. That's a good question. To	0	24. (Shakes head) No	0
5. rubber plant plant source	1	15. Snakes.	1	25. artery, vein, + capilary.	1
6. ken. Nix, Rose Tru. since 1900?	1	16. the home of the Cath. Diocese Home	1	26. a book. Jewish, like Jewish Torah.	0
7. poet	1	17. no idea (guess?) No, must 3 months	0	27. got me there.	0
8. 52	1	18. next to Bethleham + Jerusalem	1	28. (repeat) I don't know this.	0
9. Chic. to fa? I'd say Southwest.	1	19. forms a bacteria	0	29. has something to do w/ Greek mythology	0
10. just above s. pole in S. America	1	20. 13 million... I was discussing that	0	20. 2 months ago.	17

OBSERVATIONS: runs along... (?) in S. Amer.

13. (mumble) heat doesn't penetrate white but does dark... (?) white not penetrated

14. winter. February... (guess) you're got me there.

15. of Cath. religion.

17. by merchant steamer; 5½ hr. by plane.

24. sounds like catipillar (laugh) as close as I can come.

26. scroll. A book on the same subject as the Torah.

2. COMPREHENSION		SCORE 2, 1 or 0
1. Clothes	—	2
2. Engine	—	2
3. Envelope I'd put it in the mailbox.		2
4. Bad company uh.... to stay out of trouble. If I were going out w/ a girlfriend... if they were stealing I couldn't steal cause I had nothing in common w/ them if they were killing I		1
5. Movies I would get up till the owner might went to know or one of the people in charge here so why. they would put them out so as not to kill them. Not to cause a panic.		2
6. Taxes So that we have a police dept., a fire dept., so our children have schools, to maintain needs for the community.		2
7. Iron If you're angry, jump right in. (?) that's the first thought that came into my mind.		1
8. Child labor because people years ago would take advantage of children -- work long hours + abuse them.		2
9. Forest Uh.. that's a good question. Start marking trees that I past so if I went in a circle, I would at least know I'd been there before. Faith, the sun. As		0-1
10. Deaf long as it was in front of me I'd keep going in that direction because they can't hear the sounds		1
11. City land uh.. I think politics has a lot to do w/ that (laugh) That's a good question. Because land in the city		1
12. Marriage is closer to conveniences eg the 1st floor costs more than the top floor. But that's not bec. of the lissstemanket--symdis...drive up high rises.		0-1
13. Brooks because - they don't (disease) run deep, Deep water is still. Shallow water bounces around more. Not as solid as a large mass of water.		0
14. Swallow uh-- well, uh, just because you see one sign, it doesn't mean -- it isn't always the way it looks. (paraphrases the saying)		2
		19

4. SIMILARITIES		SCORE 2, 1 or 0
1.	citrus fruits	1
2.	wearing apparal.	2
3.	both have a cutting edge.	1
4.	both in the animal kingdom.	2
5.	they're not. Same points on a compass.	2
6.	they're part of a human body. One hears, one sees.	1
7.	oxygen. They both have to function w/ oxygen. O₂ B?	1
8.	they're alike. . . .both are eating facilities.	1
9.	an egg and a seed. They're both fetuses seed into a flower. Egg hatches into a chicken	2
10.	they both have a history of time before	0
11.	they're wood alcohol. Both have the same base in certain drinks (?) The tree gives out sap +	0
12. feelings. 2 different feelings. Not really alike.	sometimes the sap is made into wood alcohol.	0
13. they're not.	More like paper than alcohol.	0
		13

3. ARITHMETIC			
	& or W	Time	SCORE
1. 15"	—	—	0 ①
2. 15"	—	—	0 ①
3. 15"	R	5"	0 ①
4. 15"	R	2"	0 ①
5. 30"	W	+	① 1
6. 30"	R	30'	0 ①
7. 30"	W/R	+	① 1
8. 30"	R	5"	0 ①
9. 30"	WX	+	0 ①
10. 30"	R	13'	0 ①
11. 60"	R	17"	0 ① 1-10 2
12. 60"	R	2"	0 1 ①
13. 60"	W	+	① 1 1-10 2
14. 120"	W	—	① 1 1-10 2
			10

(rpt) — corrected automatically

I really have to concentrate on these

25 t. I think I'm going to ruin its problems w/ these questions.

1-16 which I don't think is right 1½ but I say say "½" Perhaps 2.

5. DIGIT SPAN	SCORE
Digits Forward	Circle
5-8-2	③
6-9-4	3
6-4-3-9	④
7-2-8-6	4
4-2-7-3-1	⑤
7-5-8-3-6	5
6-1-9-4-7-3	⑥
3-9-2-4-8-7	6
5-9-1-7-4-2-8	⑦
4-1-7-9-3-8-6	7
5-8-1-9-2-6-4-7	8
3-8-2-9-5-1-7-4	8
2-7-5-8-6-2-5-8-4	9
7-1-3-9-4-2-5-6-8	9
Digits Backward	Circle
2-4	②
5-8	2
6-2-9	③
4-1-5	3
3-2-7-9	④
4-9-6-8	4
1-5-2-8-6	⑤
6-1-8-4-3	5
5-3-9-4-1-8	6
7-2-4-8-5-6	6
8-1-2-9-3-6-5	7
4-7-3-9-1-2-8	7
9-4-3-7-6-2-5-8	8
7-2-8-1-9-6-5-3	8
F 7 + B 5 = 12	

Highest numbers circled

It's hard to concentrate doing this too

PICTURE ARRANGEMENT
- tells each series aloud spontaneously; laughter.

3. hold up, caught, punish.
4. Ran to grab funny book. Fighting. Man separates them. Made them shake hands. Watch. Leave. He reads it. (laugh.)
5. Walking up to the door. Opening the door. Oh, he couldn't get the door open. So he walks away. Scratches his head. No. Standing here scratching his head + the other man opens it. He was opening it the wrong way. (lots of laughter.)
6. She's walking down the street, right as the little king pulls up in car. Stops + notices the girl. She stops. They walk away together.
7. Sitting here fishing. He pulled one fish up. Then pulls another fish up. Skindiver comes up + tips hat. King yells back thank you. No — fishing. First catches 1 fish. fishing. 2nd fish. Yelling down to butler. Butler comes up, tips hat to say you're welcome.
8. Hails a cab. Gets in sitting like that. Looks and realizes. Looks behind — no. Hails cab, carrying. Why don't I shut up til I do it. - like you say (re earlier talk about not stopping thinking while you're talking.) Pushes her away so it looks right. Embarrassed. Relieved he found it out.

OBJECT ASSEMBLY
(what are they?)
1. little boy -- in hot pants (laugh)
2. a woman
3. hand
4. I have no idea. Man in Greek mythology; half animal + half human psychedelic.
(uses trunk (or tail) (never changes it, but sticks w/ task overtime.) "He's out of proportion.

	SCORE 2, 1 or 0	6. VOCABULARY
1.	2	
2.	2	
3.	2	
4.	2	It's part of spring, fall, + summer. (?) weather gets colder + the heating bill goes up. Just a different season of the year. Summer's hot, winter's cold.
5.	1	(laugh) rich people yet carpenters + — Sometimes uncomfortable. Sometimes nice. plumbers. When something's broken 15month in the house -- family.
6.	2	you repair it to make it usable again -- like me. what you eat in the morning when you get up.
7.	2	material. A material you make clothes to wear. Drapes.
8.	1?	slice of pie, of bread, of meat.
9.	1	a group, a gathering. Or you assemble your things together to take inventory.
10.	2	like I hide my shape of the candy up on the closet shelf. Probably still up there. Hide or put out of sight.
11.	2	very large.
12.	2	to hurry. to hurry up.
13.	1	a group of wording or a group in itself -- you know, serving a different. -- (stretches but arm + laughs)
14.	1	you regulate your time. Like a schedule or regulate something you're doing. Cooking, handling a stove.
15.	0	coming together.
16.	1	like wonder. Wondering.
17.	1	like.. (jumble, jumble). Geyser, cliff, Yellowstone Park has them. Geyser an indentation
18.	0	not too sure (?) to do.
19.	2	home, household, household chores, housewife.
20.	2	eat
21.	2	to stop, to end to bring to a close.
22.	2	(rpt.) to make something go in another direction. Obstruction in the way of something. I'll leave that one there. (laugh)
23.	2	something like regret.
24.	1	like a Church.
25.	1	probably priceless. Something that doesn't match. 2 things that aren't alike
26.	2	you don't want to do something or you're doing something you don't want to do!
27.	0	chaos.
28.	2	strength -- of character.
29.	2	a quiet state. A quiet state of mind. It's quiet.
30.	0	(shakes head) (guess?) No.
31.	2	sympathy, kindness, love to fellow man.
32.	0	changeable.
33.	0	a lever or a level, (gestures a surface w/ hand). I'm probably off base on that too.
34.	1?	(rpt.) would be... (long pause) obstinant.
35.	0	I'll take a guess. friendly. I'm lost on that one.
36.	1	something like a fight. or a temper tantrum.
37.	0	encumber? you come on to something you want to understand.
38.	0	you've got me (laugh)
39.	1	ugh! like put a fork in a roast. ugh! (laugh) I don't know what I'd say to that.
40.	0	I'd have a wild guess. Something to do w/ the Church. I don't know.
	48	

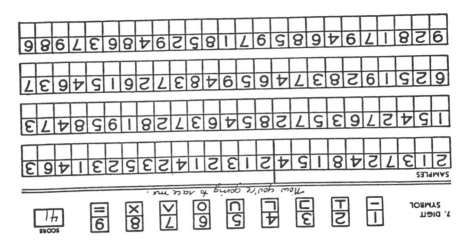

7. DIGIT SYMBOL

1	2	3	4	5	6	7	8	9
—	⊥	L	⊐	∪	∩	∨	X	=

SAMPLES

SCORE [41]

Now you're going to race me.

---

8. PICTURE COMPLETION	SCORE 1 or 0
1. Knob	1
2. Tail	1
3. Nose	1
4. Handles	0
5. Diamond	1
6. Water	0?
7. Nose piece	0
8. Peg	1
9. Oar lock	1
10. Base thread	1
11. Stars	0
12. Dog tracks	0
13. Florida	1
14. Stacks	0
15. Leg	1
16. Arm image	1
17. Fingers	1
18. Shadow	0
19. Stirrup	0
20. Snow	0
21. Eyebrow	1
	12

9. BLOCK DESIGN

	Time	SCORE
1.	60" 9"	0 2 ④
2.	60" 55"	0 2 ④ I did that wrong
3.	60" 10"	0 ④
4.	60" 15"	0 ④
5.	60" 50"	0 ④
6.	60" 13"	0 ④
7.	120" 35"	0 4 ⑤ 1-20 6
8.	120" 65"	④ 5 6
9.	120" 90"	0 ④ 5 6
10.	120" (laugh)	0 4 5 6

10) 1' holds head + concentrates. At 2½ still has problem + prongs — 38

10. PICTURE ARRANGEMENT — see attached sheet

talks each story out aloud

		Order	Time	SCORE
1. Nest	60"	WXY	15"	0 2 ④ WXY
2. House	60"	PAT	12"	0 2 ③ PAT
3. Hold up	60"	ABCD	13"	④ ABCD
4. Louie	60"	ATOMIC	25"	④ ATOMIC
5. Enter	60"	opens	30"	0 ④ OPENS
6. Flirt	60"	ajnet	35"	0 ③ 4 JANET JANET AJNET
7. Fish	120"	efghij	40"	0 2 4 ⑤ 6 EOFGHI EFGHIJ
8. Taxi	120"	samuel	55"	0 2 ④ 6 SALMUE SAMUEL AMUELS

5) 1st try lots like a negative w/red.)
7) 1st did it w/ whole th center then spontan. ∆)
8) works systematically " " to be funny.
9) when solo puts hands head to be funny. Has trouble but spontan. corrects.

SCORE 31

11. OBJECT ASSEMBLY — see attached sheet

	Time	SCORE
Manikin	120" 15"	0 1 2 3 4 5 6 ⑦ 8
Profile	120" 40"	0 1 2 3 4 5 6 7 8 9 ⑪ 12 13
Hand	180" 45"	0 1 2 3 4 5 6 7 8 ⑨ 10 11
Elephant	180" †	0 1 2 ③ 4 5 6 7 8 9 10 11 12

WAIS INTERPRETATION

Test Behavior: With structure Mrs. R stuck with the tasks and responded quickly and cooperatively. Her style was self-deprecating, self-doubting, and apologetic with a little nervous laughter.

Mrs. R earned a verbal IQ of 102, performance IQ of 101, and full-scale IQ of 102, indicative of average intelligence or about that of 50 percent of Wechsler's sample. Her verbal and performance IQ scores are almost identical so there is no reason to expect depression of motor skills relative to verbal skills or vice versa. All scaled scores of subtests fall within a moderate range of 6 points (8-13) indicating no outstanding strengths or weaknesses. However, both the highest and lowest scaled scores are on performance tests, suggesting that for tasks with motor involvement Mrs. R's intellectual functioning is more variable than in tasks which utilize verbal skills (which fall within a narrow range of 3 points, 9-11).

When Mrs. R's performance on each test was compared with that of people her own age using Wechsler's norms in the score manual, it was found that her ability to acquire new learning and use it in a visual-motor task (DIGIT SYMBOL) (Burik, 1950) was slightly below average, as were her familiarity with common objects and alertness for detail (PICTURE COMPLETION) and her ability to visually and spacially identify the relationship of parts to whole (OBJECT ASSEMBLY). Mrs. R could also do simple arithmetic problems in her head and could conceptualize the basic similarities between objects only slightly less ably than the average person of her age-group. She was slightly above average in her general fund of information, in the extent of her vocabulary, and in her comprehension of the proper response to and meaning of everyday affairs of life. She appeared capable of concentrating and applying auditory memory better than the average person her age, as evidenced by ability to repeat back from memory a string of digits. However, her performance on several tests (such as, the spottiness of her ARITHMETIC and PICTURE COMPLETION) indicate she either does not or cannot consistently use her ability to attend and be alert. For example, her lowest subtest score (DIGIT SYMBOL) suggests she may have trouble concentrating and applying herself for any length of time (Dennerll et al., 1964). This could also indicate an organic condition, as an alternate hypothesis (Ladd, 1964).

Mrs. R can synthesize abstract concepts in a visual-motor problem (BLOCK DESIGN) slightly better than average. Her highest subtest score was on PICTURE ARRANGEMENT where she outperformed 84 percent of Wechsler's population in her age-group, suggestive of ability to comprehend and size up a situation and to interpret social situations according to custom (Krippner, 1964). This is good evidence that she has the ability to judge her home situation with some rationality. Wechsler (1958, p. 77) believes this "social" intelligence is actually just general intelligence applied to social situations. In addition, he writes that, "People who do well on Picture Arrangement seldom turn out to be mental defectives, even when they do badly on other tests." In summary, Mrs. R demonstrated about average intelligence for her age, and her intelligence should not keep her from being an adequately functioning person in society.

Analysis of the internal patterns of Mrs. R's test reveals information for hypothesis-building about her functioning that is not provided by simple comparison of her test results with Wechsler's group norms. Mrs. R's verbalized thinking became jumbled and rambling unless the situation was well-structured and she was reminded to stick with the topic at hand (e.g. INFORMATION item 10: Brazil. "Just above the South Pole in South America . . . [mumbled jumble] . . . runs along the . . . [mumbled jumble] . . ." (?-summarize) . . . "in Southern America.") Her highest score was attained on a test where she structured the situation herself and constantly reminded herself to stick with the task by spontaneously talking out a story step-by-step to each card of PICTURE COMPLETION. The direction of her mental rambling is tangential and concrete. She was willing to guess at questions she did not know but her guesses were very immediate, often sounded like the question (clanging), and were generally wrong: (e.g. INFORMATION item 28: ethnology. "ethics"; VOCABULARY item 32: tangible. "changeable"; INFORMATION item 18: Egypt. "next to Bethlehem and Jerusalem.") Her grabbing at the first thought that enters her mind instead of entertaining alternate hypotheses makes for poor problem-solving ability and lack of insight-forming mechanisms when she is faced with new and unfamiliar situations: (e.g. OBJECT ASSEMBLY: elephant. Identification as animal but total time spent with trunk and tail in same wrong places without these locations having any particular significance for her, as indicated by later inquiry.) This tendency could compete with her "social" intelligence inferred from PICTURE ARRANGEMENT and hamper her ability to handle unexpected problems that arise at work and home. Although Mrs. R sometimes has trouble thinking in abstractions and becomes too concrete too soon for accurate thinking to take place (e.g. SIMILARITIES item 1. "citrus fruits"; INFORMATION: she missed all the questions with numerical answers, 11, 14, 17, 20, 21, 23), she nevertheless has the ability to organize nonverbal concepts (Cohen, 1957a, 1957b, 1959), as evidenced by a decent BLOCK DESIGN score.

A striking feature of Mrs. R's test performance was the spottiness of her scores in individual subtests. There is evidence to suggest that this is due to one of, or a combination of, several factors. The possibility of brain damage or perceptual difficulties cannot be ruled out (e.g. PICTURE COMPLETION items missed, 4, 6 "hand holding the thing," 11, 12, 14, 18, 19, 20). Because the test items of each scale are generally supposed to be in an approximate order of increasing difficulty,[5] spotty scores could indicate not inability but rather some impairment of functioning, also suggesting that Mrs. R's present intellectual functioning is below the actual potential she has (e.g. at times systematic in approaching BLOCK DESIGN tasks, at times not). There is also a strong possibility of a problem of alertness and concentration, of which she actually complained during testing, making her scores spotty. At several points during testing Mrs. R's performance also appeared to falter with sexual stimuli, which seemed to be anxiety producing for her (e.g. SIMILARITIES item 9. "An egg and a seed. They're both fetuses. Seed into flower. Egg hatches into a chicken" after which Mrs. R missed all four subsequent items of the subtest, in two cases rejecting the idea that there was any similarity between the test items; VOCABULARY item 39: impale. expression of disgust "ugh! like to put a fork in a roast ugh! I don't know what I'd say to that.") With such anxiety her defenses were not sufficient to avoid hampering of intellectual functioning. It appears that Mrs. R tries to block out anxiety using rejection of the problem or, if flustered or stumped, by using withdrawal into a dazelike state in efforts to either remove herself from the stimulus or to get the stimulus to

[5] Order of difficulty of test items was generally derived from frequency tables of items passed or failed by Wechsler's standardizing population. Order of test items is revised in the WAIS-R to reflect changes in item difficulties.

withdraw from her (e.g. following flustering at the beginning of BLOCK DESIGN, by item 5 Mrs. R was in a glassy-eyed, dazelike state, but resumed work). Thoughts of children or household are positive for her, aid in recovery from anxiety, and are associated with high scores and good intellectual functioning (e.g. 2 scores for items 6 and 8 on COMPREHENSION). The importance of social situations to her is suggested by her highest score being on PIC-TURE ARRANGEMENT, which she seemed to enjoy and verbally relish. Cohen (1959) calls PICTURE ARRANGEMENT the performance subtest which best measures general intelligence, with VOCABULARY and INFORMATION, in that order, the best subtests in general for measuring general intelligence (Cohen, 1957b, 1959). Since Mrs. R's relatively high scores occur on all three of these subtests, it is plausible that she has better intelligence than the other subtest scores suggest, and poorer performance on the latter due to incumbrances like inattention, drugs, etc.

Several hypotheses about some positive features of Mrs. R's personality as revealed by WAIS performance are: She knows when she is wrong and "rambling"; she is highly motivated to stick with a task or problem (e.g. overtime on several items), even when her efforts are nonproductive or frustrating, apparently at least in part to satisfy dependency needs (please tester.)

Several other features of her test results which deserve mention, but from this test alone are not yet used for hypothesis-building: spontaneous mention of food; superstition(?) by use of the number "13" in INFORMATION items 20 and 23.

None of the features of Mrs. R's scatter pattern are particularly outstanding (the highest and lowest scores have already been commented upon) and her scattergram did not fit any of Schafer's (1948) diagnostic summaries nor any of Wechsler's (1958) "Test Characteristics for Various Clinical Groups" particularly well. Thus, although Rapaport et al. (1968) report that in their opinion the scattergram is definitely diagnostic in 30 to 40 percent of cases, offers diagnostic directions and hints in another 30 to 40 percent, and in the rest is inconclusive, we have not had to face the problem of scattergram analysis and its contradictory research, because Mrs. R's pattern simply does not fit well any of those that I have available for comparison.

CHAPTER 8

BENDER-GESTALT

REVIEW OF LITERATURE

B ENDER'S (1938) Visual Motor Gestalt Test is a simple copy-ing test procedure based on extensive research into the ability of children and adults with various personality disorders to reproduce figures.[1] Interpretation of the Bender-Gestalt, or B-G, depends on knowledge of gestalt principles, personality dynamics manifested in graphic media, and maturational factors affecting visual-motor activity. The development of visual-motor reactions was studied extensively by Bender, and she standardized her test for children of different ages. There also exist test standards for adult-hood and old age. The test product is supposed to be an indication of how the stimulus is perceived, organized, and what it means to the subject. The latter meaning is determined by what the subject does to simplify the stimulus, what s/he adds to it, or how s/he otherwise modifies it. The B-G is also supposed to tap the subject's capacity to produce his percepts, his level of visual-motor coordination, and his action patterns. The way an individual handles B-G tasks is thus a function of the degree of biological visual-motor development and all the behavior patterns s/he has developed (such as age, ability, emo-tional stability, mood).

In his review of the B-G literature from 1950-1961, Billingslea (1963) reports that the methods of evaluating performance on the B-G have been relatively subjective means, such as introspection as used by Bender (1938) and Hutt (1945, 1969), and relatively objec-tive scoring as used, for example, by Koppitz and Pascal and Suttell. One major problem of scoring, says Billingslea, is that it utilizes the stimulus design as a standard referent against which to judge the subject's protocol, but this is based on the untenable assumption of a constant stimulus. For example, rotation of copied figures is supposed to indicate brain pathology. Yet Billingslea reports that rotation oc-curs in the protocols of subjects carrying other diagnostic labels

---

[1] Figures were originated by Wertheimer (1923).

who appear to be free of any brain pathology; and B-G reviewer Blackmore (in Buros, ed., 1965) reports that studies have shown rotation to be largely due to stimulus variables. In one study Hannah (1958) gave two groups matched for age, sex, and psychological diagnosis the B-G. One group was given the B-G designs on cards printed horizontally; the other group received cards with designs printed vertically. In copying the designs the latter group produced fewer rotations, significant at the .01 level. Hannah concluded that one way "abnormalities" are produced in B-G protocols is a function of the way the stimulus design is oriented on the card on which it is presented. Griffith and Taylor (1961) did a later replication of Hannah's experiment, but instead of giving each group vertically or horizontally oriented designs on the cards, they rotated the copying paper so that for one group both the design cards and paper were oriented lengthwise left-to-right; for the other group the design cards were oriented lengthwise, but the paper was oriented vertically up and down. They found that "many of the rotations of the B-G figures may be attributed to the accidental circumstance that the long axis of the test card is oriented at 90° to the long axis of the paper upon which the figure is usually drawn." Blackmore also suggests that it could be that a particular stimulus factor, such as, orientation, only has meaning to a certain type of patient. Lack of standardization of B-G stimulus variables and conditions of testing not only probably effects validity of the B-G but also casts doubt on apparent group differences on the B-G, which are supposed to be related to neurological or psychiatric diagnosis. Both Blackmore and Billingslea express concern with regard to this and other aspects of the validity of the B-G; much research seems to remain to be done with regard to the validity and usefulness of the B-G in general.

Although not generally effective in differential diagnosis much above chance level, performance on the B-G has been shown to vary to an extent with age and biological maturation. Reasonably valid MAs (mental age) can be obtained with it for children age four to twelve and for adults with equivalent MAs, but not for adolescents or adults with higher MAs. Billingslea (1963) also comments on a more recent trend away from using the B-G to produce diagnostic classification of subjects and instead toward evaluation of mental processes, such as, perception and problem solving, as is more in keeping with Bender's original conception of the test. But validation of the B-G in these respects still remains to be clearly demonstrated.

With regard to reliability the B-G fares quite well. With Pascal and Suttell's scoring method, test-retest reliability coefficient is about .70, interjudge reliability about .90. The B-G also seems less prone to variance due to the influence of the tester in both testing and interpretation than most other tests used in this battery (Paella, 1962).

The B-G may be helpful in this battery of tests for Mrs. R in providing clues for possible presence of organic pathology (see additional comments on this topic in interpretation subsection of this chapter). Although quite reliable, the standard objective methods of scoring the B-G have not proven to be any more valid than the test itself. Thus I have stayed with a simple inspection of Mrs. R's B-G à la Bender (1938) for hypothesis-building. Halpern (in Murstein, 1965) has also been useful in this respect.

BENDER-GESTALT

RAW DATA

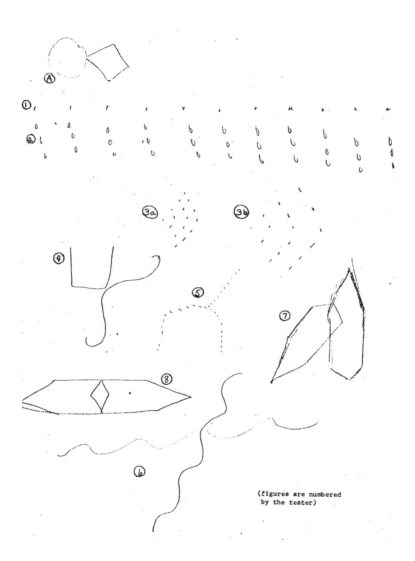

(figures are numbered
by the tester)

INTERPRETATION OF MRS. R's BENDER-GESTALT

I administered Mrs. R the B-G using Bender's instructions (1946, p. 6), "Here are some figures for you to copy. Just copy them as you see them." Her copies are about the same size as the models and organized well on the paper with good, free use of the space available (indicative of good planning?). But copying the designs did not seem an easy task for her, and her productions do not look too good in light of her purported "artistic" abilities.

Mrs. R. was not meticulous regarding detail (e.g. 1, 2, 3, 5 — not counted; use of lines for dots in 1, 3, 5), and her work looks a bit sloppy or tentative. Yet the fact that she was trying hard (e.g. as evidenced by her test behavior and two attempts at 3) rules out the hypothesis that she was haphazard, nonchalant, or did not care about her performance on the test. The generally mediocre quality of her drawings could be due to (1) emotionality, (2) poor motor control, and/or (3) perceptual problem.[2] With regard to emotionality factors, a space where lines should meet, or "closure difficulty" (A, 4), suggests lack of closure or hesitancy, difficulty in maintaining interpersonal relationships, self-doubt, anxiety (Hutt, 1969). Difficulty with angles (e.g. reduction of pointedness and trouble with 3, problem with points of 7 and 8) and the sketchiness of the points in 7 in particular indicates not only uncertainty, timidity, or avoidance but also point to a psychodynamic hypothesis: that of anxiety raised by phallic imagery and/or aggression and penetration.

But the hypothesis of a problem with an organic basis must be considered. Inability to draw dots (e.g. Mrs. R uses lines or loops and note also no dots in her DAP in Chapter 9) suggests poor motor control. Substitution of dashes for dots could be an effort to conserve energy and unwillingness to exert herself, but this seems not likely in light of her motivation to do well on the tasks. Her use of dashes could instead be seen to support the emotionality hypothesis: Halpern (in Murstein, 1965) relates use of dashes instead of dots to impulsivity; Hutt (1969) suggests it is a primitive form of the gestalt. Difficulty with angles in the angular effects of A, 3, 4, 7, 8 is, however, additional evidence that can indicate a problem with visual-motor coordination rooted in an organic disorder. But because her

---

[2]See useful catalogues of interpretive hypotheses drawn from varied literature for the B-G, TAT, Rorschach, WAIS, and Human Figure Drawing in Gilbert (1978) and Ogden (1967).

problems with angles occurred only on a specific set of designs (that is, the more phallic-looking, sharp, or "aggressive" 3, 7, 8), it looks like this too is support for a personality or emotional problem instead of an organically based one. Because she made no verbal or other indication about her inaccuracies with regard to knowing they were wrong, we must also consider the problem of a perceptual problem. In summary, it looks like a possible perceptual problem and an emotional problem, particularly with regard to phallic and/or aggressive factors.

An indication of an aspect of her intellectual style of functioning, we note perseveration, or repetition of the same idea in subsequent tasks (e.g. in 1 and 2 where parts of one pattern influence the next). This could have either organic or emotional significance and resembles schizophrenic functioning.

With regard to the ability of the B-G to discern organic brain pathology, Goldberg (in Murstein, 1965) investigated to see if the B-G could differentiate between organics and nonorganics, by comparing judges' estimates of presence or absence of organicity in the Bender protocols of thirty patients. Fifteen of these patients had been diagnosed previously as organic following neurological examinations with the results indicative of clearcut cortical impairment, and fifteen others had been independently diagnosed as nonorganic based on negative cortical impairment by several standards. His judges averaged a 68 percent "hit" rate and one Bender "superexpert" judged 83 percent correctly. He concludes that the Bender is at best only middling in diagnosing organicity and is best used as part of a composite measure in the company of other tests of organicity. These results do not help us place additional confidence in the hypothesis of organicity for Mrs. R, and it must remain purely hypothetical. Incidentally, Goldberg's judges were experienced clinicians, trainees, and hospital secretaries (who had no experience with the B-G beyond having been administered the test once themselves). All did equally well making judgments with the Bender!

CHAPTER 9

DRAW-A-PERSON

REVIEW OF LITERATURE

I N the Draw-A-Person Test (DAP)[1] it is hoped that by holding the stimulus situation constant (that is, to "Draw a person."), varia- tion in the responses by different subjects will be accountable in terms of the internal organization of each subject's personality. The DAP is a highly unstructured test. With this lack of structured stimulus is associated the hypothesis of Stone and Dellis that there is an inverse relationship between stimulus structure in each projective technique and the level of personality tapped by the test such that highly structured tests are readily susceptible to conscious control, while unstructured tests are least subject to control.

To test this hypothesis, Stone and Dellis (1960) predicted that the order of increasing ability of a test to tap lower or more primitive levels of impulse control would be: Wechsler-Bellevue and/or WAIS, Forer Sentence Completion Test, TAT, Rorschach, DAP. Using a population of patients diagnosed as schizophrenics, they found that patients showed the least pathology on the Wechsler, with decreasing control on the other tests in order according to the hypothesis. But results were significant only for two of the four tests run at the .05 level. Unfortunately, this study employed no control groups, and Murstein (1963, p. 67) criticizes the study on the basis that most projective scoring systems emphasize "unhealthy" traits, and thus the DAP (versus, for example, the WAIS treated as a pro- jective) is more likely to be scored "unhealthy."

Donald Fiske (in Murstein, 1965, p. 73) reports on the reliability of the DAP, from a personal communication with Shanan, that the correlation between the total area used for two figures over a six- month period is only .66. Swensen's (1957) review of the DAP litera- ture cites similarly low reliability correlations, although Swensen also cites Wagner and Schubert who report a stability of .86 in ratings of overall quality of DAP drawings.

---

[1] Related titles are the House-Tree-Person (H-T-P) and Human Figure Drawing Tests.

In his article Swensen (1957) attempts to review all the empirical literature on the DAP from its first publication by Machover in 1949 through December 1959; he also tries to examine Machover's basic hypotheses about the DAP in light of this literature.[2] As regards validity of the test, Swensen finds little in support of the bases of the test (such as, for the basic premise that drawing any part of a human figure involves projection of important psychological characteristics.) But it should be noted that many of Machover's hypotheses have not been directly tested in the literature, and Swensen often had to draw his conclusions from inferences made from studies two or three steps removed from the DAP hypothesis in question.

Although there is a lack of standardized methods of analyzing the DAP drawings, there are a lot of suggested working hypotheses provided by Machover for use with an introspective approach. In trying to interpret Mrs. R's drawings, Swensen's information on the empirical success of some of Machover's hypotheses and also an article by Bell (1948), who tabulated 182 articles through 1947 on literature on the elements of the analysis of drawing and painting and their clinical significance, were useful as aids in hypothesis building. Gilbert (1978) provided a useful catalogue of classic hypotheses.

Before proceding I would like to introduce a note of caution about the possible distortion in interpretation that is likely due to the effects of the biases of my own projections as interpreter of Mrs. R's DAP. Hammer and Piotrowski (1953 in Murstein, 1965), using simple ratings of hostility in the House-Tree-Person drawings of 400 patients, found a .94 correlation between these ratings, which were made by psychologists, and ratings of hostility made on these psychologists by their supervisors. Let us hope I do not project too much of myself into my estimate of Mrs. R's pictures.

---

[2] Test reviewer Dale Harris (in Buros, ed., 1974) found that in addition to Machover (1949), Jolles (1952) also provides particularly useful suggestive hypotheses for the DAP.

DRAW-A-PERSON

RAW DATA

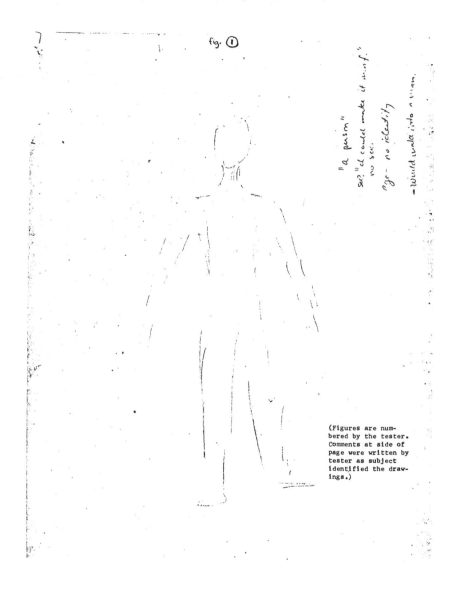

fig. ①

(Figures are num-
bered by the tester.
Comments at side of
page were written by
tester as subject
identified the draw-
ings.)

fig. ②

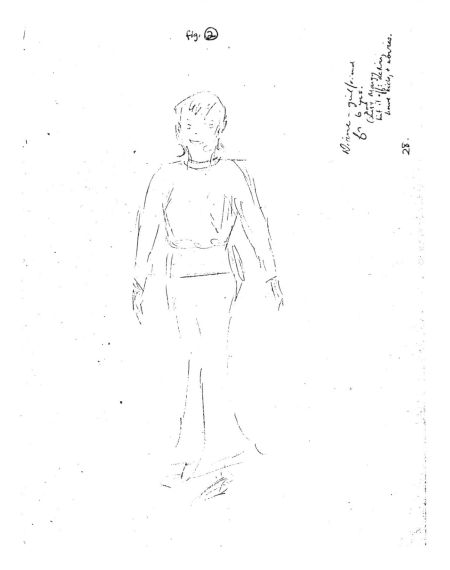

Fig. 3

fig

Sm
Paul - 6.
age

fig. ⑤

fig. 6.

boat
[spontaneously
drawn]

INTERPRETATION OF MRS. R's DAP

Test Behavior: During testing Mrs. R was cooperative, solicitous, and worked quickly and conscientiously. She made several self-deprecating comments about her poor drawing ability and the decline in said ability that has come about since her high school peak.

In Mrs. D's protocol there are six pictures, numbered 1 to 6 by myself in their order of rendition. After standard instructions Mrs. R literally drew what she called "a person." This first figure had no sex, nor age, nor identity. When asked to identify the sex of the figure, she said, "I could make it male or female" depending on my (tester's) preference. In a second run with the same instructions Mrs. R drew "Diana," a girlfriend whose home Mrs. R had gone to with her children just prior to hospital admittance because she thought someone had broken into the basement of her house. When then asked to draw a person of the opposite sex, Mrs. R drew her daughter, but upon identifying the picture as such exclaimed, "Oh, I started to draw my son, you said opposite sex, but it became her." On another try with the opposite sex Mrs. R drew her youngest son, age six. She then was asked to do a free-drawing with the instructions, "Draw anything." She replied, "I see your hat." (My hat was on the table before us with a lot of other hospital books and papers.) "But that wouldn't be 'anything.'" When I told her it was up to her, she drew picture 5, which is actually a good resemblance of my rather shapeless woolen hat. Finally Mrs. R spontaneously began to draw another picture and said, "I'd like to do a boat. I like one with big masts. Like on Salem." (a harbor town).

Concreteness, or uncritically grabbing onto an immediate aspect of her surroundings, is evidenced in the two cases where Mrs. R took the instructions literally and also in her choice of an object that was immediately before her for the free drawing. In these cases she hung onto immediate external cues possibly to avoid the anxiety and doubt a vague, unstructured situation calls forth in her. While drawing the sailboat, her comments were concrete or "clanging" in her use of the word "Salem," which is homonymic for "sail" (or even for "sail 'em"). Her concrete responses all aptly served a need in that they appeared to be solicitous, dependent behavior aimed to please me and gain approval.

Three sets of hypotheses associated with Mrs. R's pictures are discussed in turn below.

Hypotheses: poor body image and poor picture of self; sense of inadequacy; self-effacement; vague, lost, almost invisible self without 'feet on the ground'; unclear sexual identity.

Mrs. R's first drawing in particular, and the others also, are striking for the vague boundaries and the associated poor body image. Machover suggests that when the feet of the figure do not rest on some kind of ground, there is associated the hypothesis of precarious stability. In support of this hypothesis, Swensen (1957) cites Goldworth who found that increasing numbers of floating figures are found from normals (none lack equilibrium; none floating), to neurotics, to schizophrenics, to brain-damaged patients. Also in support of this hypothesis is Gutman's finding (cited in Swensen) that a firm and assertive stance is associated with improvement in therapy. Machover says that a subject draws a figure that represents himself in his first drawing and that scrambled sex characteristics on that figure represent sexual maladjustment, e.g. sexless identity, mixed identity, or fear of males. There has not been any direct support for this hypothesis; however, all three possibilities regarding unclear sexual identity can stand as hypotheses regarding Mrs. R.

Machover (1949) says that the type of line used in figure drawing indicates the kind of wall between the self and the environment. Mrs. R's dim, sketchy, fragmented lines suggest timidity, inadequacy, self-effacement, and uncertainty. To Machover, lines fading in and out with spotty reinforcement also indicate the possibility of hysterical reactions. There is not empirical evidence in support of Machover's hypotheses about type of line used in drawings. For example, Swensen cites Royal, who found no significant difference between normals and anxiety neurotics on pencil pressure, and Wexler, who found no differences between normal females and schizophrenic females in their use of light sketchy lines. Bell (1950) citing Bricks reports a study of children in which use of thin lines in drawings was associated with repression. Such evidence, however, is too scant to permit more than use of Machover's observations as hypotheses about Mrs. R.

Machover also says that a stance with legs close together, e.g. Mrs. R's figures 2, 3, 4, signifies tensions, self-consciousness, repression, and possibly fear of sexuality. For further support of the latter fear of sexuality, in particular, for Mrs. R, see the second set of hypotheses below. Swensen found no direct evidence to support Machover's hypotheses about stance on the DAP.

Hypotheses: sexuality trouble and fear of males; pulls self through trouble by placing herself in the role of mother.

Mrs. R had great trouble drawing a male. Her first effort after two previous drawings turned into a female, and the male she finally produced is an ineffectual-looking, castrated little boy with a stunted lower half of the body. It seems that the only way she could get a male down on paper was to minimize his size (e.g. figure 4 is her smallest human figure) and minimize his age (e.g. figure 4 is prepubescent and nonsexual). By the poor quality of the body in figure 4, we see it is even hard for her to deal with a little male (or with a little maleness). Also, as she approaches this male through figures 3 and 4 there is increasing emphasis on head relative to body size. To help her through this anxiety-producing task, Mrs. R relied on the role of mother as a way to relate to the male figure. It is possible, in fact, that her customary, and perhaps only, way of relating to males is by taking on a maternal role with them.

From her drawings it appears that Mrs. R would like to see females as larger and stronger than the fearful males (e.g. compare the sizes of her male and female drawings). Machover hypothesizes, though it is unsupported in the empirical literature, that in drawings of both sexes by the same subject, the smaller figure stands for the weaker sex to the subject. But for Mrs. R, on the contrary, we already have strong evidence that males evoke great fear in her, even if she would like to see them as ineffectual. Difficulty in confronting both her own sexuality and external sexual stimuli is suggested by Mrs. R's efforts to avoid the sex in drawing figure 1, by the relatively unfeminine figure 2, and by the unisex children of figures 3 and 4. If one is widely speculating, perhaps the "big masts" of the spontaneous final figure 6 were Mrs. R's own way of trying to complete the task of drawing a sexual, particularly masculine-sexed, figure: she was highly motivated to do the task well and finally produced phalluses in the best, most distancing way she could. Machover hypothesizes that wide and massive shoulders on a female (e.g. Mrs. R's figure 2) represents feelings of physical inadequacy. We suspect that the rather massive female represents some of the power Mrs. R would like to feel. Empirical studies of this hypothesis are not clearcut either pro or con.

Hypotheses: poor contact with outer environment; lack of confidence in social contacts; approval-seeking; inhibited aggression?; paranoid features.

With regard to what Machover calls "contact features" or those parts of the body with which a person makes effective contact with the outside world, the stiff and poorly developed arms and legs of Mrs. R's figures suggest hesitancy to make contact with surroundings. Swensen's review of literature, however, fails to find support for these hypotheses of Machover, although Goldworth did find that normals drew arms and legs more accurately in proportion and in more natural poses than did neurotics, whose work was more rigid; than schizophrenics, whose work was even more rigid; and than brain-damaged patients, whose work was most inaccurate of all. Machover also thinks that contact features such as legs and feet have aggressive implications, but Swensen could find no research relevant to this hypothesis.

Machover hypothesizes that the face is the most expressive part of the body and the center of communication; any deliberate omission of facial features, e.g. in Mrs. R's figure 1, is supposed to suggest frictional interpersonal relations. Swensen reports that Holtzberg and Wexler found no significant differences between normal and schizophrenic subjects for presence or absence of facial features in their DAPs. With regard to facial expression, Goldworth reports that patients diagnosed as neurotic had fewer happy, and more unhappy-looking faces on their figures than normals and schizophrenics, whose figures often had "most peculiar doll-like" expressions. (Compare Mrs. R's figures 3?, 4?.) Machover also thought a grinning mouth, e.g. figures 2, 3, 4, could represent forced congeniality and an effort to win approval, but there is no supporting empirical data on this. With regard to these authors, it is difficult to know whether the facial expressions on Mrs. R's figures are better described as happy, doll-like, or grinning. In any case, the hypothesis about seeking approval does seem fitting in her case, and she does seem to try to make her figures look congenial.

Machover claims that eye emphasis, large grandiose figures,

speared fingers, large head, rigid stance, and large ears are signs of paranoia. In light of Mrs. R's paranoid-sounding account of the events immediately preceding her entrance into the hospital (see history of subject in Chapter 6), it seems worthwhile to check for the presence of these features in her drawings. All her human figures have a rigid stance; eye-emphasis and large head only occur as she approaches the male in figure 4d. If these are indications of paranoia, it is likely she feels such with reference to males. The empirical literature cited by Swensen, although by no means providing a complete test of Machover's hypotheses about the DAP features that indicate paranoia, still provide no convincing support of the hypothesis. Fisher and Fisher (cited in Swensen, 1957) found that only thirteen of thirty-two patients diagnosed as paranoid schizophrenic drew DAPs with as many as three of the above DAP signs of paranoia present. (This is the same number of signs Mrs. R has present in her sketches.) Other studies found no difference between the head size of patients diagnosed as paranoid versus others, and Holtzberg and Wexler found no significant difference between normals and patients diagnosed paranoid schizophrenic in any aspect of the eyes. However, if we do put any faith in Machover's hypothesis, in light of Fisher and Fisher's results, the presence of as many as three of the DAP indicators of paranoia could be considered to be rather high. From what we already know of Mrs. R and her feelings about males, the hypothesis of paranoia, especially with regard to males, does not seem inappropriate. We may speculate that such fear of males could have arisen from the observation of her father's assaultive behavior, and its parallel in her second husband. Although such fear of males could be based on real occurrences in her life, the paranoid aspect of her personality is that which generalizes the fear to all males and makes the fear take form in unrelated situations and beyond the bounds of rationality.

CHAPTER 10

TAT

REVIEW OF LITERATURE

IN 1935 Morgan and Murray (1935, and Murray, 1938, p. 530) described the purpose of the Thematic Apperception Test (TAT) in these words: "to stimulate literary creativity and thereby evoke fantasies that reveal covert and unconscious complexes..." They elaborated their conception of the test: "The test is based on the well-recognized fact that when a person interprets an ambiguous social situation he is apt to expose his own personality as much as the phenomenon to which he is attending. Absorbed in his attempt to explain the objective occurrence, he becomes naively unconscious of himself and of the scrutiny of others and, therefore, defensively less vigilant. To one with double hearing, however, he is disclosing certain inner tendencies and cathexes: wishes, fears, and traces of past experiences." *The Sixth Mental Measurements Yearbook* (Buros, ed., 1965) alone cites 897 references for the TAT. I will not attempt to comment on the test as a whole here in any depth but will present some general conclusions about the validity and reliability of the test, as drawn from test reviewer Adcock (in Buros, ed., 1965) and Lindzey (1952), both of whom have been helpful to me in deciding how to best employ the TAT in the case of Mrs. R.

With regard to the reliability of the TAT, Adcock reports that interscorer agreement ranges from .54 to .91 depending upon the scoring system that is used. Average internal consistency, however, is only about .13; thus caution must be exercised in using summed scores derived from several cards. Test-retest reliability is difficult to estimate because of the tendency of subjects to remember and repeat the same stories, and tends to be not too high because the TAT is likely to tap some aspects of personality that are only temporary. Adcock also reports that although there is much literature on the TAT (and it is still growing) there is a lack of reassuring validative studies.

Lindzey (1952) has made explicit some of the implicit assumptions involved in the clinical use of the TAT and has discussed them in a review of empirically relevant literature. He concludes:

(1) The assumption that motivational factors are revealed in completing unstructured situations seems clearly warranted;

(2) The assumption that a subject identifies with the first person or another figure in the story and thereby reflects and describes himself cannot be clearly demonstrated at present, although empirical evidence suggests that identification figures can be established with reasonable reliability;

(3) There is some evidence that subjects tend to represent their dispositions and conflicts symbolically;

(4) There is little empirical evidence pertinent to the assumption that certain crucial stories depict a subject's impulses and conflicts better than others;[1]

(5) Empirical evidence seems to support the assumption that stimulus-bound responses are less diagnostic than responses that do not depend as much on stimulus constraint;

(6) There is little evidence to support the assumption that recurrent themes are indicative of important features of personality;

(7) There is excellent empirical evidence indicating that stories are responsive to both situational and enduring motivational factors;

(8) Available empirical data appear to support the assumption that particular events remembered by the subject are diagnostic of his dispositions and conflicts;

(9) What little evidence is available supports the assumption that stories reflect the sociocultural group membership of an individual;

(10) Empirical evidence clearly supports the notion that fantasied behavior is not always a direct predictor of overt behavior, and the relationship between the two is not yet clearly specified.

In general, more research is needed to further clarify the status of these assumptions (and additional work has been done, such as some of the studies cited later in this chapter) and the conditions under which they are valid, but in all, the validity of most of the TAT assumptions looks quite good.

---

[1] →

With regard to Mrs. R, there seems to be no reason why all her more basic personality factors should not be represented on the TAT protocol, but unfortunately there is no guarantee that they will be present and even less certainty that they will be present to a degree to make reliable measurement possible. Although some scoring systems exist for a limited number of presses, tendencies, needs, etc., I would like to take advantage of the breadth of the TAT. In this respect there is lacking, to a large extent, empirical research that would make clear the specific meaning of Mrs. R's particular responses. It therefore seems best to treat the TAT not as a direct measure of any particular *a priori* feature of personality but rather as a stimulus, from the responses of which can be gained clinical insight into the workings of Mrs. R. Once again, for purposes of assessing the personality of an individual, we have found it best to treat the personality test in question as an aid to hypothesis-building. We cannot expect any ready-packaged information out of it.

It seems that the best way of trying to estimate the degree, or "level," of projection in a story by Mrs. R is to assess her protocol in light of available internal and external evidence about the meaning of the stimuli to her. The crucial role of the stimulus in determining content of TAT stories has been documented numerous times.[2] As an aid to making hypotheses and for information about what each card tends to elicit and what tend to be normal responses to each card, I have used Henry's (1956, p. 337-366) description of the stimulus properties of the pictures; Holt's *An Analysis of TAT Cards*;[3] and Rapaport, Gill, and Schafer (1968, p. 487-489, 505-521). The ten TAT cards used in testing Mrs. R were recommended by my test supervisor as being particularly appropriate if a patient has mentioned the possibility of suicide during the intake interview. I do not have independent verification of this assertion.

[1,2] Although Lindzey (1952) did not find sufficient evidence to support this contention, later writers did. For example, see one of the first major critical studies of the TAT by Leonard Eron entitled, "A Normative Study of the Thematic Apperception Test" (in Murstein, 1965).
[3] Unpublished material.

TAT

RAW DATA

Mrs. R's TAT:
beginning time: 3:15pm
ending time: 3:45pm

(Mrs. R brings in a glass of water; says she has been thirsty all day; asks me to shut window because of the cold; inquires if her smoking bothers me; does not smoke until I ask her if she would like to.)

Card 1 5" ⁴ His mother told him he had to take violin lessons. He's not very happy but will wind up doing what she says. He has the expression "am I going to get stuck doing this?" Funny, I have a boy who did take the violin. . .till he took up drums. That's all. Mother and him and the violin. (1' 20")

Card 2 8" Oh! woman's liberation like from the days of yore. Now it's woman. (mumble, tester cannot understand) . . .this woman worked the fields with husband while in childbirth. Standing in the fields looking at— Now is the lady's liberation that only it—education for future women. (1' 35")

Card 3BM 15" He's not bleeding, so I'll say he shot something. So I'd say now he's in deep grief. So of course he'll go to jail—if that's what he's done. (45")

Card 4 5" Looks like they were talking very deeply about something and he wants to leave but she doesn't. I don't know what kind of ending I can come up with. She wants to console him from doing something. I don't know what it is. But I can't think of an ending. (1')

Card 17GF 15" I'm stumped on this one. It looks awful dreary and macabre. That's about all I can say about this one. I'm stumped— I don't know what to say about it. (45")

(Mrs. R is sitting calmly, legs crossed at ankles, hands in lap—on this card and previous one.)

Card 10 6" I'd say they *were* married. They're happy—they're close. And their lives will probably end that way really. (40")

---

⁴The ' and " are abbreviated notations for minutes and seconds of time, respectively. The indication of time next to each TAT card number indicates the time interval that passed before the subject responded to the card stimulus. The indication of time at the end of the paragraph for each card denotes the total amount of time the subject spent with the stimulus card. Card 15 also elicited a 20-second pause during the story.

Card 13MF 15" I'm pretty well stumped on this one too. Looks like a Bible. They went to a motel — someplace — he's showing remorse over it. That's all I can — (shrugs shoulder) (1')

Card 6BM 2" She looks like the mother and now she's standing at the window and I wonder if he wants to leave home and she's saying, "Well, where are you going? Are you going to leave me?" and he feels badly. He might leave. I don't know. He could be leaving home. (1')

(Mrs. R has been holding cigarettes and matches but not lighting up. I say it is all right to smoke if she wants to. She replies: "Oh, good. I'm smoking less here. Cut coffee consumption too. From one and one-half packs a day to one-half a day. Would you like to open a window a little, you'll turn green.")

Card 15 2" Oh my God! 20" Not unless somebody — oh, I don't know — not unless somebody dear to him had died. The way the picture's taken shows the heartbreak or how he's feeling. The picture presents his mood. (She shows me.) Unless he's a ghoul (laughs). Wow! One picture like that in my room and I don't think I'd ever go to sleep. (1' 30")

Card 14 11" I don't know. Looks to me like a man standing in the room looking out the window (I cough. She moves, puts out cigarette, says "You'll turn green.") (?-continue) My son and I had a telescope and we'd sit on the porch and look at the stars and see how far we could see or light on the beach or some unsuspecting passerby.

Inquiry: (What do the pictures tell about yourself?) I don't know how to do that. (Any picture tell about yourself or your feelings?) I don't know. I just said what came into my head when I saw them. (Brevity because she is concerned about being at a ward group meeting).

INTERPRETATION OF MRS. R'S TAT

Test Behavior: During TAT administration Mrs. R tended to be self-deprecating, solicitous, and orally dependent. For example, she came into the test room holding a glass of water, commented on cigarettes and food, inquired if her smoking bothered me and did not smoke when holding cigarette and matches in her hand until I invited her to do so. Her general style of response to the TAT cards was nonintrospective and she seemed to have trouble making up stories: her voice was very soft and hard to understand, and she often mumbled verbalizations. Much was left vague and unidentified with no endings to stories, no looking into the future.

Although Mrs. R showed strongly dependent behavior during the TAT, there is no firm evidence of overt expression of strong dependency needs in her protocol. This nonetheless is fitting with some research data. For example, Fitzgerald (1958) in evaluating TAT protocols for prediction of overt dependent behavior found no evidence that TAT responses, as measured by frequency of response according to scores from his own n Dependency code, are related to interview or sociometric indices of dependent behavior. Using the same code he did find that TAT responses are significantly related to an interview measure of importance of conflict in n Dependency. If from her interview behavior we assume that Mrs. R does have strong needs for dependency, her responses to cards 4 and 6BM suggest ambivalence over dependent ties because they carry a theme of abandonment, especially of women by males. Therefore, we infer conflict over dependency needs: she wants to be dependent on a male but expects abandonment and disappointment of the need.

Mrs. R also appears to fear males and feels helpless in male-female relationships: males hurt you, make you feel bad, and have the upper hand (cards 4, 17GF, 13MF, 6BM). Her interpersonal relationships in general do not look very successful and her relationships with others are not deep but at their best only formally or institutionally defined by a label (card 1- mother not liked by son; card 2-she does not/cannot bring the 3 people together except through marital tie and by "work"; card 3BM- the male relates to the "something" by shooting it and feeling grief.) The protocol has no indications of well-developed relationships with others except for the couple in card 10, and this story sounds like it represents wishful thinking much more than knowledge of cause and effect about how to build good relationships in the real world.

Sexuality gives her big problems on the TAT (card II- flustered and rambling; card 13MF; depression mixed with aggression, etc. as aftereffects in stories following card 3BM and card 13MF). Her defenses are generally weak and give her little room to maneuver in the face of anxiety such as that caused by sexuality. At first she tries to be concrete focusing on immediate details (card 3BM- gun; card 13MF- Bible; card 14- literal description of the card); she also tries unsuccessfully to withdraw the trouble-producing stimulus (brevity and rejection of cards 17GF, 13MF); but cannot stop the stimulus from impinging on her by denial or other defenses, nor can she withdraw herself successfully from it, and she falls into deep depression mixed with aggression. The depression shows in the gloominess of stories and paucity of production. Even when things are going pretty well she retains some depression (e.g. soft voice, relative paucity of production) and is pessimistic about the future. We saw that she has planning ability on the WAIS; it looks here more like she does not want to look ahead because of the unpredictability of the world around her and the bleakness of the future, e.g. card 6BM. The only way for her to make the future look good is to resort to fantasy and wishful, fairy-tale thinking (card 10).

On the TAT Mrs. R dealt with aggression largely by denying it in herself and projecting it onto males (cards 3BM, 4, 13MF, 15). Mixed with her paranoid expression of aggression are themes of guilt, remorse, and punishment in addition to the general depression. Note she uses a male identification for this aggressive, ugly side of herself, e.g. card 3BM.

Mrs. R is capable of strong emotional responses but is affectively labile to the extent that she has trouble controlling strong emotion, and it can block her more rational mode of responding (strong emotional reactions to card 15; only description of mood and affect tone on card 17GF; "Oh my God" in 2″ on card 15).

A positive device for anxiety reduction and recovery of stability and good functioning was use of the idea of herself in the role of mother. Mrs. R relied on this device heavily, making intelligent, versatile use of it (e.g. brings self into test as mother on card 1; quick attempted recovery from 13MF on 6BM- 2″; card 14). But even in the role of mother Mrs. R sees herself successful only in the short-run, e.g. card 1, and the device only maintains her for a short while. She thus cannot maintain herself at her best level of functioning for very long, but continually makes attempts to try to keep from slipping too far too long (into anxiety, uncontrolled emotion, and loosened contacts with reality).

One aspect of the TAT that has been empirically investigated in some depth is the relationship between fantasied aggression on the TAT and overt expression of aggression in behavior. We have already seen evidence of projected aggression in Mrs. R's protocol. What is the extent to which she expresses aggression in overt behavior? From the small sample of behavior the interview and testing situations provide, the only indications of overt aggression were small, indirect, apologetic, friendly and joking utterances of annoyance, such as "You'll turn green;" therefore we can hypothesize that overt expression of aggression in Mrs. R is strongly inhibited. Lindzey and Tejessy (in Murstein, ed., 1965) found that subjects' self-ratings on aggression showed much higher correlation with TAT aggression than diagnostic council ratings of aggression in the subjects. This suggests that subjects are able to censor or control hostile content of TAT stories so that it is in accord with their self-concept. Since Mrs. R's use of aggression on the TAT was limited to projection onto males, we can infer that in self-concept she sees herself as nonagressive, but not so her surroundings and particularly the males in her surroundings. In efforts to maintain this self-concept we would expect inhibition of direct, overt aggression in behavior by Mrs. R. Card 15 is known to evoke aggressive fantasies. In it Mrs. R sees "somebody dear to him dies," and he feels "heartbreak" but then becomes a "ghoul." This response suggests that besides projection, depression, remorse, and guilt are also manifestations of the inhibition of aggression in Mrs. R. In reviewing studies on TAT aggression and overt behavior, Murstein (1963) reports a study of a sample of college students in which projection of hostile content varied with feelings of guilt; direction of aggression varied with feelings of guilt and the stimulus value of the TAT cards. For example, with highly structured cards, hostility tended to be turned inward (internal punishment), with individuals with hostile self-concepts (much guilt) projecting more internal punishment than persons with friendly self-concepts. From these results we can hypothesize that Mrs. R's constant use of females as the victims of male aggression implies a hostile self-concept and a lot of guilt. We suspect that although Mrs. R expresses much aggression by projection of it onto males, the major victim of her aggression at present is herself; her major expression of aggression in overt behavior would thus be limited to suffering as the victim of her own paranoia.

CHAPTER 11

RORSCHACH

REVIEW OF LITERATURE

THE Rorschach (1921) is the oldest and probably still the most commonly used projective technique. There is reportedly more publication on the Rorschach than on all the other projectives combined, and it has been a rather bewildering experience to try to get even an overview of the literature on the test as a whole. For example, the *Sixth Mental Measurements Yearbook* gives 3030 references for the Rorschach, and reviewer Jensen (in Buros, ed., 1965) states that between 1955 and 1965 Rorschach publications averaged three per week in the United States and at that point the rate of publication was accelerating!

It has been discouraging in my reading on the Rorschach to see the great contrast between the bravos of the clinicians versus the boos of the researchers. Many of the latter seem ready to throw the Rorschach out for its poor reliability and shakcy validity, both in part, e.g. specific responses and scores, and as a whole, i.e. in terms of overall impressions garnered from the Rorschach technique. Jensen (in Buros, ed., 1965), citing Sundberg (1961), makes a good though overstated argument against the Rorschach in terms of its questionable validity. Sundberg asserts that, (1) it is one of the most time-consuming psychological tests and probably requires the most extensive training of practitioners of all the psychological assessment techniques; (2) Sundberg reports that the Rorschach is administered to over 1,000,000 persons per year in the United States and consumes about 5,000,000 clinical man-hours at a cost to clients of $25,000,000; (3) as yet, forty-five years of massive research effort on the Rorschach has yielded little that is promising in terms of the validity and reliability of the test. Thus Jensen finds it hard to justify the effort and credulity that have been lavished on the Rorschach and prefers to measure the rate of progress with the Rorschach by how fast it is gotten rid of!

But this point of view overlooks some of the major clinical advantages of the Rorschach. The Rorschach need not be seen solely as a psychometric instrument in need of empirical validation. It can be viewed and treated as a framework for testing hypotheses, with the consistent stimuli of the technique serving to minimize the tester's own biases in his attempts to form an approximation of another person's personality.[1] In open-ended, projective tests like the Rorschach and TAT, the most commonly used scoring is a count of salient features of a subject's responses and not direct measure of any one variable. Thus these tests cannot be treated as inventories and require clinical judgment to make sense of a specific set of salient features and the contexts in which they occur.[2] Zubin et al. (1965) make the interesting suggestion of treating the Rorschach as a standard interview procedure. This would seem to fit the above conception of the Rorschach, might make some researchers more cognizant of what clinicians really do with the Rorschach, and could help avoid the type of fruitless validation studies which measure the Rorschach against its ability to measure a multitude of specific variables which may not be tapped in a specific setting, administration, and person.

Rorschach content, for example, has not fared well in validation studies that seek to use it as a measure of specific variables. But content has stood up well in reliability and in validity studies where it is employed to yield information about an individual. Draguns, Haley, and Phillips (1967) systematically covered past research on traditional Rorschach content in light of interpretive statements found in several Rorschach guidebooks, such as, Klopfer et al.'s *Developments in the Rorschach Technique* (1954). They found that although "no single content category is uniquely indicative of a specific diagnostic category, a personality variable, or a situationally induced factor," indications were found that content variables provide information on "the nature and adequacy of an individual's relationship to external reality, his social interaction, and his attitude toward his impulse life."

I cannot pass final judgment on the Rorschach, but found it interesting and useful with Mrs. R. I scored her protocol with Klopfer (1954) and used the detailed analysis of the protocol such scoring requires and Klopfer's associated hypotheses as aids to facilitate ap-

---

[1] The idea of the Rorschach as a constant stimulus can nonetheless be misleading because of varying effects of stimuli due to influences of the tester (cf Schafer, 1954).
[2] The salient features are often nonindependent, such as the Rorschach F and R scores.

praisal of what happened in Mrs. R's test. The meaning of the symbols used in scoring the Rorschach is presented in Table IV.

TABLE IV

MEANING OF SYMBOLS USED IN SCORING RORSCHACH

Component	Symbol
Whole Response	W, w
Common Details	D, d
Uncommon Details	dr, dd, de, di
Space	S
Form	F +, F, F –
Human Movement	M
Animal Movement	FM
Object Movement	Fm
Form Dominant Color	FC
Form Secondary Color	CF
Pure Color	C
Form Dominant Shading	FC', Fk
Form Secondary Shading	KF, kF, C'F
Pure Shading	K, C'
Form Dominant Texture	Fc
Form Secondary Texture	cF
Pure Texture	c
Form Dominant Vista	FK

Table adapted from Gilbert (1978, p. 237).
Taken from system used by Kloper *et al.* (1954, vol. 1).

RORSCHACH

RAW DATA AND SCORING

THE RORSCHACH
METHOD OF
PERSONALITY DIAGNOSIS

INDIVIDUAL RECORD BLANK · REVISED EDITION

Bruno Klopfer
University of California at Los Angeles
Helen H. Davidson
School of Education, City College of New York

Name_____ Sex _____ Date of Birth _____ Age_____

Address_____ Phone _____ Date of Administration _____

If subject is adult: Marital Status _____ Occupation_____

Highest School Grade Completed _____

If subject is a child: Occupation of Parent _____

School _____ Grade _____

Examiner_____

REMARKS

.

time in ( ) is total time to card.

TABULATION AND SCORING SHEET

Card No., Response No. and Position	Reac. Time	LOCATION Main Response W	D,d	Dd,S	Add.	DETERMINANT Main Response Movement	Vista Depth	Form	Texture Ach. Color	Color	Add.	CONTENT Main	Add.	P–O Main	Add.	FLR
I ①	7"	W				M						H				1.0
(45") ②		W						F				A		P		1.0
+ ③		DW						F⁻				A				-1.5
II ①	10"	W*							Fc		FM	A		P		1.0
②			D					F⁺				A				1.5
(1'15") ③			D					F⁺				H				1.5
add ④					W				Fc⁻				A			-1.0
III (50")①		W*				M					CF	Hd		P		1.0
IV ①	6"	W						F				(H)				1.0
(1'15")②		W				M						H		O⁻		1.0
V (60")①	2"	W						F				A		P		1.0
VI ①	25"	W				FM					cF	Pl	A			.5
(1'30")②		W							Fc			Aobj		P		1.0
add ④					W						cF	N				0.0
VII(1'45")①	10"	W		S		M						H				1.5
VIII ①	15"	W*				FM					CF	A	N	P		1.0
(2'50")②				Dd				F⁺				Hd				1.5
IX (45") 20"		reject														
X ①	6"		D					F				(Hd)				
②		W						F				A	N	P		1.0
③			D					F				A				1.0
④			D					F				A				1.0
(1'15") add					D						F		(A)			1.0

Total Time T=		W+D+d+Dd+S=R				M+FM+m+k+K+FK+F+Fc+c+C'+FC+CF+C=R						H (S) 4	0	P 7		
No. of Responses Main		13+5+0+1+0=19				4+2+0+0+0+0+11+2+0+0+0+0+0=19						Hd (3) 2	0	O ?		
Add.		2 1 0 0 8				0 1 0 0 0 0 0 1 2 0 0 2 0						A 9	2 (3)0-／1			
Sum FLR												Ad 0	0			
Average FLR																

form level   W < D / Dd   M > FM rest about equal   lowest of all   ( ) includes content in parentheses.

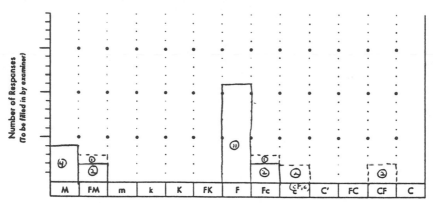

I. BASIC RELATIONSHIPS: Main Responses Only

Total Responses   R _19_

Total Time   ca 30 min.   T _____ sec.

Average Time per Response   T/R _____ sec.

Average Reaction Time:

    Achromatic Cards (I, IV, V, VI, VII)   _10_ sec.

    Chromatic Cards (II, III, VIII, IX, X)   _10_ sec.

$\dfrac{F}{R}$ _58_ F%

$\dfrac{FK + F + Fc}{R}$ _68_ %

$\dfrac{A + Ad}{R}$ _47_ A%

(H + A) : (Hd + Ad)   (_14 : 3_)   _13 : 2_

Popular Responses   P _7_

Original Responses   O _?_

$\dfrac{FC + 2CF + 3C}{2}$ sum C _0_

M : sum C   _4 : 0_

(FM + m) : (Fc + c + C')   _2 : 2_

$\dfrac{\text{Responses to Cards VIII + IX + X}}{R}$ _32_ %

W : M   _13 : 4_

II. SUPPLEMENTARY RELATIONSHIPS: Main + $\frac{1}{2}$ Add.

M : FM   _4 : 2½_

M : (FM + m)   _4 : 2½_

$\dfrac{FK + Fc}{F}$ _2/11_

(Fc + cF + c + C' + C'F + FC') :   _3.5 : 1_
(FC + CF + C)

(FK + Fc + Fk) : (K + KF + k + kF + c + cF)   _2.5 : 1_

FC : (CF + C)   _0 : 1_

III. MANNER OF APPROACH

		Main Responses		
	No.	Actual %	Expect. %	No. Add. Scores
W	13	68	20-30	2
D	5	26	45-55	1
d	0	0	5-15	0
Dd+S	1	5	< 10	0 1

IV. ESTIMATE OF INTELLECTUAL LEVEL

Capacity _____

Efficiency _____

V. SUCCESSION

Rigid _____

Orderly _✓_

Loose _____

Confused _____

VI. FORM LEVEL SUMMARY

Average Unweighted FLR _____

Average Weighted FLR _____

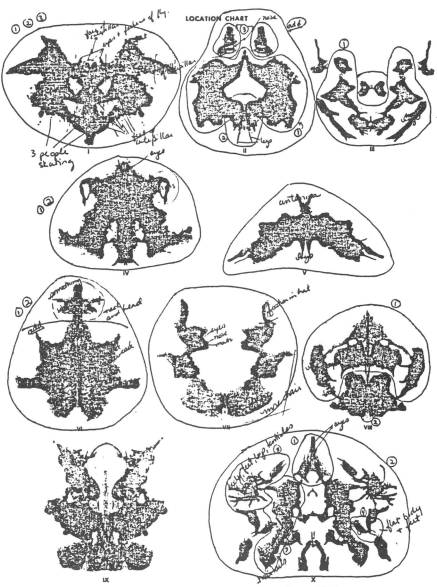

Rorschach: PSYCHODIAGNOSTIK. Copyright 1921 (renewed 1948)
Verlag Hans Huber Bern

Mrs. R's Rorschach: (She was generally very soft spoken. There were many requests made by the tester that she repeat what she had said.)

Beginning time: 4:30PM
Ending time: 5:00PM

Card I (Mrs. R is thirsty again because of medication; smoking)

INQUIRY

1. (Sitting back relaxed in chair, then looks closer.) 7″ At first it looks like 3 people skating. You know how the coats flair out, the capes.

1. Border between the people is all blended in. Cape, face, hat, jacket. (?) in the middle is a smaller person they're helping along trying to skate. (Gestures with arm up) Looks like this. (?-sex) the outer ones are women. I don't know about the middle one. That's just a random guess. I just said what came into my head. (Reassure) the first thing I saw were 2 heads and capes, then inward to skating.

2. On second look, it looks like a housefly. (?) That's about all. I've been shuffling things I did last week, thinking back, and it's a wonder the police didn't bag me! A mature woman!—or immature. (Tester about to change cards) 45″

2. Thinking of fly. Legs, face.

3. Or a caterpillar with big feet. (Laugh) That's all I can do with that one.

It's so dry that you can hardly breathe.

3. (Describes and points out feet and face on card. Body is rest of card.)

Card II

1. (Leans forward) 10″ Looks like 2 bears.

1. Heavy, thick. 2 bears doing the dance of Zorba the Greek.

2. I'm trying to figure out what this is (finger on lower red). That looks like a moth.

2. Big wings, legs, shape of body.

3. (Lifts up and puts down card; touches and points with finger.) They look like the faces of 2 little children.

That's all I can do on that one.
1′ 15″

3. Nose, eyes, mouth (defined by shading). Big woolen hat on them.

add. or 2 baby moths just coming out of their cocoon.

Card III

1. (Leans forward; touches lower right, then upper red spot) Looks like (leans closer) looks like 2 men carrying something. But I don't know what these red ones are (points to red bow). (Sitting back) or trying to catch something in the sack.

1. Carrying something to catch whatever that is.

50″ That's all on that one.

Card IV (Still smoking)

1. (Makes a grimace) 6″ That's some kind of monster. (Leans back) It's all that I

1. Plain monster. I've never sat so much in my life. Arms, legs.

can come up with on that one. (Hard to hear—had to repeat 3 times.) (Picks up card, laughs.)

2. Me sitting at the kitchen table over a cup of coffee or waiting for the coffee water to boil.

1' 15"

Card V

1. 2" That looks like a bat. That's all I can...(hand gesture) Nothing, just a bat. 10"

Got a glimpse of supper tonight and there's no rush. They do have exceptionally good food here though. Can't please everyone all the time, right?

Card VI

1. (Frowns, concentrates)
   20" It looks like uh...
   25" I...um. I'm lost on this. (scratches leg) I don't know what it would be. Looks like something coming out of a piece of seaweed.
2. Or it looks like some kind of a rug like a hunter would have in his house. Like some kind of strange game he would come across.

1' 30"

Card VII

1. (Picks up, laughs)
   10" Forgive me but the first thing that struck my mind is 2 old biddies sitting in their rocking chairs discussing the neighborhood problems.

I don't know what else. (Picks card up, puts down) although these 2 here (fingers on card) look like faces. The first one is the one that struck me. That's it.

1' 45"

Card VIII

1. (Straightens picture on table, leaning forward with chin on hand) 15" Looks like 2 what-do-you-call it...weasels. You know, water weasels, building a dam over something. You know like this (gestures) with water and they breed in the hut. (Shakes head) That's all I can think of. I've never seen one go straight up though. If it were one half I could say he was walking, climbing up over.

2. "Coffee crouch"; one eye down, the hair, the monster.

1. (Gradually, annoyance has developed around inquiry for cards II and III. She tactfully wants to leave. Later, impatience subsides and she is cheery toward the end of the inquiry.)

1. (Seaweed?) mushy.
   (Why coming out?) looks like wings.

2. Some wild animal he killed. First I saw the top. Looks like an animal, then bottom, seaweed, sand [*add.*], or a piece of fur.

1. Posture (gestures and imitates). I've seen them over my backyard fence over their tables. (laugh—idea to defy them) but I dislike gossip. So many women's wasted lives. Shame on them...talking about... not busy with their own lives. Like, "You've got a big boy there. How long have you been married? 8 years? What?"

1. Tail, legs. (dam?) green and gray.

2. There's a little something down there (laughs and points it out). That looks like Bozo the Clown.

(Sips water) I have nothing (softly) That's probably enough! (laugh)

2′ 50″

Card IX

1. (Picks up, shakes head, puts down) 20″ You've got me on that one. (Chin on hand) I have no idea. None whatsoever.

45″

Card X (Leans forward)

1. 6″ They look like something from outer space. (Touches card)
2. They look like underwater fish. Like from the ocean. Heavily populated area.
3. Sea horses.
4. Crabs. (Lifts and touches card) I've never seen anything like him before though. (Laughs, touches card, puts card down, picks card up, puts down.)

That's all. 1′ 15″

2. The hair sticks up, eyes, head and shoulders. (F)

1. Face, eyes.
add. My first impression really was sea monsters. Just one. Crabs.
2. 3. 4. (Describes features named.) The rest is part of the scenery.

INTERPRETATION: NOTES ON MRS. R's RORSCHACH

Because the amount of raw and scored data from Mrs. R's Rorschach is sizeable, its interpretation is divided into two parts, each a separate subsection of Chapter 11. The Rorschach interpretation starts with this subsection entitled, "Notes on Mrs. R's Rorschach." This subsection provides lists of (1) my observations about her Rorschach responses based on a quantitative analysis; and (2) associated hypotheses drawn from Klopfer et al. (1954), which constitutes a traditional text on Rorschach interpretation.[3] In addition to these hypotheses are some inferences of my own plus some empirically based comments regarding several hypotheses. This subsection is organized into the following five divisions based on the types of information derived from the Rorschach interpretation:

(1) The Psychogram
(2) Inner Resources and Impulse Life
(3) Organization of Affectional Need
(4) Emotional Reactivity to Environment
(5) Intellectual Manner of Approach

The second part of the Rorschach interpretation consists of an integration and summary of findings. This is provided in the subsequent and final subsection of this chapter entitled, "Integration and Summary of Mrs. R's Rorschach."

The Psychogram

Observations	*Hypotheses*
1. Bulk in middle	1. Can be impersonal and matter-of-fact.
2. Left and right sides about equal, but many additionals on right.	2. About equal access to inner and outer determinants, but more hesitant to use outer determinants (or extra available from stimulus) than to use her own inner resources and impulses in perceiving reality.

---

[3] For other major scoring systems see Beck (1951, 1952, 1962) and Phillips and Smith (1953).

Inner Resources and Impulse Life

Observations	*Hypotheses*
1. M > FM	1. Good balance between impulse life (under control) and value system.
2. M = 4[4]	2. Can empathize; can deal with frustration (deny immediate impulses); can use imagination, e.g. can use escapist fantasies when in trouble(?)[5]

M scores tend to be reliable. Holzberg and Wexler (in Buros, ed., 1965, p. 496) got reliability coefficients of about .70 for M, F, and content, and about .30 for color and shading in retest of twenty schizophrenic subjects over three weeks. Kagan found that only M and content showed statistically significant stability in a long-term study of thirty-seven males and thirty-eight females tested at ages ten, thirteen, sixteen, and thirty-five.

Regarding M scores and empathy, it looks like Ms tend to be a good predictor of empathy in light of the empirical literature. For example, Geishune (1961) cites that King could significantly predict at a better than chance level the adequacy of some social work students' effectiveness in forming interpersonal relationships, by independent measures, using the number of Ms on Rorschach protocols. Holt (cited in Geishune, 1961) found the eight psychiatric residents rated highest in empathy produced significantly more Ms than the eight psychiatric residents rated lowest in empathy. King (cited in Geishune, 1961) seemed to find that M scores could be used to measure patients' insight into interpersonal conflicts by using schizophrenics disturbed in interpersonal relationships, as measured by interview rating. Of these patients, the higher M scorers tended to recognize problems involving interpersonal relationships more than the low M scorers, who were more lacking in such insight.

With regard to M scores and denial of immediate impulses, there is some evidence that introversion, or tending to take thought and

---

[4] Average M is about 2.9 (Buros, ed., 1965, p. 504).

[5] But note the failure of a relationship between high M scores and creativity to be borne out in empirical studies.

not action, as measured by high M scores is supported in research. For example, there is some evidence that M is related to inhibition of actual physical movement and to the use and sensation of kinesthetic fantasies (Buros, 1965, p. 496).

Observations	*Hypotheses*
3. Ms are pretty well integrated and differentiated.	3. Capable of same; intelligence; good tie with external reality.
4. FM = 2 + 1 additional, but no m.	4. She *feels* impulses but is not aware of threats or conflicts with "external" forces; cessation of the struggle toward integration(?)

Organization of Affectional Need

Handling of surface use of shading is based on hypotheses related to ways of handling primary security needs, and the derived need for affection, affiliation, and belongingness. But reliability for shading is quite low according to Holzberg and Wexler, for example .30 in retests of schizophrenics over three weeks. Also there is a lack of any clear-cut research evidence that shading is significantly related to the above personality functions traditionally assigned to it (Geishune, 1961, p. 53; Buros, ed., 1965, p. 496). Note that Mrs. R's lack of any K responses is still within the normal range.

Observations	*Hypotheses*
1. FK + Fc < 1/4 F	1. Denied, repressed, or underdeveloped need for affection. Could be serious enough to warp personality such as from serious rejection experiences, according to Klopfer et al. (1954, p. 292).
2. cF = 2 additionals low form level	2. Immaturity and lack of control. But since Mrs. R only gave these responses hesitantly as additionals, it looks like the immaturity, etc., is controlled (like Fc) and subordinate to other determinants.

Therefore, Mrs. R may not actively seek physical contact to satisfy a continued early need for closeness and fondling with infantile dependence on others. She may only feel the craving. Possible serious early frustration of the need or great repression and anxiety over the need.

There is some empirical evidence that indefiniteness and inaccuracy of form are indications of impulsivity and poor reality testing. In Mrs. R's case, her poor form level scores are particularly associated with shading responses, suggesting her dependency need tends to loosen her tie with reality and to give her a problem with controlled expression of it. But here, as in many of the other Rorschach scores, because the average frequency for each determinant on a protocol tends to be low, it is hard to discriminate among people in terms of what is a high and what is a low score: There is only a small amount of variation over many subjects. It is hard to believe that 2 cFs is really a very high score, but relative to her other scores, and from what we already know of Mrs. R's behavior, performances on other tests, and family history, Klopfer's shading hypotheses do not seem at all unfitting for her.

Observations	*Hypotheses*
3. Fc = 2 + 1 additional but not too good form level, e.g. Fc $^-$	3. The affiliation-dependency need is controlled. Awareness and acceptance of the affection need, experienced in terms of desire for approval, belongingness, response from others. Less immediate, more indirect satisfaction than with cF; sensitivity to others' needs too (?) But her low form level tempers the positive aspects of the above hypotheses, indicating a serious distortion of perception by a strong affectional need

that is poorly integrated within
the total personality.

Emotional Reactivity to Environment

The way color is handled in the Rorschach is traditionally related
to hypotheses about the subject's mode of reacting to emotional chal-
lenges from the environment and especially to the impact of chal-
lenges from interpersonal relationships. Unfortunately, the color
hypotheses have not fared very well in empirical studies of them,
and Geishune (1961) concludes that "color shock" cannot be due to
the disturbing effects of the color of the cards *per se*. I have listed the
traditional hypotheses about color responses to help analyze
Mrs. R's protocol. However, these hypotheses about Mrs. R will be
treated with an extra degree of caution.

Observations	*Hypotheses*
1. $Fc + cF + c + C' + C'F + FC'$ $= 2(FC + CF + C)$ (achromatic: chromatic)	1. "Burnt child"; responsiveness to outside stimulation has been inter- fered with by some kind of trau- matic experience and withdrawal has resulted. -or- The need for affectionate response from others is so great that it re- sults in inhibition and toned-down overt reactions to others for fear of being hurt or repulsed. Over- cautious in emotional contacts.
2. Reject card IX	2. Possible color trouble, especially in light of hypothesis 4 below, but more likely the difficulty was with the complexity of the card, its dif- ficulty, etc. Mrs. R did not have trouble with color cards (For ex- ample, there is no difference in her average reactivity times to col- or. Also, her number of responses to cards VIII(?) IX(?) X(?)/R is 32 percent or about average.)

3. FC = 0
    C = 0[6]

3. Cannot say much because the average is so low anyway.[7] Just average.

4. CF = 2 additionals
    FC < CF + C

4. Uncontrolled reaction to emotional impact. But for Mrs. R this reaction is modified and she does not lose all control, as indicated by the additionals.

5. Sum C < 3
    = 0

5. Very low emotional responsiveness.

Intellectual Manner of Approach

Observations	*Hypotheses*
1. W% > 30% With medium form level but organizational effort.	1. Tries to make sense of experience; seeks relationships; need for intellectual achievement; need to superimpose generalizations of facts; organizational interest and ability.
DW = 1	But weakness in link with reality; overgeneralization; not enough intellectual criticism to prevent jumping to erroneous conclusions on the basis of little evidence.
2. W > 3M	2. Aspiration too high for her resources, or it interferes with her intellectual capacity, so that her efforts to gain an integrated view of the world are ineffective.
Constrictive Control (?) 3. F% = 58% moderate % with ok form level	3. Can be impersonal and matter-of-fact, but may avoid acknowledging her own needs and strong emotional impact for her environment.

[6,7] Average FC is .9; average C is .2 (Buros, ed., 1965, p. 504).

4. D% < 45%

4. Capable of differentiation but lacks recognition of everyday problems and facts.

5. d% < 5%

5. Low level of interest in the minutiae of experience.

6. Responses generally given easily and sometimes enthusiastically.

6. Perceptual responsiveness; receptivity to world around her.

7. P higher than average.

7. Ok tie with reality but emphasizes conventionality.

8. H + A > (Hd + Ad)

8. Absence of highly over-critical attitude.

9. A% — tendency is high.

9. Tendency toward a sterotyped view of the world; too narrow a range of interests.

10. Succession = orderly

10. Systematic but flexible approach to situations.

INTEGRATION AND SUMMARY OF MRS. R's RORSCHACH

Mrs. R does not focus on detail and is not meticulous. Although capable of noting the details of her environment, she does not dwell on the minutiae of everyday facts and problems of her life (D and d low; H + A > 2(Hd + Ad)). In efforts to understand what goes on around her, she is prone to overgeneralization (W and DW; a few have low form level); to draw conclusions based on inadequate evidence; and to produce a rather stereotyped, conventional view of the world (A% and Ps high). Thus her aspirations to view the world in an integrated way can be ineffective and beyond her present resources (W > 3M).

She knows what healthy mental functioning, with firm ties to reality, is (first responses to cards I and II) and is strongly motivated to function in this manner. But maintenance of this level is at present beyond her capability, and she falls quickly to a state of weak tie with reality, e.g. confabulated caterpillar on card I and minus form level of 3rd response to card II. She can nevertheless recover quickly and well from psychotic-looking breaks with reality and depends on such means as oral dependency and the thought of herself as a mother in relation to home and children as aids for recovering good contact with reality (two little children on card II; supper comment in reaction to card IV).

Although Mrs. R can employ being nurtured in a positive way, her needs for affection and affiliation, which she experiences as the desire for approval and belongingness, are not well-integrated within her personality and can distort her perceptions (low Fc form levels). Much of her need for dependency may be strongly repressed, inhibited and controlled; but very near the surface, ready to burst forth uncontrollably, is a strong primitive craving for contact from others. She only hesitantly recognizes the existence of this need, and its strong impact on Mrs. R can block her ties with reality (cF low form level and additional). Fear of the distorting power of these dependency needs or important rejection experiences in her past are likely to have made her only hesitantly admit to these strong needs and have made her try to control and inhibit their overt expression, resulting in an emotionally toned-down reaction to others.

Mrs. R is capable of emotional response to people who are important to her, but tries to avoid these responses and keep them to a minimum (CF only given as an additional). When she does respond she has trouble maintaining control and thus is hesitant to let loose; she inhibits expression of these responses. Mrs. R is nonetheless sensitive to the feelings of other people (4M) but sees people in general as dangerous, and males, in particular, as aggressive and threatening. (It is easier for her to give animal than human responses: A > H; and she uses more distancing in the human responses she does give than in her animal responses: (H) + (Hd) > (A) + (Ad); in card III she mixes people and bugs; phallic male cards IV, VI are associated with threatening aggression: monster and hunter who kills...but note this male monster also turns into herself, reminiscent of male identification and projection of aggression on the TAT).

Mrs. R is concerned and troubled with reference to sexuality, and sees herself in a poor light in this respect (card VIII: breeding to Bozo; softly muttered comment, "I have nothing" following). She also suffers from depression and very low self-esteem (self as monster in card IV; note phallic identification for the more aggressive, ugly, monster side of herself.) If shading is an accurate indication of dependency needs, in Mrs. R's case the strongest aspects of this need are associated with sexuality and with reference to males (use of cF on cards VI and VIII.)

Mrs. R approached the Rorschach test responsively, flexibly, and generally used her intelligence well. Unfortunately the force of her emotions at times outdid the strength of her control of them and could block her otherwise good contact with reality.

CHAPTER 12

MMPI

REVIEW OF LITERATURE

THE Minnesota Multiphasic Personality Inventory (MMPI) is a structured inventory free of subjective scoring. It is built on the concept that the 550 or so test items can form numerous potential scales such that new scales only require the additional equipment of a new scoring key. Over 200 new scales have been added to the original scales of Hathaway and McKinley (1940, 1943), making the test indeed "multiphasic." For Mrs. R, I have scored for only the basic fourteen scales:[1]

VALIDITY SCALES

    Cannot Say score. . . . . ?

    Lie. L

    Infrequency . . . . F

    Correction . . . . K

CLINICAL SCALES

    Hypochondriasis . . . . Hs

    Depression . . . . D

    Conversion hysteria. . . . . Hy

    Psychopathic deviate. . . . . Pd

    Masculinity-femininity . . . . Mf

    Paranoia. . . . . Pa

    Psychasthenia. . . . . Pt

    Schizophrenia . . . . Sc

    Hypomania . . . . Ma

    Social introversion. . . . . Si

The MMPI subtests were constructed to distinguish definite criterion groups from a "normal population." The items for each scale were chosen accordingly to separate the normals from the abnormals. In fact, in the *MMPI Manual* (1967) Hathaway and McKinley say the MMPI's chief criterion of excellence is the test's valid predic-

---

[1] See Dahlstrom, Welsh, and Dahlstrom (v. 1, 1972, p. 4).

tion of clinical cases, as independently measured by neuropsychiatric diagnosis. The MMPI's population of "normals" for test construction consisted of 724 males and females who accompanied or visited patients at the Psychiatric Unit of the University of Minnesota Hospital. This pre-World War II sample was not selected as carefully, nor does it merit the same degree of confidence, as the stratified national sample of the WAIS. Nonetheless, it has so far stood up fairly well to checks on the external validity of this sample to the population in general. For example, Dahlstrom and Welsh (1960) report that the means and variances of scores of later samples used in the 1950s are close to those of the pre-World War II Minnesota sample. Interpretation of each scale of the MMPI would seem best done in light of the criterion group to which each scale refers, and this is the procedure I have generally followed in the interpretation section of this chapter. Consequently the descriptions of the abnormal criterion groups used in constructing the scales relevant to Mrs. R are not discussed here but in the interpretation part of this chapter.

The MMPI seems fairly well able to differentiate those who have from those who do not have emotional and adjustment problems, in a wide variety of settings. But there is conflicting evidence regarding its ability to significantly differentiate either *within* the normal range or *within* the abnormal range. For example, Lingoes (in Buros, ed., 1965) reports that character disorders, psychotics, and maybe some psychosomatics can be broadly and reliably separated from normals and from one another, but that finer distinctions within these groups cannot be made. The only MMPI validity study Hathaway and McKinley cite in their manual (revised 1967, p. 8) shows a 60 percent correspondence between a high score on a scale and final clinical diagnosis of new psychiatric admissions. This seems a strange choice for them to use as the only validation study to report in their manual because this study does not make as strong a case as some other studies have for the MMPI doing what it was constructed to do, i.e. to separate normals from abnormals. Their population was already to an extent preselected by virtue of the need for testing and would thus seem to inflate the chances of the test to pick out a new admission since it did not really have to pick out abnormals from clearcut "normals." The more interesting result of this study, however, was the finding that even when a new admission was not made, a high score on a scale was noted to almost always indicate an abnormal degree of the trait in question. I have used the MMPI for Mrs. R in this sense: not to make a diagnosis, but to see the extent to which there is strong evidence, i.e. a high score, that she shares certain features in common with criterion groups, i.e. features found to characterize each criterion group.

Test-retest reliability measures of the subscales used for Mrs. R look quite decent in the *MMPI Manual* (Hathaway and McKinley, revised 1967, p. 8). It should be noted though that reliability studies quoted in the manual were mostly conducted over a relatively short time period, about a week on the average. Dahlstrom and Welsh (1960) note that test-retest reliability on the basic scales seems to decrease with time, e.g. K at 1 week = .92; at 4 years = .44 to .47. But retest reliability is better discussed in the context of the individual subscales since in not all the scales would stability be expected over long spans of time.

The interpretation of Mrs. R's MMPI is presented in two sections of this chapter. The first section contains a discussion of her scores on individual MMPI subtests. It is entitled, "Interpretation of the MMPI: Analysis of Mrs. R's Scores on the MMPI Scales." The second part of the interpretation is the section entitled, "Interpretation of Mrs. R's MMPI Based on Cookbooks." In the latter section some of the "cookbooks" available on the MMPI are referred to for interpreting the patterns of Mrs. R's scores.[2]

---

[2] See Meehl (1956) regarding the term "cookbook."

MMPI

MRS. R's MMPI SCORES

Mrs. R's MMPI Scores

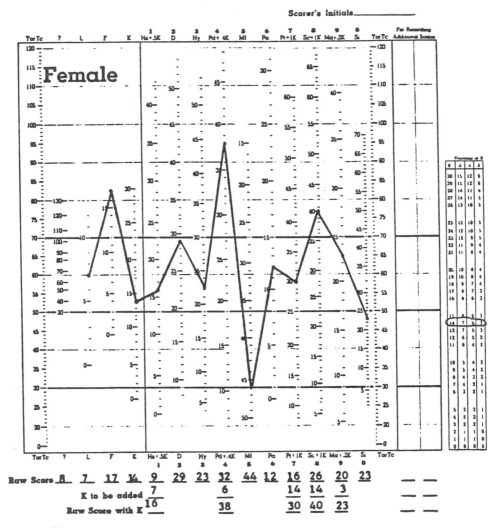

The Minnesota Multiphasic Personality Inventory
Starke R. Hathaway and J. Charnley McKinley

Printed in U.S.A.

INTERPRETATION OF MMPI:
ANALYSIS OF MRS. R's SCORES ON THE MMPI SCALES

Validity Scales: L, F, K, ?

The MMPI has four internal validity scales to enable the tester to check for fraudulent profiles. They are the L, F, K, and ? scales. The effects of faking on a protocol are demonstrated in a study by Exner, McDowell, Pabst, et al. (1963) in which it was found that all scores except L were significantly raised when college subjects were asked to deliberately fake in an abnormal direction. Attempts to fake in the normal direction were less significant, and the major significant differences in scores occurred on L, F, K, and Pd, in that order. Regarding the ability of the validity scales to detect faking, Exner et al. (1963) cite Ellis (1953) who reported in a summary of literature on faking that twenty-two of twenty-five studies of faking showed the MMPI fakable in spite of the validity scales. Cofer, Chance, and Judson (1949, cited in Exner) found that college students attempting to malinger on the test have significantly higher F scores than those not so doing; they also found that trying to fake in the normal direction could be detected by a combination of L and K scores. Calvin and McConnell (1953, cited in Exner, 1963) refer to eight studies where faking on the MMPI could be significantly detected using the validity scales.[3] But more recent evidence indicates that a high score, such as $T \geq 70$, on a validity scale does not necessarily invalidate the clinical scales or the diagnostic patterning used in the cookbooks. For example, Gynther (1961, cited in Exner, 1963) found high F scores in almost all cases of behavioral disorder he studied. Heibrum (1961, cited in Exner, 1963) suggested a high K score should be interpretable only in light of the psychological adjustment of the individual.

Although Mrs. R did score higher than 98 percent of the normal sample population on the F scale, from her general test behavior, cooperation, and motivation to comply, and from a comparison of her score patterns with charts, there is no reason to think she had a

---

[3] Gough in the late 1940s was one of the first to suggest the use of a linear combination of validity scores to detect faking, and now tables for comparison are available to help check if score patterns are likely to have resulted from random-sorting, falsifying in a "bad" direction, in a "good" direction, etc.

response set to false-bad, false-good, malingering, or random-sorting. There is, however, the possibility of exaggeration.

Studies on the configuration of validity scales have found them to be correlated with various diagnostic features. Dahlstrom and Welsh (1960) report that a sharp F spike with the rest of the validity scores near the mean, as in Mrs. R's case, is generally found in a person with an acute disorder in which the F scale responses reflect part of the emotional upset.[4] Their conclusion is based largely on a study of MMPI L-F-K relationships by Gross (1959), which indicates that the validity scales do indeed measure personality characteristics. Gross used fifty male and fifty female patients in a VA hospital who were diagnosed as schizophrenic. These patients were rated *a priori* from their clinical records on "behavioral disturbance" (BD: rated "mild" or "severe") and "social adjustment" (SA: rated "poor" or "good"). Gross found that patients rated as having severe BD had an MMPI L-F-K configuration with an upward pointing F spike ∧ and that patients rated as having mild BD had an L-F-K configuration with an F trough ∨ . In addition, BD in combination with SA produced three distinct L-F-K profiles, depicted in Table V.

Because the MMPI has not yet proven clearly valid in differentiating among normals, in this discussion and interpretation of individual scales we will emphasize only Mrs. R's highly elevated or submerged scores, or those scales on which her scores significantly differ from those of most of the normal sample. For example, with regard to Mrs. R's K score of 14, which is near the mean for normals, it is difficult to say much except that on that scale she performed like about 50 percent of the normal sample did. The K subscale was designed to catch the abnormals the MMPI had missed with its other scales. A group of psychiatrically disturbed patients who had achieved scores in the normal range were used as the criterion group. Items included in the construction of the scale were those on which the criterion group answered differently than the normals. To these items were also added eight more which involved high denial of problems or constant admission of problems. Dahlstrom and Welsh (1960) report that this scale tests significantly at the .001 level, but only for extreme scores when the K score is greater than 19 or less than 11, neither of which cases fits Mrs. R's score. Mrs. R's L score

---

[4]For example, there is a great frequency of F spikes, ∧ and not ∨, among the clinical cases in Hathaway and Meehl's *Atlas* (1951).

TABLE V

L-F-K CONFIGURATIONS

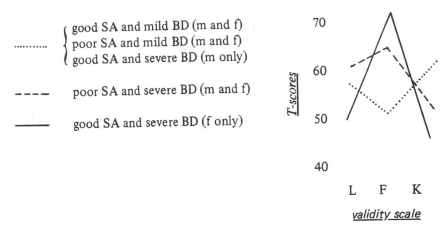

··········· {	good SA and mild BD (m and f)
	poor SA and mild BD (m and f)
	good SA and severe BD (m only)
- - - -	poor SA and severe BD (m and f)
————	good SA and severe BD (f only)

Mrs. R's L-F-K configuration fits the good SA and severe BD group of females, and we will retain these features as hypotheses for her.

similarly is not extreme. But it does tend upward, being greater than 84 percent of the Minnesota normal sample. My test supervisor's "Handy-Dandy Guide through the Darkest MMPI," which is based on her clinical experience and training, says an L upwards of 5 or 6 (Mrs. R's is 7) begins to reveal a trait of wishing to be seen as conforming, often accompanied by religiousness and a strong sense of morality.

Mrs. R's F score of 17 is very high. The items in the F scale were selected as those rarely endorsed by the Minnesota normals (90% did not endorse them.) Hypotheses associated with the "deviants" who did score high on F involve carelessness, confusion, illiteracy, inability to understand test items, deliberate lack of cooperation, "odd person" or "odd thoughts," overstatement or a loud signal for help. Dahlstrom and Welsh (1960) cite the IPAR studies of Gough, McKee, and Yandell (1955) and of Block and Bailey (1955), in which normal subjects were rated on adjective checklists and on a

Q-sort by an assessing staff. It was found that subjects with very low F scores tended to be rated: unpretentious, sincere, calm, dependable, honest, moderate, simple, slow, unassuming, loyal, patient, spunky. Subjects with very high F scores tended to be rated: more complex and restive, affected, curious, moody, opportunistic, changeable, complicated, dissatisfied, opinionated, talkative, unstable, lacking in conformity. Dahlstrom and Welsh say that the degree of super-elevation of F is an indication of the severity of an emotional upset; scores as high as 16-20, e.g. Mrs. R's, are usually produced by patients with frank psychoses, but may be from subjects who are resistive to the test and to assessment. With regard to Mrs. R, we have already stated that it is unlikely that she had an uncooperative response set to elevate her F score.

Other evidence in support of a high F score indicating severe emotional disturbance appears in the work of Kazan and Scheinberg (1945) and Brozek and Schiele (1948). Kazan and Scheinberg found that thirty-seven of 170 soldier patients who took the MMPI had high F scores ($T = 70+$). Of these thirty-seven, they claim that thirty-five had MMPIs which presented valid pictures of the patients. They concluded that "a number of badly neurotic and psychotic subjects obtain F scores validly." Brozek and Schiele obtained observations in support of Kazan and Scheinberg. With increasing experimental starvation of male subjects, they found pronounced personality deterioration reflected not only in elevated neurotic and, in some cases, psychotic scales but also in critical F scale items. However Schneck (1948) found F scores no more able to indicate personality disturbances than the inventory as a whole, based on impressions from interviews with and study of MMPI protocols of several hundred prisoners.

In Mrs. R's case, it looks likely that her high F score indicates she has an emotional disturbance, but we will also retain the hypothesis that the high F could indicate exaggeration of her troubles in efforts to call for help. It should also be noted that F elevation tends to result in the elevation of other clinical scales, and that a high F score is correlated with a high Sc score.

D

Mrs. R's Depression T score is almost at seventy, or almost

above the scores attained by 98 percent of the normal sample, putting her at the upper limits of normality on this scale. The criterion group for the D scale was fifty as-pure-as-possible cases of depression. Hypotheses associated with high D score are pessimism of outlook on life and the future; moodiness, self-deprecation; feelings of hopelessness, worthlessness, slowing of thought and action, apathy, preoccupation with death and suicide (Dahlstrom, Welsh, and Dahlstrom, 1972, p. 184, etc.). The item with the highest correlation with the rest of the scale by item analysis (.78), Mrs. R checked true for herself ("I feel weak all over much of the time.") From previous information and test results of Mrs. R, depressed seems an appropriate description of Mrs. R. The last two aspects of depression listed in the above hypotheses, however, seem less fitting for her than the other aspects listed.

Pd

The criterion group for the Pd scale, on which Mrs. R scored extremely high, consisted of 100 males and females age sixteen to twenty-two with histories of delinquency. The personality features which characterized them should be considered possible hypotheses with regard to Mrs. R: trouble maintaining satisfactory personal relationships; superficially genial but easily angered or irritated; bright but unable to profit from experience as other people do; poor anticipation of the consequences of behavior and little anticipatory deterrent anxiety; projection of blame onto others so as to be paranoid-looking; nervousness and concern over a threat perceived to be real.[5]

Mf

Mrs. R's score on the Masculinity-femininity scale is quite low, lower than almost 90 percent of the sample population, and deserves comment. The criterion group used in constructing the MMPI Mf scale was "homoerotic male inverts;" the purpose of the scale was to identify male sexual inversion. The builders of this scale were not concerned immediately with females; there were later unsuccessful attempts to make a similar female sexual inversion scale. If the

---

[5] See Dahlstrom, Welsh, and Dahlstrom, 1972, p. 195-201.

criterion group for this scale were considered useful for generating hypotheses about females, which is doubtful, then a low raw score should indicate passivity and dependency.[6,7]

It should be noted that masculinity-femininity is not a clearly defined construct in psychological tests and should be used with caution. For example, Barrows and Zuckerman (1960), in support of a previous study of college students by Nance (1949), found low but highly significant correlations between masculinity-femininity measures of 2,296 male employees of a Canadian company using the Guilford-Zimmerman Temperament Survey M-F scale (G-Z), the MMPI Mf scale, and the Strong Vocational Interest M-F scale. These intercorrelations are depicted in Table VI below.

TABLE VI

CORRELATIONS BETWEEN MASCULINITY-FEMININITY MEASURES

	MMPI	Strong
G-Z	.31	.34
MMPI		.33

Pa

Mrs. R's Paranoia score is relatively high, being above 84 percent of the Minnesota sample population. The criterion group for this scale were paranoid patients who featured ideas of reference, suspiciousness, interpersonal sensitivity, rigid and inflexible adherence to ideas and attitudes, and feelings of persecution and grandiose ideas.[8] Because 75 percent of the patients diagnosed as paranoid in Hathaway and Meehl's *Atlas* (1951) have Pa T scores below 70 (and 30 percent of their paranoid patients have *no* scores at all above 70), it is hard to judge what Mrs. R's T score of 62 is likely to signify. It almost looks as if she is more likely to have paranoid traits because

<hr/>

[6] See Dahlstrom, Welsh, and Dahlstrom (1972, p. 201-206.)
[7] My test supervisor's "Handy Dandy Guide through the Darkest MMPI" says that in females this dependency is likely to look masochistic, and the low Mf combined with a high Pd makes for a "castrating bitch" who uses femininity to manipulate. This information is largely based on her clinical experience and training.
[8] See Hathaway (1956) and Dahlstrom, Welsh, and Dahlstrom (1972, p. 206-211.)

her T score is less than 70! And a case can be made for this stance by speculating that paranoids may be too wary to get caught here with a high score.[9] Some paranoia does seem to be an appropriate hypothesis for Mrs. R.

Sc

Mrs. R's score on the Schizophrenia scale is higher than that attained by 98 percent of the normal sample population, putting her upwards of, if not beyond the limits of, normality. It is harder to determine the meaning of this scale than most of the others; even though much time has been devoted to its development, it is one of the weaker scales.[10] Even with the K-correction, the detection rate for fifty criterion schizophrenic cases is only 60 percent. This low criterion validity is probably due to the difficulty of capturing the rather elusive phantom "schizophrenia." The diversity of schizophrenia is reflected in the little homogeneity of the item content of the Sc scale.

Although the scale cannot be used to diagnose schizophrenia, it may tap some of its symptoms. The criterion group was supposed to have the following features, which can stand as hypotheses to consider for Mrs. R: incongruity of affect and thought content, fractionalization of thought processes, inadequate family relations, interest withdrawn from the outside world, emotional isolation. In light of what we have already seen of Mrs. R in other tests, it is likely that she is at times characterized by most of these features, but not continuously, and at her best, probably quite infrequently. Her family relations, however, are probably always pretty bad. Note also that her Sc score may have been elevated by a cry for help in her F score since the two scores are correlated.

Ma

Mrs. R's Ma score was higher than that of over 84 percent of the normal sample population and deserves comment. The criterion group for Ma was twenty-four "pure manics" (McKinley and Hatha-

---

[9] My test supervisor offers her clinical judgment (which in this instance is based on her clinical experience) that a score over 60 is likely to be diagnostically significant.
[10] See Hathaway (1956) and Dahlstrom, Welsh, and Dahlstrom (1972, p. 215-220.)

way, 1944).[11] Features associated with this group, which serve as hypotheses against which to compare Mrs. R's personality, are generally mild aspects of elevated moods, hyperactivity, restlessness, easy distractibility, unstable elation, insomnia, overoptimism, emotional excitement, flight of ideas, much activity but frequently inefficient and unproductive, undertaking more than one can handle. In its positive aspects this trait can be manifested as vigor, ambition, and energy. High Ma often goes with a high D score. In Mrs. R neither of these scores is extreme. We have already seen a fair amount of evidence of depression in her, particularly at this period of great stress in her life. Perhaps the manic side of her behavior shows itself when things are going better for her. From Mrs. R's life history, there is evidence that she is apt to take on more than she can handle and to do so with energy, e.g. trying to support her family, raising her children, running a duplex.

INTERPRETATION OF MRS. R's MMPI
BASED ON COOKBOOKS

Meehl (1954, 1956) has presented some of the advantages of "cookbooks:" he stresses the representativeness of the behavioral sample to which a cookbook "recipe" refers; its accuracy in recording and cataloging data from research studies; and the cookbook's enabling the professional to economize the amount of time spent on analyzing and interpreting data. Several major cookbooks used in the field are described below, accompanied by an interpretation of Mrs. R's MMPI scores according to each book.

Marks and Seeman's *An Atlas for Use with the MMPI* (1963)

In their cookbook the authors use actuarial description, whereby explicit rules delimit specific descriptive attributes which are to be assigned to an individual on the basis of quasi-experimentally demonstrated associations between MMPI profiles and sets of attributes. Their atlas was constructed using patients seen at the Department of Psychiatry at the University of Kansas Medical Center. But it is not really experimentally based because in method it largely relies on the investigators' judgments and not on any experimentally controlled

---

[11] See Dahlstrom, Welsh, and Dahlstrom (1972, p. 220-224.)

manipulation of variables.

Mrs. R's MMPI scores did not fit any of Marks and Seeman's profiles perfectly nor did they follow most of the rules associated with the profile to which they came closest in fit. Although goodness of fit was therefore only approximate, the characteristics of the authors' 482 mean profile nonetheless sound quite descriptive of Mrs. R. This profile type is pictured in Table VII below; a list of the Q-item Characteristics that Marks and Seeman ascribe to this type is also provided in Table VIII.[12] These characteristics sound like a summary of the personality characteristics of Mrs. R that we have already described based on the previous tests, and lend good support to the general line of hypothesis building that has been taken on the previous tests.

Hathaway and Meehl's
An Atlas for the Clinical Use of the MMPI (1951)

This is not really a cookbook, although it is at times referred to in this context, but a collection of case summaries which provide a cross-section of the authors' clinical experience with the MMPI in the Psychiatry Unit of the University of Minnesota Hospitals between 1937 and 1949.

Hathaway and Meehl employ a nomenclature which codifies each subject's MMPI scores. According to their system, Mrs. R's profile code is 48′ 296 *73* 1 -50 7:17:14. This does not fit the codes of any of the cases they give for comparison very well. The two closest codes were both those of two young males with the following features: paranoid thinking, suicidal, pathological sex activities, alcoholism, failure to comply with social disapproval, psychosis (schizophrenic, catatonic features).

Dahlstrom, Welsh, and Dahlstrom's
An MMPI Handbook (v. 1, 1972)

This is also not really a cookbook in Meehl's sense. The authors provide some major MMPI configural patterns based on an eclectic

---

[12]Marks and Seeman (1963, p. 172-174). The set of Case History Characteristics and Psychometric Characteristics that Marks and Seeman (p. 174-177) list as descriptive of this profile type are contained in Appendix B.

TABLE VII

482 MMPI PROFILE

Mean Profile for Atlas Code: 4-8-2/ 8-4-2/ 8-2-4

(Female: solid line; Male: broken line)

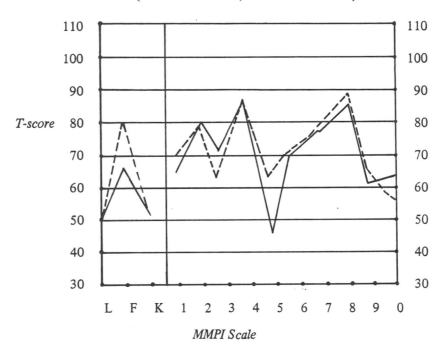

MMPI Scale

Rules for Profile

4, 8, and 2 above 70 Ts
4 minus 2 less than 15 T-scores
4 greater than 7 (or 7 minus 4 less than 5 T-scores)
8 minus 2 less than 15 T-scores
8 minus 7 more than 5 T-scores
8 minus 9 more than 10 T-scores
9 below 70 Ts
L and K less than F, F below 80 Ts

P.A. Marks and W. Seaman; *An Atlas for Use with the MMPI: Actuarial Description of Abnormal Personality*, 1963, The Williams & Wilkins Company. Reproduced by permission.

TABLE VIII

Q-ITEM CHARACTERISTICS ASSOCIATED WITH 482 PROFILE

> (I have marked characteristics that
> seem to fit Mrs. R, based on her
> other tests, with a check mark ($\sqrt{}$)).

Most Descriptive:

    Is distrustful of people in general; questions their motivations.
$\sqrt{}$ Keeps people at a distance; avoids close interpersonal relationships.
$\sqrt{}$ Utilizes projection as a defense mechanism.
    Utilizes rationalization as a defense mechanism.
$\sqrt{}$ Is afraid of emotional involvement with others.
$\sqrt{}$ Genotype has paranoid features.
$\sqrt{}$ Has inner conflicts over sexuality.
    Complains of weakness or easy fatigability.
$\sqrt{}$ Genotype has schizoid features.
    Is resentful.
    Is argumentative.
    Is sensitive to anything that can be construed as a demand.
$\sqrt{}$ Possesses a basic insecurity and need for attention.
    Is unpredictable and changeable in behavior and attitudes.
$\sqrt{}$ Reacts to frustration intropunitively.
    Utilizes acting-out as a defense mechanism.
$\sqrt{}$ Has feelings of hopelessness.
$\sqrt{}$ Seems unable to express own emotions in any modulated adaptive way.
$\sqrt{}$ Tends to be ruminative and overideational.
$\sqrt{}$ Has an exaggerated need for affection.
$\sqrt{}$ Has inner conflict about emotional dependency.

Least Descriptive:

$\sqrt{}$ Is "normal," healthy, symptom free.
$\sqrt{}$ Is cheerful.
$\sqrt{}$ Would be organized and adaptive when under stress or trauma.
$\sqrt{}$ Has the capacity for forming close interpersonal relationships.
$\sqrt{}$ Appears to be poised, self-assured, socially at ease.
$\sqrt{}$ Exhibits good heterosexual adjustment.
    Accepts others as they are; is not judgmental.
$\sqrt{}$ Has good verbal-cognitive insight into own personality structure and dynamics.
$\sqrt{}$ Presents self as being physically, organically sick.
$\sqrt{}$ Defenses are fairly adequate in relieving psychological distress.
    Is socially extroverted (outgoing).
$\sqrt{}$ Has a resilient ego-defense system; has a safe margin of integration.
$\sqrt{}$ Psychic conflicts are represented in somatic symptoms.

TABLE VIII (Cont'd)

√ Has "diagnostic" insight; awareness of the descriptive features of own behavior.
   Is able to sense other person's feelings; is an intuitive, empathic person.
√ Manifests hypochondriacal tendencies.
√ Has multiple neurotic manifestations.
√ Presents a favorable prognosis.
   Has a need to affiliate with others.
√ Is perfectionistic; is compulsively meticulous.

gathering of information and on general characteristics of people studied by Hathaway and Meehl.

Two of their patterns are relevant to Mrs. R's scores (1972, p. 270, 273.):

48's Frequently described by others as odd; unpredictable, impulsive, nonconforming; schizoid personality; underachievement, marginal adjustment, and uneven performance in school and jobs; nomadism, social isolation, delinquency; crimes committed by such people are often senseless, poorly planned and executed and may involve very vicious sexual and homicidal assault. Females with this pattern: vague physical complaints, changes from doctor to doctor and lack of follow-up visits; lack of frankly bizarre behavior; tend to be early psychotic reactions.

42's Alcoholism; situationally produced and short-lived depression; guilt and self-deprecation but usually not sincere; females tend to be pre-psychotic.

Gilberstadt and Duker's *A Handbook for Clinical and Actuarial MMPI Interpretation* (1965)

Another actuarial cookbook, this handbook provides nineteen basic profile types. Once again, Mrs. R's profile did not fit any of the nineteen very well, but the closest fit suggested looking for paranoia, immaturity, alcoholism, and sexual deviancy.

CHAPTER 13

SUMMARY REPORT
AND RECOMMENDATIONS

THIS final chapter of our volume presents the psychological report for Mrs. R. The report is typical of those prepared by psychologists in field settings in the course of their work with clients in terms of the type of material covered and the manner in which findings are presented. Its degree of detail and lengthiness, however, are not typical of most psychological reports, which generally must be prepared rapidly, in terse fashion, and are frequently written so as to address a specific referral question.

The report integrates the findings from each test we have covered in Chapters 7 to 12 into a total picture, or formulation, of Mrs. R's personality. It has five divisions: (1) an introduction containing demographic and referral information; (2) a summary of Mrs. R's behavior during test administration; (3) a description of her intellectual functioning; (4) the main body of the report describing the organization of her personality and its characteristic manners of functioning; and (5) brief recommendations regarding her treatment.

PSYCHOLOGICAL REPORT

Tester: Carol Deinhardt
Testing Dates: April 3, 19__, 2 hours
April 8, 19__, 2 hours
Subject: Mrs. R
Sex: Female
Race: Caucasian
Nationality: U.S.A.

Materials: WAIS, Bender-Gestalt, DAP, TAT, Rorschach, MMPI
Age: 33
Marital Status: Legal separation
Education: 10th grade
Occupation: Secretary/housewife

Mrs. R is a sleepy, matronly, plain-looking woman of average height with short, curly, dull-brown hair. Following her second unsuccessful marriage, she has been legally separated from an alcoholic husband for the past three years and is now largely self-supporting of herself and three children ages six, nine, and fifteen. She became pregnant with her first child before her first marriage and entered a

185

marriage of convenience (not natural father). The other two children were born during her present marriage.

Mrs. R was referred for testing having entered the hospital because, in her words, her job, home, and responsibilities had become "too much." Immediately prior to entrance she had moved with her children from her duplex home because she thought that someone had gone through the basement and that her new subletters in the other half of the duplex had taken pictures at the company where she is secretary to a security agent. Police reports seem to have been negative, and Mrs. R is aware that the problem might rest with herself.

Test Behavior

At the first session it was difficult to get information from Mrs. R. Her thinking was spotty and run-on; her mind wandered off tangentially into jumbled tales with unidentified people and events. However, with constant verbal reminders she could stay with a topic and respond appropriately. She was cooperative and made attempts to be friendly that were interjected with nervous laughter. She was dependent, apologetic, self-deprecating, and depressed. In the second session she was much more verbally coherent and much less rambling. She was still depressed, dependent, and self-doubting. She spoke very softly (bordering on mumbling) so I often could not understand her and continually had to ask her to repeat what she had said. She smoked frequently, complained of thirst, and often mentioned food and hunger. Generally she seemed tired, sad, and listless.

Intellectual Functioning

Mrs. R's intelligence scores were "average" based on a verbal IQ of 105, performance IQ of 98, and full scale IQ of 102. She uses her intelligence quite resourcefully and with a high degree of motivation. She can be objective and can spontaneously spot and correct her own errors. But her style of thinking is concrete, personalized, and tangential, and she is apt to give jumbled, perseverated, unthought-out responses unless she is working in a structured situation that reminds her to stick with the topic at hand.

Although capable of noting the details of her environment, Mrs. R does not focus on detail, is not meticulous, and does not dwell on the minutiae of everyday facts and problems. In efforts to understand what goes on around her she is prone to overgeneralize, draw conclusions based on inadequate evidence, and produce a stereotyped picture of the world. Thus her aspirations to view her surroundings in an integrated way can be ineffective and beyond her present capabilities. She can approach problems systematically and is motivated to stick with a task or a new problem even if she is getting nowhere with it, but she flusters easily and withdraws into herself to try to get the troublesome area to stop impinging on her.

Mrs. R has good comprehension of the proper response to and meaning of everyday affairs but has poor problem-solving skills when faced with new or novel situations: she lacks insight-forming mechanisms and does not entertain alternate hypotheses but instead makes concrete, usually wrong, guesses when in doubt and uncritically grabs at whatever the immediate aspects of her surroundings suggest to her.

Mrs. R has adequate verbal skills but some problem working with abstractions, particularly with numbers. She also has trouble concentrating especially over a sustained period of time, and may have a problem with visual-motor coordination. There is evidence that her intelligence may have deteriorated from a once higher level of functioning and the possibility of a perceptual problem cannot be ruled out at this point. Mrs. R has more than adequate intelligence resources for functioning well in society. It is her weak control over all that she does have to work with that can grossly hamper her good functioning.

Personality

Mrs. R has low self-esteem and generally feels inadequate, pessimistic, and uncertain in the face of what looks to her like a bleak world. Lack of insight into herself combined with passivity and poor anticipation of the consequences of her behavior makes for unsuccessful outcomes of the important activities she undertakes; she sees little hope for improvement in her own sad and unsatisfactory life. She has the energy to tackle problems but usually takes on more than she can handle, becomes overwhelmed, ineffectual, and feels all the more helpless. She lacks knowledge of how to satisfy her needs and desires and instead tries to attain them in passive wishful thinking.

Mrs. R's needs for affection and affiliation, which she experiences as a desire for approval and a sense of belongingness, are not well integrated in her personality. She lacks confidence in social contacts, has poor capacity to form and maintain close interpersonal relationships, and sees people as generally threatening to her. She especially fears males and, because she is unsure of her femaleness and feels guilty about and frightened by sexuality, she feels helpless in male-female relationships. She has a confused, primitive picture of herself as a sexual being and experiences herself sexually as phallic, incompetent, and monsterlike.

Much of her need for dependency is strongly repressed and inhibited; yet, very near the surface ready to burst forth uncontrollably is a strong infant-like craving for physical contact with others. She only hesitantly recognizes the existence of this need, and its strong impact on Mrs. R can block her ties with reality and distort her perceptions. She also feels conflict over her strong need to be dependent on other people and expects to be abandoned by them. Important rejection experiences in her childhood by her parents are likely to have kept her from developing mature ways of expressing this need: she looks for a great deal of attention but in inappropriate and devouring ways; she uses people to care for her but is unable to respond to them. She has not yet learned adult ways of relating to others and is unable to express her primitively experienced emotions in any modulated, adaptive way. She consequently lives in what amounts to a state of emotional isolation.

Feeling ineffectual and frustrated, Mrs. R carries a rage deep inside her which is seldom relieved by outward aggression, which she sees as inconsistent with her image of herself. Instead her anger is manifested in depression, guilt, and remorse. Some is relieved by the projection of aggression onto males, but she is the unfortunate victim of this aggression and punishes herself with her own paranoia.

Mrs. R knows what healthy mental functioning with firm ties with reality is, and is strongly motivated to function in this manner. But maintaining this level is at present beyond her capabilities. Her poor defenses give her little maneuvering room in the face of anxiety. When stress she perceives is not severe she relies on denial of her impulses or of the troublesome external input. But under heavier strain she becomes panicked and disorganized, tries to withdraw into herself in a dazelike fashion, or resorts to concrete psychotic-looking thinking; but she does all of these unsuccessfully and she sinks into a deeper depression.

She can nonetheless recover quickly and well with the aid of support from others. She also uses the thought of herself as a mother to help her recover and maintain her stability. This is the one role she sees herself as having carried out somewhat successfully, and it is the positive center of her life and a major source of desperately sought affection. It is not surprising that the time her youngest child began school has been concomitant with the decline of her personality functioning.

In summary, Mrs. R has resources and abilities but she does not know how to make the best use of them. She can be responsive and sensitive to the world around her and wants to take part, but she has not learned how to relate successfully to other people as an adult. The force of her emotions at times outdoes the strength of her control over them and breaks her otherwise good contact with reality. Although her personality frequently vacillates and decompensates even under minimal stress, with much needed support she can recover quickly and effectively.

Recommendations

Mrs. R needs to learn alternate ways of behaving. She needs to develop adult responses to life and learn to respond to other people and not use them only to care for her. Treatment for her should be planned step-by-step with realistic goals set which she can be encouraged to see as attainable by her own efforts. Thus she can gain confidence in her ability to change her way of life and increase in sense of adequacy. Mrs. R needs successful, long-term, warm relationships on which she can rely for support, affection, and advice. A case worker could be effective, but there is the danger of a change in personnel having disastrous effects on Mrs. R. Therefore, a long-term group situation would probably be best, and in addition to the above functions, could help her improve her self-esteem. Employment involving contact with children should also be helpful for her by capitalizing on her role as mother.

APPENDICES

SURVEY OF PERSONALITY ASSESSMENT TEXTBOOKS CURRENTLY IN PRINT

Questions regarding the extent to which each book covers how to interpret raw data for constructing the psychological report.

Name of Book:

Author:

Publisher:

Copyright Date:

No. of Pages:

Type of Book:

(1) Does the textbook give models or methods of how to prepare high quality psychological assessment reports from raw data?

(2) What are the models or methods?

(3) Does the textbook discuss how to interpret raw data?

(4) Does the textbook discuss the scientific mode of thinking?

    a. type of thinking to use, e.g. forming hypotheses from raw data using hunches, experience, lore, information regarding tests, literature.

    b. using hypothesis testing for interpretation of data.

    c. discuss relevance of test literature to data.

    d. discuss relevance of other research literature to data.

    e. discuss testing alternate hypotheses.

(5) Does the textbook demonstrate how to apply the above in a case study or studies?

    a. type of thinking to use.

    b. hypothesis testing.

    c. relevance of using knowledge of test literature in drawing up hypotheses and evaluating them.

    d. relevance of using other knowledge of other research literature to evaluate hypotheses and interpretations.

e. testing alternate hypotheses.

f. provide sample psychological reports based on raw data to demonstrate above.

(6) Does the textbook include case studies or samples from case studies that show an explanation of the sources of each interpretation made?

(7) Does the textbook provide an extended case study using a battery of tests for personality assessment?

a. with interpretation test by test?

b. with psychological assessment report for each test?

c. with grand summary psychological report?

d. with reference to test literature?

(8) Does the personality assessment textbook lump personality assessment together with psychological testing and diagnosis so that the student is unlikely to develop assessment skills using interpretation from this book or be aware of the nature of assessment, its modes of thinking, its uses, advantages, limitations?

CASE HISTORY CHARACTERISTICS AND PSYCHOMETRIC CHARACTERISTICS OF THE 482 PROFILE

V. Case History Characteristics

Presenting Illness

Areas of Manifestation

Personality	85.0	
Marital	82.4 + + +	
Social	60.0 +	
Home	35.0	
Occupational	25.0	
Sexual	20.0	
Educational	10.0 + + +	
Religious	0.0	

System Involvement

Musculoskeletal	20.0
Genitourinary	15.0
Cardiorespiratory	5.0 –
Gastrointestinal	5.0 –

Age of Onset

Mean age (years)	28.6 –
Range	15:54

Length of Onset

Less than a week	10.0
A week to a month	10.0 –
A month to a year	35.0
Over a year	45.0 +

Duration of Illness

Less than a week	0.0
A week to a month	10.0
A month to a year	25.0 –
Over a year	65.0 +

Previous Episodes

None	55.0
Similar	30.0
Other	15.0

Personal History

Birth

Abnormal	5.0
Illegitimate	10.0 +

Childhood Health

Behavior problem	35.0 +
Physical Illness	5.0 –

School Achievement

Above average	10.0 –

Sibling Status

Only child	20.0 +
Youngest	33.3
Middle	20.0 –
Oldest	26.7

Number of Children

Mean number	2.4
Range	1:5

P.A. Marks and W. Seaman, *An Atlas for Use with the MMPI: Actuarial Description of Abnormal Personality*, 1963, The Williams & Wilkins Company. Reproduced by Permission.

Average	50.0 –	Extramarital Relations	25.0
Below average	40.0 + + +	Marital Adjustment	
Social		Poor	69.2 +
Withdrawal	65.0	Good	30.8 –
Participation	35.0	Gynecology	
Menarchal Age		Abortions	10.0
Mean age (years)	12.3 –	Hysterectomy	0.0 –
Sex Instruction		Parental Home	
Family	45.0 + +	Poverty	0.0 –
Dating		Disruption	35.0 –
Often or steady	57.1 –	Alcoholism	15.0
Rarely or never	42.9 +	Father	15.0
Delinquency		Mother	0.0 –
Sexual	30.0 +	Physical illness	10.0
Other	10.0 +	Father	0.0 –
Criminal Record	5.0	Mother	10.0
Education		Mental illness	10.0
Grade school	35.0 +	Father	0.0 –
High school	35.0 –	Mother	10.0 +
Junior college	20.0 +	Death	10.0 –
College	10.0 –	Father	10.0 –
Marital Status		Mother	5.0 –
Married	50.0 –	Paternal Relations	
Single	33.3 +	Indifference	43.8 +
Divorced	11.1	Affection	37.5
Separated	5.6	Rejection	12.5
Widowed	0.0 –	Domination	6.2
Length of Courtship		Neglect	0.0
Less than a week	14.3	Overprotection	0.0
A week to a month	14.3 –	Discipline	
A month to a year	14.3 –	Permissive	30.0
Over a year	57.1 + +	Strict	15.0
Marital Age		Maternal Relations	
Mean age (years)	19.1 –	Rejection	47.0 + +
Range	17:25	Domination	29.4
Parental Consent	10.0 –	Indifference	17.6 +
Attitude and Behavior		Neglect	6.0 +
Apathetic	30.0	Affection	0.0 – –
Agitated	25.0 –	Overprotection	0.0 –
Tearful/crying	20.0 –	Discipline	
Dishevelled	15.0	Strict	45.0
Poor cooperation	10.0 –	Permissive	0.0 –
Illegitimate Births	0.0 –	Gestures	5.0 –

Stream of Thought		Poor Judgment	40.0
Irrelevant	35.0	Poor Memory	15.0
Incoherent	10.0	Feelings	
Retarded	10.0 −	Inferiority	40.0
Emotional Tone		Guilt	30.0 +
Depressed	80.0	Unreality	30.0
Anxious	40.0 −	Perplexity	15.0 −
Labile	30.0 +	Doubt	10.0
Irritable	15.0		
Disoriented	5.0		

Symptoms and Complaints

Depression/despondent	80.0	Worrisome	25.0 +
Tense/nervous	75.0	Excitability	20.0
Anxious	75.0	Immaturity	20.0
Irritability	70.0 + + +	Impulsivity	20.0
Hostile	65.0 +	Insomnia/sleep disturb	20.0 −
Suspicious	55.0	Loss of interest	20.0
Withdrawn	50.0 +	Manipulative	20.0 +
Suicidal attempts	45.0 + + +	Passivity	20.0 +
Ideas of reference	40.0 +	Amorality	15.0 + + +
Moodiness	40.0 + +	Constipation	15.0 +
Sexual difficulty	40.0 +	Dependent	15.0 −
Emotional inapprop	40.0 +	Homicidal	15.0 +
Disturbance of thought	35.0 +	Indecisive	15.0
Suicidal ruminations.	35.0 +	Religious	15.0
Delusions	30.0	Alcoholism	10.0
Somatic complaints	30.0	Anorexia	10.0 −
Difficulty concentrating	25.0	Headache	10.0
Fatigue	25.0	Ruminative	10.0
Hallucinations	25.0 +	Secondary gain	10.0
Paranoid	25.0	Suicidal threats	10.0 +
Phobic/fearful	25.0	Weight loss	10.0
Schizoid	25.0 + +		

Course in Treatment

Length		Prognosis	
Mean days	60.5	Good	18.7
Range	7:178	Fair	50.0 +
		Poor	31.3 −

Type		Disposition
Psychotherapy only	70.6 +	Committed	30.0 + + +
Plus tranquilizers	23.5	Referred clinic Op	30.0 –
Plus energizers	5.9	Terminated	25.0
Plus ECT	0.0 –	Referred hospital Ip	15.0
Response		Terminated ATA	0.0 –
No change	22.2 –	
Small improvement	38.9	
Decided improvement	38.9 +	

VI. PSYCHOMETRIC CHARACTERISTICS

Shipley
113.0 | IQ | 85:131 | 93.5 + | CQ | 67:118
WAIS

111.2	FS	96:128						
105.	VS	95:122	10	13	9	11	10	11
108.0	PS	96:130	12 +	11 +	10	12 +	11	

Wittenborn
I 6 + | II 4 | III 3 | IV 4 | V 2 – | VI 2 – | VII 2 | VIII 1 – | IX 5 +
MMPI

Adm/Fe	3.9	11.8	13.5	66	79	72	85	45	69	77	86	62	64
Adm/Me	3.8	15.9	13.6	70	80	65	86	64	69	77	89	68	57
Pro	9.0	5.6	22.0	52	55	59	71	56	56	55	64	68	47
Dis	5.2	9.2	14.8	52	73	67	77	49	64	65	73	60	59

BIBLIOGRAPHY

Aiken, L.R., Jr. *Psychological Testing and Assessment.* 3rd ed. Allyn, 1978.

Ainsworth, M.D. "Problems of Validation," in B. Klopfer, M.D. Ainsworth, W.G. Klopfer, and R.R. Holt, eds. *Developments in the Rorschach Technique.* v. 1 Yonkers: World Book Co., 1954, p. 405-500.

Allison, J., et al., eds. *The Interpretation of Psychological Tests.* New York: Harper and Row, 1968.

Allport, G.A. *Pattern and Growth in Personality.* New York: Holt, Rinehart, and Winston, 1961. A revision of earlier book, *Personality: A Psychological Interpretation.* (Holt, Rinehart, and Winston, 1937).

American Psychologist., 1981, 36, No. 6, p. 633-686.

American Psychologist. Special Issue, "Testing: Concepts, Policy, Practice, and Research." 1981, 36, No. 10, whole issue.

Anastasi, A. *Psychological Testing.* 5th ed. New York: Macmillan, 1982.

Anderson, J.K., Parenté, F.J., and Gordon, C. "A Forecast of the Future for the Mental Health Profession," *American Psychologist.* 1981, 36, p. 848-855.

Andrulis, R.S. *Adult Assessment: A Source Book of Tests and Measures of Human Behavior.* Springfield, Ill.: Charles C Thomas, Publisher, 1977.

"APGA Ethical Standards, 1974," in R. Callis, ed. *Ethical Standards Casebook.* 2nd ed. Washington, D.C.: American Personnel and Guidance Association, 1976.

Appelbaum, S.A. "Science and Persuasion in the Psychological Test Report," *Journal of Consulting and Clinical Psychology.* 1970, 35, p. 349-355.

Barnett, D.W. *Nondiscriminatory Multifactored Assessment.* New York: Human Sciences Press, 1982.

Barrows, G.A., and Zuckerman, M. "Construct Validity of 3 Masculinity-Femininity Tests," *Journal of Consulting Psychology.* 1960, 24, p. 441-445.

Bazhenov, L.B., and Samorodnitski, P.Kh. "The Role of Experience and Logical Thinking in Constructing Scientific Knowledge," (Russ.) *Voprosy Filosofii.* 1976, 6, p. 93-103.

Beck, S.J. "The Rorschach Test: A Multi-dimensional Test of Personality," in H.H. Anderson, and G.L. Anderson, eds. *An Introduction to Projective Techniques.* New York: Prentice-Hall, 1951.

Beck, S.J. *Advances in Interpretation.* New York: Grune, 1952.

Beck, S.J. *Rorschach's Test: v. 1.* New York: Grune, 1962.

Bell, J.E. *Projective Techniques.* New York: Longmans, Green, and Co., 1948.

Bender, L. *A Visual Motor Gestalt Test and Its Clinical Use.* New York: American Orthopsychiatric Association, 1938.

Bender, L. *Instructions for the Use of Visual Motor Gestalt Test.* New York: American Orthopsychiatric Association, 1946.

Bersoff, D.N. "'Current Functioning' Myth: An Overlooked Fallacy in Psychological Assessment," *Journal of Consulting and Clinical Psychology.* 1971, 37, 391-393.

Bersoff, D.N. "Silk Purses into Sow's Ears: The Decline of Psychological Testing and a Suggestion for its Redemption," *American Psychologist.* 1973, 28, p. 892-899.

Bersoff, D.N. "Professional Ethics and Legal Responsibilities: On the Horns of a Dilemma," *Journal of School Psychology.* 1975, 13, p. 359-376.

Bersoff, D.N. "Testing and the Law," *American Psychologist.* 1981, 36, p. 1047-1056.

Billingslea, F. "The Bender-Gestalt: A Review and Perspective," *Psychological Bulletin.* 1963, 60, p. 233-251.

Blake, R.M., et al. *Theories of Scientific Method: The Renaissance through the Nineteenth Century.* Seattle: University of Washington Press, 1960.

Bourne, L.E., Ekstrand, B.R., and Dominowski, R.L. *The Psychology of Thinking.* Englewood Cliffs, New Jersey: Prentice-Hall, 1971.

Braithewaite, R.B. *Scientific Explanation: A Study of the Function of Theory, Probability, and Law in Science.* Cambridge: University Press, 1968.

Breuer, J., and Freud, S. "Case Histories," (Orig. publ. 1895; trans. by J. Strachey) In J. Strachey, ed. *The Standard Edition of the Complete Psychological Works of Sigmund Freud.* v. 2 London: Hogarth Press, 1955, p. 19-181.

Brewer, J., and Owen, P. "A Note on the Power of Statistical Tests in the *Journal of Educational Measurement*," *Journal of Educational Measurement.* 1973, 7, p. 258-271.

Bromley, D.B. *Personality Description in Ordinary Language.* New York: Wiley, 1977.

Brown, W.R., and McGuire, J.M. "Current Psychological Assessment Practices," *Professional Psychology.* 1976, 7, p. 475-484.

Brozek, J., and Schiele, B.C. "Clinical Significance of the Minnesota Multiphasic F Scale Evaluated in Experimental Neurosis," *American Journal of Psychiatry.* 1948, 105, p. 259-266.

Bryan, W.L., and Harter, N. "Studies on the Telegraphic Language. The Acquisition of a Hierarchy of Habits," *Psychological Review.* 1899, 6, p. 345-375.

Burik, T.E. "Relative Roles of the Learning and Motor Factors Involved in the Digit Symbol Test," *J Psychol*, 1950, 30, p. 33-42.

Buros, O.K., ed. *Fifth Mental Measurements Yearbook.* New Jersey: Gryphon Press, 1959.

Buros, O.K., ed. *Sixth Mental Measurements Yearbook.* New Jersey: Gryphon Press, 1965.

Buros, O.K., ed. *Personality Tests and Reviews.* New Jersey: Gryphon Press, 1970.

Buros, O.K., ed. *Tests in Print II: An Index to Tests, Test Reviews, and the Literature on Specific Tests.* Highland Park, New Jersey: Gryphon Press, 1974.

Buros, O.K., ed. *Mental Measurements Yearbook.* 8th. v. I-II. Highland Park, New Jersey: Gryphon Press, 1978.

Caine, T.M. "Personality and Illness," in P. Mittler, ed. *The Psychological Assessment of Mental and Physical Handicaps.* London: Methuen, 1970.

Campbell, D.T., and Fiske, D.W. "Convergent and Discriminant Validation by the Multitrait-Multimethod Matrix," *Psychological Bulletin.* 1959, 56, p. 81-106.

Campbell, D.T., and Stanley, J.C. *Experimental and Quasi-Experimental Design of Research.* Chicago: Rand McNally, 1963.

Carlson, R. "Where is the Person in Personality Research?" *Psychological Bulletin*. 1971, 75, p. 203-219.

Carr, A.C. "Psychological Testing and Reporting," *Journal of Projective Techniques and Personality*. 1968, 32, p. 513-521.

Cattell, R.B. *Personality and Motivation Structure and Measurement*. Yonkers: World Book, 1957.

Cattell, R.B. *Description and Measurement of Personality*. Johnson Repr., 1969 repr. of 1946 ed.

Chambers, G.S., and Hamlin, R. "The Validity of Judgments Based on 'Blind' Rorschach Records," *Journal of Consulting Psychology*. 1957, 21, p. 105-109.

Chan, D.W.O. "Inferential Judgment and Implicit Theory of Psychopathology," *Diss Abstr Int* 1979 (Mar), 39(9-B), 4570-4571.

Chapman, L. and Chapman, J. "Genesis of Popular but Erroneous Psychodiagnostic Observations," *Journal of Abnormal Psychology*. 1967, 72, p. 193-204.

Chapman, L., and Chapman, J. "Illusory Correlations as an Obstacle to Use of Valid Diagnostic Signs," *Journal of Abnormal Psychology*. 1969, 74, p. 271-280.

Chassan, J.B. *Research Design in Clinical Psychology and Psychiatry*. 2nd ed. New York: Appleton-Century-Crofts, 1979.

Cohen, J. "A Factor Analytically Based Rationale for the Wechsler Adult Intelligence Scale," *Journal of Consulting Psychology*. 1957a, 21, p. 451-457.

Cohen, J. "The Factorial Structure of the WAIS between Early Adulthood and Old Age," *Journal of Consulting Psychology*. 1957b, 21, p. 283-290.

Cohen, J. "The Factorial Structure of the WISC at Ages 7-6, 10-6, and 13-6," *Journal of Consulting Psychology*. 1959, 23, p. 285-299.

Cohen, J. "The Statistical Power of Abnormal-Social Psychological Research," *Journal of Abnormal Social Psychology*. 1962, 65, p. 145-153.

Cox, B., and Sargent, H. "TAT Responses of Emotionally Disturbed and Emotionally Stable Children: Clinical Judgment vs. Normative Data," *Journal of Projective Techniques*. 1950, 14, p. 61-73.

Cronbach, L.J. "The Two Disciplines of Scientific Psychology," *American Psychologist*. 1957, 12, p. 671-684.

Cronbach, L.J., *Essentials of Psychological Testing*. 2nd ed. New York: Harper, 1960.

Cronbach, L.J., *Essentials of Psychological Testing*. 4th ed. New York: Macmillan, 1976.

Cronbach, L.J., and Meehl, P.E. "Construct Validity in Psychological Tests," *Psychological Bulletin*. 1955, 52, p. 281-302.

Dahlstrom, W.G., and Welsh, G.S. *An MMPI Handbook: A Guide to Use in Clinical Practice and Research*. Minneapolis: University of Minnesota Press, 1960.

Dahlstrom, W.G., Welsh, G.S., and Dahlstrom, L.E. *An MMPI Handbook. v. 1 Clinical Interpretation*. Minnesota: University of Minnesota Press, revised ed., 1972.

Daily, C.A. *Assessment of Lives: Personality Evaluation in a Bureaucratic Society*. San Francisco: Jossey-Bass, 1971.

Dawes, R., and Corrigan, B. "Linear Models in Decision Making," *Psychological Bulletin*. 1974, 81, p. 95-106.

Dennerll, R.D., Broeder, J., and Sokolov, S.L. "WISC and WAIS Factors in Children and Adults with Epilepsy," *Journal of Clinical Psychology*. 1964, 20, p. 236-237.

Dewey, J. *Logic: The Theory of Inquiry*. New York: Holt, 1938.

Diagnostic and Statistical Manual of Mental Disorders. 4th ed. (DSM-III). Washington, D.C.: American Psychiatric Association, 1980.

Dollard, J. *Criteria for the Life History: With Analysis of Six Notable Documents*. New Haven, Conn.: Yale University Press, 1935.

Dollard, J. *Criteria for the Life History*. New York: Peter Smith, 1949.

Draguns, J.G., Haley, and Phillips. "Studies of Rorschach Content: A Review of the Research Literature Part I: Traditional Content Categories," *Journal of Projective Techniques*. 1967, 31, p. 3-32.

Dukes, W.F. "N = 1," *Psychological Bulletin*. 1965, 64, p. 74-79.

Ebbinghaus, H. *Über das Gedachtnis*. Leipzig: Duncker and Humblot, 1885.

Ebel, R.L. "And Still the Dryads Linger," *American Psychologist*. 1974, 29, p. 485-492.

Einhorn, H.J. "Expert Measurement and Mechanical Combination," *Organizational Behavior and Human Performance*. 1972, 7, p. 86-106.

Einhorn, H.J., and Hogarth, R.M. "Confidence in Judgment: Persistence of the Illusion of Validity," *Psychological Review*. 1978, 85, p. 395-416.

English, H.B., and English, A.C. *A Comprehensive Dictionary of Psychological and Psychoanalytic Terms: A Guide to Usage*. New York: Longmans, Green, and Co., 1958.

Erikson, E. "The Nature of Clinical Evidence," *Daedalus*. 1958, 87, p. 65-87.

"Ethical Principles of Psychologists," (American Psychological Association) *American Psychologist*. 1981, 36, p. 633-638.

Ethical Standards of Psychologists. Washington, D.C.: American Psychological Association, 1977, revised 1979.

Exner, J.E., McDowell, E., Pabst, J., et al. "On the Detection of Willful Falsifications in the MMPI,"*Journal of Consulting Psychology*. 1963, 27, p. 91-94.

Eysenck, H.J., and Eysenck, S.B. *Personality Structure and Measurement*. Knapp, 1969.

Fitzgerald, B.J. "Some Relationships among Projective Tests, Interview, and Sociometric Measures of Dependent Behavior," *Journal of Abnormal Psychology*. 1958, J6, p. 199-204.

Ford, J.D. "Research on Training Counselors and Clinicians," *Review of Educational Research*. 1979, 49, p. 87-130.

Fowler, M.G., and Epting, F.R. "The Person in Personality Research: An Alternative Lifestyle Case Study," *Journal of Clinical Psychology*. 1976, 32, p. 159-167.

Freud, S. (1887-1902) *The Origins of Psycho-analysis: Letters to Wilhelm Fleiss, Drafts and Notes: 1887-1902*. London: Images, 1954.

Freud, S. "Fragment of an Analysis of a Case of Hysteria," (orig. publ. 1905) *Standard Edition*, v. 7. London: Hogarth Press, 1953.

Garett, K. "The Relationship between Critical Thinking, Ability, Personality, and Academic Achievement in Graduate Students in the School of Education at the University of Southern California," *Dissert Abstr Internat* 1978 (Jun), 1.38(12-A), 7226.

Garfield, S.L. *Introductory Clinical Psychology*. New York: Macmillan, 1957.

Garfield, S.L. "The Clinical Method in Personality Assessment," in J.M. Wepman and R.W. Heine, eds. *Concepts of Personality*. Chicago: Aldine, 1963, p. 474-502.

Geishune. *The Rorschach Technique*. Harvard memeo (1961).

Gilberstadt, H., and Duker, J. *A Handbook for Clinical and Actuarial MMPI Interpretation*. Philadelphia: W.B. Saunders, 1965.

Gilbert, J. *Interpreting Psychological Test Data*. v. 1 New York: Van Nostrand, 1978.

Glasser, J.M. "An Investigation of the Process of Perceiving Nonverbal Behaviors with Implications for Clinical Judgment," *Dissert Abst Internat* 1979, 39(12-B), 6195.

Goldberg, L.R. "The Effectiveness of Clinicians' Judgments: The Diagnosis of Organic Brain Damage from the Bender-Gestalt Test," *Journal of Consulting Psychology*. 1959, 23, p. 25-33.

Goldberg, L.R. "The Effectiveness of Clinicians' Judgments: The Diagnosis of Organic Brain Damage from the Bender-Gestalt Test," in B.I. Murstein, ed. *Handbook of Projective Techniques*. New York: Basic Books, 1965.

Goldberg, L.R. "Simple Models or Simple Processes? Some Research on Clinical Judgments," *American Psychologist*. 1968, 23, p. 483-496.

Goldberg, L.R. "Some Recent Trends in Personality Assessment," *Journal of Personality Assessment*. 1972, 36, p. 547-560.

Golden, C.J. *Clinical Interpretation of Objective Psychological Tests*. Grune, 1979.

Goldstein, M., and Goldstein, I.F. *How We Know: An Exploration of the Scientific Process*. New York: Plenum, 1978.

Grant, M.Q., Ives, V., and Ranzoni, J.H. "Reliability and Validity of Judges' Ratings of Adjustment on the Rorschach," *Psychological Monograph*. 1952, 66, No. 334.

Griffith, R.M., and Taylor, V.H. "Bender-Gestalt Figure Rotations: A Stimulus Factor," *Journal of Consulting Psychology*. 1961, 25, p. 89-90.

Gross, L.R. "MMPI L-F-K Relationships with Criteria of Behavioral Disturbance and Social Adjustment in Schizophrenic Population," *Journal of Consulting Psychology*. 1959, 23, p. 319-328.

Guralnik, D.B., ed. *Webster's New World Dictionary*. 2nd college ed. New York: Simon & Schuster, 1982.

Haccoun, D.M., and Lavigueur, H. "Effects of Clinical Experience and Client Emotion on Therapists' Response," *Journal of Consulting and Clinical Psychology*. 1979, 47, p. 416-418.

Hall, C.S. and Lindzey, G. *Theories of Personality*. New York: Wiley, 1957.

Halpern, F. "The Bender Visual Motor Gestalt Test," in B.I. Murstein, ed. *Handbook of Projective Techniques*. New York: Basic Books, 1965.

Hammer, E.F., and Piotrowski, Z.A. "Hostility as a Factor in the Clinician's Personality as it Affects his Interpretations of Projective Drawings (H-T-P,)" (1953) in B.I. Murstein, ed. *Handbook of Projective Techniques*. New York: Basic Books, 1965.

Hammond, K.R., Hursch, C.J., and Todd, F.J., "Analyzing the Components of Clinical Inference," *Psychological Review*. 1964, 71, p. 438-456.

Haney, W. "Validity, Vaudeville and Values," *American Psychologist*. 1981, 36, p. 1021-1034.

Hannah, L.D. "Causative Factors in the Production of Rotation in the Bender-Gestalt Designs," *Journal of Consulting Psychology*. 1958, 22, p. 398-399.

Harrower, M. *Appraising Personality: An Introduction to Projective Techniques*. New York: Simon and Schuster, 1952, 1964.

Hathaway, S.R. "Scales 5 (Masculinity-Femininity), 6 (Paranoia), and 8 (Schizophrenia)," in G.S. Welsh and W.G. Dahlstrom, eds. *Basic Readings on the MMPI in Psychology and Medicine*. Minneapolis: University of Minnesota Press, 1956.

Hathaway, S.R., and McKinley, J.C. "A Multiphasic Personality Schedule (Minnesota): I. Construction of the Schedule," *Journal of Psychology*. 1940, 10, p. 249-254.

Hathaway, S.R., and McKinley, J.C. *The Minnesota Multiphasic Personality Schedule*. Minneapolis: University of Minnesota Press, 1943.

Hathaway, S.R., and McKinley, J.C. *MMPI Manual*. The Psychological Corporation, revised 1967.

Hathaway, S.R., and Meehl, P.E. *An Atlas for the Clinical Use of the MMPI*. Minneapolis: University of Minnesota Press, 1951.

Hays, W.L. *Statistics*. New York: Holt, Rinehart and Winston, 1963.

Henry, W. *The Analysis of Fantasy*. New York: Wiley, 1956.

Hoffman, P.J. "The Paramorphic Representation of Clinical Judgment," *Psychological Bulletin*. 1960, 57, p. 116-131.

Hollis, J.W., and Donn, P.A. *Psychological Report Writing: Theory and Practice*. 2nd ed. Muncie, Indiana: Accelerated Development, 1979.

Holt, R.R. *Assessing Personality*. Harcourt-Brace J., 1971.

Holt, R.R. *Methods in Clinical Psychology. v. 1, Projective Assessment*. Plenum, 1978.

Holt, R.R. *Methods in Clinical Psychology, v. 2, Prediction and Research*. Plenum, 1978.

Holt, R.R. *An Analysis of TAT Cards*. (xerox of unpublished manuscript).

Holt, R.W. "The Information Acquisition Process in Causal Attribution," *Dissert. Abstr. Internat.* 1978, 39(5-B), 2570.

Holtzman, W.H. "Statistical Models for the Study of Change in the Single Case," in C.W. Harris, ed. *Problems in Measuring Change*. Madison, Wisconsin: University of Wisconsin Press, 1963.

Holtzman, W.H., and Sells, S.B. "Prediction of Flying Success by Clinical Analysis of Test Protocols," *Journal of Abnormal Social Psychology*. 1954, 49, p. 485-490.

Horst, P. *Personality: Measurement of Dimensions*. San Francisco: Jossey-Bass, 1968.

Huber, J.T. *Report Writing in Psychology and Psychiatry*. New York: Harper, 1961.

Hunt, W.A., and Walker, R.E. "Validity of Diagnostic Judgment as a Function of Amount of Test Information," *Journal of Clinical Psychology*. 1966, 22, p. 154-155.

Hutt, M.L. "The Use of Projective Methods in Personality Measurement in Army Medical Installations," *Journal of Clinical Psychology*. 1945, 1, p. 134-140.

Hutt, M.L. *The Hutt Adaptation of the Bender-Gestalt Test*. 2nd ed. New York: Grune, 1969.

Jackson, D.N., and Messick, S., ed. *Problems in Human Assessment*. New York: McGraw-Hill, 1967.

James, W. *The Principles of Psychology*. New York: Holt, Rinehart and Winston, 1890.

Janis, I.L., Mahl, G.F., Kagan, J., and Holt, R.R. *Personality: Dynamics, Development, and Assessment.* New York: Harcourt, Brace, and World, 1969.

Johnson, D.M. *Systematic Introduction to the Psychology of Thinking.* New York: Harper and Row, 1972.

Jolles, I.A. *A Catalogue for the Quantitative Interpretation of the H-T-P.* Beverly Hills, California: Western Psychological Services, 1952.

Kahneman, D., and Tversky, A. "Subjective Probability: A Judgment of Representativeness," *Cognitive Psychology.* 1972, 3, p. 430-451.

Kahneman, D., and Tversky, A. "On the Psychology of Prediction," *Psychological Review.* 1973, 80, p. 251-273.

Kamin, L.J. *The Science and Politics of IQ.* New York: Wiley, 1974.

Kazan, A.T., and Scheinberg, I.M. "Clinical Notes on the Significance of the Validity Score (F) in the MMPI," *American Journal of Psychiatry.* 1945, 102, p. 181-183.

Kelly, E.L. *Assessment of Human Characteristics.* Belmont, California: Brooks-Cole, 1967.

Kelly, G.A. *The Psychology of Personal Constructs.* New York: Norton, 1955.

Klofper, B., Ainsworth, M.D., Klopfer, R.R., eds. *Developments in the Rorschach Technique.* v. 1 Yonkers: World Book Co., 1954.

Klopfer, B., and Davidson, H.H. *The Rorschach Method of Personality Diagnosis — Individual Record Blank.* Revised edition. New York: Harcourt, Brace and World, 1960.

Klopfer, W.G. *The Psychological Report: Use and Communication of Psychological Findings.* New York: Grune and Stratton, 1960.

Koester, G.A. "A Study of Insight in the Diagnostic Process Through the Counselors' Use of Diagnostic Information," Unpublished Doctoral Dissertation, University of Minnesota, 1951.

Korchin, S.J., and Schuldberg, D. "The Future of Clinical Assessment," *American Psychologist.* 1981, 36, p. 1147-1158.

Korner, I.N. "Test Report Evaluation," *Journal of Clinical Psychology.* 1962, 18, p. 194-197.

Kostlan, A.A. "A Method for the Empirical Study of Psychodiagnosis," *Journal of Consulting Psychology.* 1954, 18, p. 83-88.

Krippner, S. "WISC Comprehension and Picture Arrangement Subtests as Measures of Social Competence," *Journal of Clinical Psychology.* 1964, 20, p. 366-367.

Ladd, C.E. "WAIS Performance of Brain Damaged and Neurotic Patients," *Journal of Clinical Psychology.* 1964, 20, p. 114-117.

Lanyon, R.I., and Goodstein, L.O. *Personality Assessment.* New York: Wiley, 1971.

Lastrucci, C.L. *The Scientific Approach: Basic Principles of the Scientific Method.* Cambridge, Mass.: Schenkman Publishing, 1963.

Leli, D.A. "The Prediction of Brain Damage with the Wechsler-Bellevue I: A Clinical Actuarial Investigation," *Dissert Abstr Internat.* 1979, 39(11-B), 5564-5565.

Levy, L.H. *Psychological Interpretation.* New York: Holt, Rinehart and Winston, 1963.

Levy, M.R., and Fox, H.M. "Psychological Testing is Alive and Well," *Professional Psychology.* 1975, 6, p. 420-424.

Lichtenstein, S., Fischhoff, B., and Phillips, L.D. "Calibration of Probabilities: The State of the Art," in H. Jungerman and G. de Zeeuw, eds. *Decision Making and Change in Human Affairs*. Dordrecht, The Netherlands: Reidel, 1977.

Lindzey, G. "Thematic Apperception Test: Interpretive Assumptions and Related Empirical Evidence," *Psychological Bulletin*. 1952, 49, p. 1-25.

Lindzey, G. "Seer versus Sign," *Journal of Experimental Research in Personality*. 1965, 1, p. 17-26.

Lindzey, G., and Tejessy, C. "Thematic Apperception Test: Indices of Aggression in Relation to Overt and Covert Behavior," in B.I. Murstein, ed. *Handbook of Projective Techniques*. New York: Basic Books, 1965.

Loeser, F.A. "A Revolution in Creative Thinking," *R. and D. Management*. 1978, 8 (special issue), p. 155-158.

London, H., and Exner, J.E., Jr. *Dimensions of Personality*. New York: Wiley. 1978.

Lorge, I. "The Fundamental Nature of Measurement," in D.N. Jackson and S. Messick, eds. *Problems of Human Assessment*. New York: McGraw-Hill, 1967, p. 43-56.

Lowery, C.R., and Higgins, R.L. "Analogue Investigation of the Relationship between Client's Sex and Treatment Recommendations," *Journal of Consulting and Clinical Psychology*, 1979, 47(4), p. 792-794.

Lubin, B., Wallis, R.R., and Paine, C. "Patterns of Psychological Test Usage in the United States, 1935-1969," *Professional Psychology*. 1972, 3, p. 63-65.

Lubin, B., and Lubin, A.W. "Patterns of Psychological Services in the United States: 1959-1969,"- *Professional Psychology*. 1972, 3, p. 63-65.

Lueger, R.J., and Petzel, T.P. "Illusory Correlation in Clinical Judgment: Effects of Amount of Information To Be Processed," *Journal of Consulting and Clinical Psychology*. 1979, 47, p. 1120-1121.

Machover, K. *Personality Projection in the Drawing of the Human Figure*. Springfield, Ill.: Charles C Thomas, 1949.

Mack, J. *Psychological Examination and Report Writing*. Exposition, 1978.

Maloney, M.P., and Ward, M.P. *Psychological Assessment: A Conceptual Approach*. Oxford University Press, 1976.

Marks, P.A., and Seeman, W. *An Atlas for Use with the MMPI: Actuarial Description of Abnormal Personality*. Baltimore: Williams and Wilkins, 1963.

Mayman, M. "Style, Focus, Language, and Content of an Ideal Psychological Test Report," *Journal of Projective Techniques*. 1959, 23, p. 453-458.

McArthur, C. "Analyzing the Clinical Process," *Journal of Counseling Psychology*. 1954, 1, p. 203-208.

McKinley, J.C., and Hathaway, S.R. "The MMPI: V. Hysteria, Hypomania and Psychopathic Deviate," *Journal of Applied Psychology*. 1944, 28, p. 153-174.

Meehl, P.E. *Clinical vs. Statistical Prediction*. Minnesota: University of Minnesota Press, 1954.

Meehl, P.E. "Wanted—A Good Cookbook," *American Psychologist*. 1956, 11, p. 263-272.

Meehl, P.E. "What Can the Clinician Do Well?" (1959) in D.N. Jackson and S. Messick, eds. *Problems of Human Assessment*. New York: McGraw-Hill, 1967, p. 594-599.

Meehl, P.E., "The Cognitive Activity of the Clinician," *American Psychologist*. 1960, 15, p. 19-27.

Meehl, P.E., "Seer Over Sign: The First Good Example," *Journal of Experimental Research in Personality*. 1965, 1, p. 27-32.

Miller, G.A. *Mathematics and Psychology*. New York: Wiley, 1964.

Mischel, W. *Personality and Assessment*. New York: Wiley, 1968.

Morgan, C.D., and Murray, H.A. "A Method for Investigating Fantasies: The Thematic Apperception Test," *Archives of Neurology and Psychiatry*. 1935, 34, p. 289-306.

Mueller, C.G. "Some Origins of Psychology as a Science," *Annual Review of Psychology*. 1979, 30, p. 9-29.

Murray, H.A. *Explorations in Personality*. New York: Oxford University Press, 1938.

Murray, H.A. *Thematic Apperception Test Manual*, 1943.

Nance, R.D. "Masculinity-femininity in Prospective Teachers," *J. Educ. Res.* 1949, 42, p. 658-666.

Murstein, B.I. *Theory and Research in Projective Techniques (emphasizing the TAT)*. New York: Wiley, 1963.

Murstein, B.I., ed. *Handbook of Projective Techniques*. New York: Basic Books, 1965.

National Education Association. "Code of Ethics of the Education Professional," in C.E. Beck, ed. *Philosophical Guidelines for Counseling*. Dubuque, Iowa: W.C. Brown, 1971, p. 317-320.

Naylor, J.C., and Wherry, R.J., Sr. "The Use of Simulated Stimuli and the 'JAN' Technique to Capture and Cluster the Policies of Raters," *Educational and Psychological Measurement*. 1965, 25, p. 969-986.

Novick, M.R. "Federal Guidelines and Professional Standards," *American Psychologist*. 1981, 36, p. 1035-1046.

Ogden, D.P. *Psychodiagnostics and Personality Assessment: A Handbook*. Los Angeles: Western Psychological Services, 1967.

O'Leary, M.R., Donovan, D.M., Chaney, E.F., and O'Leary, D.E. "Interpersonal Attractiveness and Clinical Decisions in Alcohol Treatment," *American Journal of Psychiatry*. 1979, 136, p. 618-622.

Oskamp, S. "Overconfidence in Case-Study Judgments," *Journal of Consulting Psychology*. 1965, 29, p. 261-265.

Pace, D.A. "Effects of Educational Level, Emotional Content Level of Arguments Containing Logical Fallacies, and Training on Logical Reasoning and Logical Behavior," *Dissert Abstr Internat* 1977, 38(6-B), 2944-2945.

Paella, "Inter-examiner Effects on the Bender-Gestalt," *Journal of Consulting Psychology*. 1962, 18, p. 23-26.

Parker, C.A. "As a Clinician Thinks..." *Journal of Consulting Psychology*. 1958, 5, p. 253-262.

Pascal, G.R., and Suttell, B.J. *The Bender-Gestalt Test*. New York: Grune & Stratton, 1950.

Pervin, L.A., and Levenson, H. *Personality: Theory, Assessment and Research*. 2nd ed. New York: Wiley, 1974.

Phillips, L., and Smith, J.G. *Rorschach Interpretation: Advanced Technique*. New York: Grune, 1953.

Piotrowski, Z.A. "Unsuspected and Pertinent Microfacts in Personality," *American Psychologist*. 1982, 37, p. 190-196.

Prince, M. *The Dissociation of a Personality*. New York: Longmans, Green, 1905.

Prunkl, P. *The Psychological Testing Workbook*. Champaign, Illinois: Institute for Personality and Ability Testing, 1979.

Ramzy, I. "How the Mind of the Psychoanalyst Works: An Essay on Psychoanalytic Inference," *International Journal of Psycho-Analysis*. 1974, 55, p. 543-550.

Ramzy, I., and Shervin, H. "The Nature of the Inference Process in Psychoanalytic Interpretation: A Critical Review of the Literature," *International Journal of Psycho-Analysis*. 1976, 57, p. 151-159.

Rapaport, D. "The Scientific Methodology of Psychoanalysis," in M.M. Gill, ed. *The Collected Papers of David Rapaport*. London: Basic Books, 1967.

Rapaport, D. Gill, M., and Schafer, R. *Diagnostic Psychological Testing; The Theory, Statistical Evaluation, and Diagnostic Application of a Battery of Tests*. Chicago: The Yearbook, 1945-6.

Reichenbach, H. *The Rise of Scientific Philosophy*. Berkeley: University of California Press, 1951.

"Responsibilities of Users of Standardized Tests (APGA Policy Statement)," October 5, 1978.

Rorschach, H. (1921) *Psychodiagnostics*. New York: Grune & Stratton, 1949.

Sanders, R., and Cleveland, S. "The Relationship between Certain Examiner Personality Variables and Subjects' Rorschach Scores," in B.I. Murstein, ed. *Handbook of Projective Techniques*. New York: Basic Books, 1965.

Sarason, S.B. "An Asocial Psychology and a Misdirected Clinical Psychology," *American Psychologist*. 1981, 36, p. 827-836.

Sarbin, T.R., Taft, R., and Bailey, D.E. *Clinical Inference and Cognitive Theory*. New York: Holt, Rinehart and Winston, 1960.

Sawyer, J. "Measurement *and* Prediction, Clinical *and* Statistical," *Psychological Bulletin*. 1966, 66, p. 178-200.

Schafer, R. *The Clinical Application of Psychological Tests: Diagnostic Summaries and Case Studies*. New York: International Universities Press, 1948.

Schafer, R. "Criteria for Judging the Adequacy of Interpretations," (1954) in D.N. Jackson and S. Messick, eds. *Problems of Human Assessment*. New York: McGraw-Hill, 1967, p. 559-574.

Schneck, J.M. "Clinical Evaluation of the F Scale on the MMPI," *American Journal of Psychiatry*. 1948, 104, p. 440-442.

Sechrest, L. "Incremental Validity," in Jackson and Messick, eds. *Problems in Human Assessment*. New York: McGraw-Hill, 1967.

Shaklee, H. "Bounded Rationality and Cognitive Development: Upper Limits of Growth?" *Cognitive Psychology*. 1979, 11, p. 327-345.

Shapiro, M.B. "Experimental Method in Psychological Description of the Individual Psychiatric Patient," *Journal of Social Psychiatry*. 1957, 3, p. 89-102.

Shertzer, B., and Linden, J.D. *Fundamentals of Individual Appraisal: Assessment Techniques for Counselors*. Boston: Houghton-Mifflin, 1979.

Simon, H. *Models of Man*. New York: Wiley, 1957.

Sines, L.K. "The Relative Contribution of Four Kinds of Data to Accuracy in Personality Assessment," *Journal of Consulting Psychology.* 1959, 23, p. 483-492.

Sloves, R.E., Docherty, E.M., and Schneider, K.C. "A Scientific Problem-Solving Model of Psychological Assessment," *Professional Psychology.* Feb. 1979, p. 29-35.

Slovic, P., Fischhoff, B., and Lichtenstein, S. "Behavioral Decision Theory," *Annual Review of Psychology.* 1977, 28, p. 1-39.

Slovic, P., and Lichtenstein, S. "Comparison of Bayesian and Regression Approaches to the Study of Information Processing in Judgment," *Organizational Behavior and Human Performance.* 1971, 6, p. 649-744.

Srimad Bhagavatam. (trans. by A.C. Bhaktivedanta Swami Prabhupada) New York: Bhaktivedanta Book Trust, 1978.

Standards for Educational and Psychological Tests. Washington, D.C.: American Psychological Association, 1974.

Steiner, H. "Freud Against Himself," *Perspectives in Biology and Medicine.* 1977, 20, p. 510-527.

Sternberg, R.J. "Testing and Cognitive Psychology," American Psychologist. 1981, 36, p. 1181-1189.

Stevens, S.S. "On the Theory of Scales of Measurement," *Science.* 1946, 103, p. 677-680.

Stone, H.K., and Dellis, N.P. "An Exploratory Investigation into the Levels Hypothesis," *Journal of Projective Techniques.* 1960, 24, p. 333-340.

Stones, M.J. "A Critique of the Clinical-Personological Approach to Idiographic Personality Study," *Journal of Clinical Psychology.* 1978, 34, p. 614-620.

Stratton, G.M. "Vision without Inversion of the Retinal Image," *Psychological Review.* 1897, 4, p. 341-360, 463-481.

Subject Guide to Books in Print 1979-1980 v. 2. New York: Bowker, 1979.

Sundberg, N.D. "The Practice of Psychological Testing in Clinical Services in the United States," *American Psychologist.* 1961, 16, p. 79-83.

Sundberg, N. *Assessment of Persons: For Understanding and Decision-Making.* Englewood Cliffs, New Jersey: Prentice-Hall, 1977.

Swensen, Jr., C.H. "Empirical Evaluations of Human Figure Drawings," *Psychological Bulletin.* 1957, 54, p. 431-466.

Taft, R. "The Ability to Judge People," *Psychological Bulletin.* 1950, 52, p. 65-68.

Tallent, N. "An Approach to the Improvement of Psychological Reports," *Journal of Clinical Psychology.* 1956, 12, p. 103-109.

Tallent, N. "On Individualizing the Psychologist's Clinical Evaluation," *Journal of Clinical Psychology.* 1958, 14, p. 243-244.

Tallent, N. *Psychological Report Writing.* Englewood Cliffs, New Jersey: Prentice-Hall, 1976.

Tallent, N., and Reiss, W.J. "Multidisciplinary Views on the Preparation of Written Clinical Psychological Reports I.," *Journal of Clinical Psychology.* 1959a, 15, p. 218-221.

Tallent, N., and Reiss, W.J. "Multidisciplinary Views on the Preparation of Written Clinical Psychological Reports II.," *Journal of Clinical Psychology.* 1959b, 15, p. 273-274.

Tallent, N., and Reiss, W.J. "Multidisciplinary Views on the Preparation of Written Clinical Psychological Reports III.," *Journal of Clinical Psychology.* 1959c, 15, p. 444-446.

Thorne, F.C. *Clinical Judgment.* Brandon, Vermont: *Journal of Clinical Psychology.* 1961.

Tolor, A., and Brannigan, G.G. *Research and Clinical Applications of the Bender-Gestalt Test.* Springfield, Ill.: Charles C Thomas, Publisher, 1981.

Tomkins, S.S. *The Thematic Apperception Test: The Theory and Technique of Interpretation.* New York: Grune and Stratton, 1947.

Vernon, P.E. *Personality Assessment: A Critical Survey.* London: Methuen, 1979.

Wade, T.C., and Baker, T.B. "Opinions and Use of Psychological Tests: A Survey of Clinical Psychologists," *American Psychologist.* 1977, 32, p. 874-882.

Watson, R.I. *The Clinical Method in Psychology.* New York: Harper and Brothers, 1951.

Wechsler Adult Intelligence Scale — Revised. and *WAIS Manual.* New York: Psychological Corporation, 1981.

Wechsler, D. *WAIS Manual.* New York: Psychological Corporation, 1955.

Wechsler, D. *The Measurement and Appraisal of Adult Intelligence.* 4th ed. Baltimore: Williams and Wilkins. 1958.

Weiner, I.B. "Does Psychodiagnosis Have a Future?" *Journal of Personality Assessment.* 1972, 36, p. 534-546.

Weiss, A.A. "Alternating Two-Day Cyclic Behavior Changes," *Journal of Clinical Psychology.* 1958, 14, p. 433-437.

Wertheimer, M. "Studies in the Theory of Gestalt Psychology," *Psychol Forsch* 1923, 4, p. 300.

White, R.W. *Lives in Progress: A Study of the Natural Growth of Personality.* New York: Holt, Rinehart and Winston, 1975a.

White, R.W., et al. *Case Workbook in Personality.* New York: Holt, Rinehart and Winston, 1975b.

Whitley, B.E. "Sex Roles and Psychotherapy: A Current Appraisal," *Psychological Bulletin.* 1979, 86(6), p. 1309-1321.

Wiggins, J.S. *Personality and Prediction: Principles of Personality Assessment.* Reading, Mass.: Addison-Wesley, 1973.

Williams, R.L. "Abuses and Misuses in Testing Black Children," *Counseling Psychologist.* 1971, 2, p. 62-73.

Winch, R.F., and More, D.M. "Does TAT Add Information to the Interviews? Statistical Analysis of the Increments," *Journal of Clinical Psychology.* 1956, 12, p. 316-321.

Woody, R.H., ed. *Encyclopedia of Clinical Assessment.* San Francisco: Jossey-Bass, 1980.

Zimmerman, I.L., and Woo-Sam, J.M. *Clinical Interpretation of the Wechsler Adult Intelligence Scale.* New York: Grune and Stratton, 1973.

Zubin, J., Eron, L.D., and Schumer, F. *An Experimental Approach to Projective Techniques.* New York: Wiley, 1965.

GLOSSARY

A number of terms which could be considered equivocal are defined here to avoid confusion about their meaning in the text.

Assessment - is any process which is employed to collect information about human beings. It can involve the use of observation, tests of skill, and intelligence, professional opinion, etc. In psychology, "assessment," when accompanied by the word "personality," takes on a slightly different meaning: Here the concern is with the evaluation of personality, typically using behavior, tests, measures, and inferences.

Appraisal - could be used interchangeably with "evaluation," except that "appraisal" means the collection, interpretation, and organization of data and relies upon the judgment of the appraiser. "Evaluation" stresses the judgment aspect of appraisal.

Axioms - are principles that are certain and acknowledged by all (Blake, 1960, p. 40).

Bounded Rationality - is a term coined by Simon (1957) to indicate the manner in which limited rational schemes of the world can be superimposed on reality and limit what is perceived.

Case Study - is the in-depth examination of one individual.

Clinical - means having to do with the direct treatment and observation of clients, and can be contrasted with more scientific or experimental studies of clients under controlled conditions.

Clinical Judgment - is synonymous with the term "human judgment" but implies a judge trained in the clinical methods of psychology. The term arose historically in discussions about Paul Meehl's book *Clinical versus Statistical Prediction* (1954).

Clinical Psychology - is that branch of psychology that deals with the study of the individual person in his totality, as opposed to studying his parts. It is often viewed as the least rigorous branch of psychology because it is always two steps removed from (some say ahead of, some say behind) empiricism in its attempts to understand the individual human being.

Criterion - is a comparison object, rule, or standard against which to test a judgment or rule in order to determine its validity.

Data - is the total accumulation of information available to study at hand.

Data Base - is the total potential information from which a sampling is made for a given study. Ultimately the confidence invested in the findings of a study must derive from the researcher's knowledge about the data base and the care taken in sampling it accurately.

Personality assessment involves the use of thousands of bits of information drawn from a data base that consists of all possible information about a given human being. When psychological tests are used to sample this data base, only a small segment of the total data base is available to study. Therefore, the inferences drawn from this sample of data must be logically sound. The sampled behavior, though only a small part of the data base, nonetheless, typically consists of thousands of bits of data gotten from raw data, scored data, observations and visual impressions about the subject garnered by the assessor in the course of testing.

Empathy - is "the projection of one's own personality into the personality of another in order to understand him better" (Guralnik, 1982, p. 458).

Evaluation - is measurement against a standard. See "appraisal."

Formulation - is the process by which definite systematic statements are developed in order to describe a client. To develop a formulation requires sifting, shortening, high-lighting, organizing, and summarizing data and inferences into a form that describes the person. It is the culmination of interpretation.

Hypothesis - is a plausible speculation about a set of data that seem to be related. It is tentative and not yet proven. This term can mean an unsubstantiated inference which requires additional evidence to support it (Blake, 1960, p. 40). It can also mean a conception, or the whole system of conceptions, applied to experience by an author as a prerequisite to the collection of data (Blake, 1960, p. 69). The term "hypothesis" is sometimes used in the psychology literature in the latter sense. However, it is misleading with regard to scientific terminology and "hypothesis" is not used with this meaning in this volume.

Inference - is a "judgment based on other judgments rather than on direct observation" (English and English, 1958, p. 260).

Interpretation - is a meaningful statement, made by an assessor about a client, which is drawn by inference from data which the assessor has collected about the client. The interpretation should be characteristic of the client and verifiable by others. This volume uses the term "interpretive hypothesis" to convey this meaning of interpretation, as contrasted with "interpretative process," and "interpretative conclusion."

Intuition - is "the direct knowing or learning of something without the conscious use of reasoning" (Guralnik, 1982, p. 740).

Judgment - is an opinion put forth by a person. In psychology the term is used in conjunction with the world "clinical" to refer to the professional opinions of clinicians about their clients.

Measurement - is the "process of determining the extent or the dimensions of an object, attribute, or trait" (Shertzer and Linden, 1979, p. 12-14). Measurement can be made directly or indirectly. In direct measurement, the thing being measured is directly in contact with the measurer's human senses. In indirect measurement, the thing being studied is hidden from view, so to speak, and its characteristics must be inferred from traces it makes or leaves behind. In personality assessment measurement is virtually always indirect. For this reason the term "measurement" is not frequently used in personality assessment. Instead, other terms are more popular which connote indirect measurement, such as, evaluation, appraisal, and assessment.

Objective - is used to mean that which exists independent of the mind of the observer and can be verified by a third party.

Personality - is the totality of a human being exclusive of. . .what? Can you think of anything that it cannot include about a person? This raises the issue, that leaving out any major distinguishing feature of the person, such as, habits, dress, mannerisms, facial expression, can do an injustice to that personality. One great task of the personality assessor is to insure that all important personality features that are not described in his report of an individual's personality are at least implied.

Studies that focus on human parts or segments of behavior, such as molecular structure, perception, or group behavior, are not personality studies as such. However, when these same topics are viewed out of isolation and as part of the functioning of a unique human being, especially as regards the degree to which they distinguish one individual from all others in terms of his characteristic thoughts, actions, and feelings, they become potential topics of personality study.

Many definitions of "personality" exist in the psychology literature. Gordon Allport listed fifty definitions of "personality," "persona," and "person"; English and English (1958, p. 382-383) list six in a standard reference dictionary of psychology terms.

Postulates - are principles not universally admitted but which an author asks the reader to concede as a basis of a given demonstration (Blake, 1960, p. 40). Different books on science list different numbers of postulates of scientific inquiry. Uniform treatment of scientific method does not yet exist (Lastrucci, 1963, p. 37).

Psychological Report - is the final formulation the assessor prepares in written form to describe a personality. Most often the psychological report is prepared in response to a referral question and does not attempt to describe the entire personality.

Psychological Test - is a tool used to measure characteristics of an individual. It is a set of standardized or controlled occasions presented to an individual to elicit a representative sample of his behavior when meeting a given kind of environmental demand (English and English, 1958, p. 547).

Reliability - is used in this volume to mean the stability, accuracy, and consistency of measurement by a test. Without a fair degree of reliability a test cannot possibly be very valid. Ideally, we would have three aspects (or coefficients) of reliability estimated for each test used in a battery: stability over time, equivalence of parallel forms, and internal consistency of items in the test (heterogeneity-homogeneity). Interscorer reliability estimates have also been included in this volume for some of the scoring systems used with the tests in Section II.

Report - is "an account of what took place, by an actor or by an observer" (English and English, 1958, p. 547). The psychological report will always contain findings based on actual interaction with the client, whether the interaction takes place between an observer and the client directly, or whether the interaction takes place between the observer and the client's test material. Hearsay, speculation, and fantasy would never be included in the report unless they were labelled as such.

Schema or *Scheme* - a plan or model that shows the important relationships between concepts or ideas and states them in an organized, systematic fashion that serves as a guide to action.

Scientific - is a phrase that has grown in popularity in modern times while it has shrunk in meaning. Traditionally, "scientific" meant that which was characteristic of the scientific method, an elaborate, time consuming, logically rigorous means to ascertain truth. It involves the collection of data, construction of hypotheses to relate the data, testing of hypotheses, retesting of hypotheses as necessary, and the description of results. Nowadays, the word "scientific" is often used loosely to put a stamp of respectability on an endeavor which might be viewed as objective, rigorous, and well-studied and understood.

Scientific Mode of Thinking - is a phrase used in this volume to mean rigorous, logical thinking characteristic of the hard sciences.

Speculation - means "thinking in which the factual basis for the hypothesis. . . is slight" (English and English, 1958, p. 316). The factual basis could even be nonexistent. Although sometimes people decry speculation, it holds an important role in generating new ideas. In personality assessment, speculation has a legitimate role when it is used to brainstorm for possible solutions, alternatives, hypotheses. Once patterns of data become logically related by means of inference, hypothesis testing, and validity efforts, speculation leaves the picture.

Validity - is a term used frequently in this volume. In Section I it is often used in the context of validating hypotheses, where it refers to establishing that the hypotheses are well-grounded on evidence, personality principles, and sound logic, and able to withstand a critical evaluation. In Section II "validity" is often used in the context of measurement. Assessing the validity of measurements involves trying to answer the question Does a measure measure what you think it is measuring? The American Psychological Association's (1974)

"Standards for Educational and Psychological Tests and Manuals" distinguishes three types of validity relevant to measurement by tests:

Content Validity - involves how well the content of a test samples the class of situations or subject matter about which conclusions are to be drawn. It thereby checks on the adequacy of definitions on which the measurement is based.

Criterion-related Validity - involves a comparison of test scores with one or more external, or operationalized, variables considered to provide a direct measure of the characteristic or behavior in question.

Construct Validity - helps to increase understanding of the psychological qualities being measured by a test and involves the degree to which certain explanatory concepts and constructs (such as, a theoretical framework) account for performance on a test. Cronbach and Meehl (1955), originators of this concept, qualify it to refer to the study of *non*operationalized sides of constructs and not operationalized sides, which would be criterion validity. Construct validity can also be viewed as dependent upon a number of criterion predictions.

NAME INDEX

217

SUBJECT INDEX

A

Abandonment, 145, 188
Abilities, 10, 33, 118, 189
Ability tests, 12, 13, 14
Abstract thinking, 83, 115, 116, 187
Accuracy of judgments, x-xi, xiii, 15-16, 41-42, 49, 52-54, 63, 104
  Goldberg's summary of research findings, xiii
  McArthur's observations regarding, 41-42
Achievement, 30, 184
Actuarial description, 184
Adjustment, 169
Administration (see Test administration)
Affection, 196
  need for, 161, 166, 183, 187-188
  in Rorschach (affectional need), 159, 161-163
Affiliation, need for, 161, 162, 187-188
Aggression, 123, 137, 145, 146, 147, 166, 188
Alcoholism, 181, 184, 197
Alertness, 114, 116
Alternate hypotheses, vi, xi, xxii, 38, 76, 79, 88, 90, 114, 115, 193-194
  generation of, 73-74, 88-90
  sources of, xxii
  use of, xx-xxi, 20, table 36, 73, 90 (see also Testing)
Ambition, 180
American Educational Research Association, 23, 31
American Personnel and Guidance Association (APGA), v, 21, 22, 26-33, 68-69, fn. 69
American Psychological Association (APA), v, 13, 14, 21, 22-26, 31, 32, 68-69, fn. 69, 93
Analysis, 31, 39, 47, 62, 73
  of data (see Data analysis)

of drawings (see Drawings)
scientific method of, 62-63
Anger, 177, 188
Anxiety, 27, 116, 117, 123, 134, 136, 146, 162, 177
APA (see American Psychological Association)
Apathy, 177
APGA (see American Personnel and Guidance Association)
Appraisal, glossary 211
Arithmetic, 48
  WAIS subscale, 109, 110, 114
Assessment, ix, xi, 22, 23, 25, 32, 33, 102, 104, 148, 176, 194, glossary 211 (see also Personality assessment)
Assessor(s), 22, 32, 44, 48, 54, 58-59, 60, 61, 62-63, 64, 69, 70, 73, 75, 76, 89, 101 (see also Interpreter(s) and Test Users)
  accuracy of, 78 (see also Judges, "good")
  bounded rationality of, 86-87
  "eclectic," 84
  as generator of hypotheses, 75
  personality of, 64, 104, effects on interpretation, 64
  pitfalls for, 42-43, 81, 84
  as problem solver, 83-84
  self-criticism in, 63
  skills of, 5-6, 64, 68, 84
    importance of knowledge of statistics and measurement to, 65, 68-72
  testing hypotheses against his knowledge, 74
  training of (see Training, of personality assessors)
Assumptions
  "clinical," 39, 44, 57, 61 (see also Clinical method)
  statistical, 68
  re study of inner person, 44, 57
  underlying TAT interpretation, 38,

223

as a process, 44-45

and the treatment of data, 10, 46-49

vocabulary of (*see* Language usage)

Clinical-personological method, 44-45

Clinical thinking, 15, 39, 44, 51, 52, 68

  criticism of, 39-40, 55

  studies regarding, xiii-xv

  validity of, 39

Clinician(s), ix-xii, 5, 13, 32, 33, 42, 45, 46, 48, 49, 50, 52, 58, 63, 124, 148, 149

  with accurate judgment (*see* Judges, "good")

  cognitive activity of, xi, 10, 45, 47, 54, 81, 83

  faulty interpretation skills among, ix-xii, 42

  flexibility of, 63

  predictive ability, x-xii, 53 (*see also* Clinical judgment)

  training of, x, xii, 40, 47

  variation in ability among, 32, 53, 55

  what can they do well?, 39

Codes of ethics and professional standards, v, 14, 21, 22-37, 69, 93 (*see also* Interpretation, and science)

  APA's, 23-26

  APGA's, 26-31

  discussion of, 31-33, 68

Cognitive theory, 39, 41 (*see also* Clinical inference)

Comprehension (WAIS subscale), 109, 110, 117

Computers, 35, table 36-37, 52, 67, 79

Concentration, 102, 114, 116, 187

Conceptualization, of client, importance to prediction, 41-42

  vs. categorization, 41-42

  formation of, 42

Conceptual validity, 33, 52, 104 (*see also* Validity)

Confidence intervals, 24

Confidentiality, 93, fn. 105

Conformity, 175, 176, 184

Construct validity, 29, 30, 105, glossary 216 (*see also* Validity)

Content validity, 29, 30, glossary 216 (*see also* Validity)

Convergent validity, 103 (*see also* Validity)

Conversion hysteria (MMPI Hy scale), 168, 172

Cookbooks, 100, 104 (*see also* MMPI, cookbooks)

Cooperation, 134, 175, 176, 186

Criterion-related validity, 24, glossary 216

  (*see also* Validity)

Critical thinking (*see* Thinking processes)

Cross-validation, 16, 29, 42 (*see also* Validity)

D

DAP (*see* Draw-A-Person Test)

Data, x-xi, xxii, 10, 19, 31, 33, 38, 39, 40, 45, 51, 54, 58, 59, 63, 65, 69, 73, 81, 84, 87-88, 101, 102, 104, 193, glossary 212

  analysis of (*see* Data analysis)

  inefficient handling of, x, 5, 77, table 77, 81, 87-88

  normative (*see* Norms)

  processing of, 25, 42, 46-49, 60, 64, 74, 83, 85, 89

  psychometric vs. nonpsychometric, 46-49

  raw (*see* Raw data)

  scored (*see* Scored data)

  sources of, 11-12

  statistical treatment of, 64-67, 69, 70-72

  use of in generating and testing hypotheses, 42, 60, 63-64, 73-74, 76, 82-83, 86, 89

Data analysis, v-vi, 5, 8, 10, 16, 35, table 36, 38, 46-47, 51, 62, 64-67, 68, 73, 75, 99-101

  clinical vs. psychometric approaches, 47

  methods of, table 36

  need for description of, xii-xiii

  principles of, 88

  use of statistics and measurement in, 64-67, 68-70

Data base, glossary 212

Decision making, vi, 25, 26, 30, 80, 85-87, 99

Deduction, 41, 42, 62, 76

Defenses, 116, 145, 146, 165-166, 183, 188-189 (*see also* Denial, Projection)

Delinquency, 177, 184, 196

Denial, 146, 160, 161, 174, 188

Dependence, 145, 162, 165, 166, 178, fn. 178, 183, 186, 188, 197

Depression, 48, 146, 184, 197

  MMPI D scale, 168, 172, 176-177

Derived scores, 27, 28

Description, of personality, vii, 9, 15, 32, 48-49, 51, 85, 90

  dependence on conceptualization, 42,